REFORM AND REVOLUTION IN COMMUNIST SYSTEMS

Reform and Revolution in Communist Systems:
An Introduction

GARY K. BERTSCH

University of Georgia

Macmillan Publishing Company
NEW YORK

Editor: Bruce Nichols
Production Supervisor: Lisa G. M. Chuck
Production Manager: Richard C. Fischer
Text Designer: Patrice Fodero
Cover Designer: Brian Sheridan
Cover Photographs: J. Langevin/SYGMA; Patrick Forestier/SYGMA; and Bigwood/Gamma-Liaison
This book was set in Palatino by C. L. Hutson, Inc., and was printed and bound by
Book Press. The cover was printed by New England Book Components.

Macmillan Publishing Company
866 Third Avenue, New York, New York 10022

Collier Macmillan Canada, Inc.
1200 Eglinton Avenue East
Suite 200
Don Mills, Ontario M3C 3N1

LIBRARY OF CONGRESS CATALOGING-IN-PUBLICATION DATA

Bertsch, Gary K.
    Reform and revolution in communist systems: an introduction /
  Gary K. Bertsch.
    p. cm.
    Includes index.
  ISBN 0-02-309125-8
  1. Communism—1945– 2. Revolutions and socialism. 3. Communist
    countries–Politics and government. 4. Revolutions—Communist
  countries. I. Title.
  HX44.B435 1991
  335.43'09'04—dc20   90-6549
                             CIP

Printing: 1 2 3 4 5 6 7   Year: 1 2 3 4 5 6 7

PREFACE

Many lectures on communism and communist states in the 1990s are beginning with the words *Who would have believed . . .?* The changes that came to the Soviet Union and the countries of Eastern Europe in the latter part of the 1980s were truly incredible and historic. Who would have believed that the decision makers of these countries would undertake the far-reaching reform programs they did? Who would have believed that many of these leaders would renounce the traditional, centralized model of communist politics and search for more democratic modes of governing? Who would have believed that in a matter of months, noncommunist governments would replace many of the traditional Communist Party dictatorships in Eastern Europe? Who would have believed that the Berlin Wall would be dismantled, that barbed wire would no longer divide East from West Europe, and that other significant efforts would be made to overcome the artificial division of postwar Europe? As we enter the decade of the 1990s, fundamental change has come to what we have traditionally called the Marxist-Leninist communist states of the Second World.[1]

Although Stalinist-type systems have been replaced this does not necessarily mean that the 1990s will be a decade of stable progression toward democratic rule and economic progress in the Second World. The Soviet Union, China, the states of Eastern Europe, and other countries of the Second World face incredible challenges. There will no doubt be setbacks to the reform programs and the democratization begun in the 1980s. We cannot anticipate exactly what will happen. Very few anticipated the historic transformations that came to many of the Second World states in the 1980s. We do not profess an ability to predict what will occur in the 1990s; in fact, we beg the reader's indulgence at the very start because many of the issues addressed in this book will be quickly overtaken by events. However, we do think it is an opportune time to examine what has happened in the Second World states that in the past so fervently proclaimed to be building communism.

The late 1980s were filled with dramatic developments related to the themes of reform and revolution in communist systems. For example, the December 13, 1989 edition of the *New York Times* alone contained the following stories:

"Gorbachev Blocks Debate on Ending Party Supremacy"

"Excerpts from Gorbachev's Moscow Speech"

"Voting Machines Baffle Soviet Lawmakers"

"Upheaval in East: Gorbachev in Charge"

"But, Soviets Ask, How Do You Shut Them Up?"

"Bush Gamble in China Trip"
"Bush Is Right on China"
"Beijing View of the Furor"
"Upheaval in East: Baker in Berlin"
"Disarmament Includes East German
   Politburo"
"Dissident Group to File Charges Against
   Krenz"
"Full Slow Ahead in Germany"
"Talks on Prague Vote Stall on How to Pick
   a President"
"New Church Role in Czechoslovakia"
"Bulgarian Dissident Asking for More"
"Walesa Proposes Plan on Economy"
"Two New Parties Formed in Serbia"

One of the chief ideologists of the Soviet Union, Vadim Medvedev, noted in *Pravda* as early as 1988 that communism was in a period of crisis around the world. These were strong words and were also being spoken by other communist leaders, not the least of whom was Mikhail Gorbachev.

What is the future of communism? What are we to make of the momentous developments taking place in the Second World? What are their meanings and implications? *Reform and Revolution in Communist Systems: An Introduction* was written to address these questions and to meet what I perceive as the need of instructors and students who want to examine the key questions surrounding these political systems during this critical period of uncertainty and change in the Second World. Although many have written about communism, there are serious deficiencies in terms of what books are available for instruction today. I would be the first to admit that this book does not overcome all the deficiencies, but I have tried to address what both I and reviewers consider five major needs.

The first need addressed is a unified conceptual scheme. This book takes a straightforward approach based on the concepts of policy

goals, actions, and outcomes. What do the leaders want to accomplish (goals)? What have they done and what are they doing (actions)? What are the consequences of their actions (outcomes)? Second, this approach needs to emphasize the critical forces of politics—the historical, ideological, and environmental settings in which policymaking occurs and the Party and government organizations within which planning, decision making, and execution take place. Third, the book needs to take a comparative approach to the study of these topics, utilizing the Soviet, Chinese, and East European systems for comparison and illustration. The fourth need this book addresses is the examination of the impact of communism on the lives of the people. To what extent, for example, did communist leaders and their policies serve the needs and aspirations of the average citizen? Finally, and most importantly, this book tries to deal with the tremendous change that has taken place in the Soviet, Chinese, and other Second World systems. These systems are in a period of dramatic transition. What happens in these states over the next decade will be of considerable importance to the international system in which we live.

In the past, Americans have been ill equipped to understand and, perhaps, overly skeptical about the possibilities for change in the Second World. We have tended to associate all communism with Stalinism and have failed to recognize that communist political systems can change. We have also failed to recognize the significant differences among the Communist Party states—for example, among the Soviet Union, China and Hungary.

However, we are better equipped to study these issues and states today, particularly when it comes to information. We have at our disposal great quantities of fairly accurate and detailed information about Second World states. To observe, compare, and evaluate, one needs such information and, although we certainly would like to have more facts and figures, particularly about recent changes, we now have access to enough information to engage in critical study and to make informed observations and judgments.

There are important issues facing us as we approach the twenty-first century. We live in an interdependent world; developments in the Soviet Union, China, and Eastern Europe affect us in the West. Approximately a third of the Earth's total population lives in the sixteen states making up the Second World. We must better understand what has happened and is going on in these states. What went wrong? How are they changing? Can they become more socially, politically, and economically viable? Can they promote human dignity, democracy, freedom, and a higher quality of life? These are some of the fundamental issues that this book intends to address.

We should recognize at the beginning of our study that these and many other important questions cannot be completely answered in a book of this sort during a period of such incredible change. It is simply impossible to anticipate what will happen from month to month in these countries. As a result of this, verb tense presented an acute problem in the writing of this book. Certainly, traditional methods of communist rule are and will continue to be employed in some Second World states for the foreseeable future. However, traditional methods are no longer being used in many Second

World states and trends indicate that their use will decline even further as the 1990s progress. For this reason, we have largely decided to employ the past tense in our discussion of traditional methods of communist rule in the Second World.

Anyone claiming to be able to predict exactly what will happen in the Second World in the future is either a prophet or a charlatan. However, students of politics must raise key questions and reexamine the past and present in view of ongoing developments. Certainly, students and faculty who use this book will want to supplement it with current periodicals, including newspapers, to try to stay abreast of the rapid pace of change in the Second World.

I would like to thank all those who have helped me over the years to better understand the politics of Second World systems. In addition, thanks are due to my former research assistants, Stephen McKelvey and Wu Zhongyi, for their aid in the preparation of this book; Jan DeFoor, Angie Wilson, and Teresa Williams for the typing; Professors John Bing, William Reisinger, and Benedict Stavis for reviewing the draft manuscript; and several additional external reviewers of this and earlier editions of *Power and Policy in Communist Systems* from which this book evolved. Finally, special thanks go to Sam Watson, who co-authored Chapters 4, 5, and 6 and made helpful suggestions on the remainder of the book.

GARY BERTSCH

Notes

1. The term *Second World* will be used to identify the countries we are covering in this book and to distinguish them from the more developed and democratic states of the First World and the less developed states of the Third World.

CONTENTS

Contents

Reform and Revolution in Communist Systems

INTRODUCTION:
STUDYING POLITICS IN
SECOND WORLD SYSTEMS

What do we mean when we refer to a political system as a "Second World" or a "communist" system? The term *communist* or *Marxist-Leninist political system* once had a clearer meaning than it does today. Richard C. Gripp noted in the 1970s that these were systems characterized by: (1) a deterministic and materialistic interpretation of history; (2) a revolutionary transformation of the former political system; (3) rule by a dictatorship of the working class, through the Communist Party; (4) egalitarianism of society; (5) anticapitalism and anti-imperialism; (6) public ownership and state control of the important economic functions of society; and (7) a commitment to a progressive/humanitarian society conducive to social welfare.[1] As we will see in the pages ahead, the political systems of the countries we are studying in this book have never fully corresponded with these features. Furthermore, given the radical changes taking place in most of these states, the lack of correspondence is growing.

That raises the question, are we studying similar political systems? And, if they are not all similar and communist, why should we be studying them together in this book? First, it must be said that significant changes came to many of the so-called communist states of the Second World, and particularly, Eastern Europe, in the latter part of the 1980s. Many of these states have clearly moved away from communism and Marxism-Leninism. It is inappropriate, therefore, to still refer to all of them as communist or Marxist-Leninist political systems. Nevertheless, we will keep this group of countries together in this book because we need to follow their stories. They all began their communist experiments by subscribing to a common ideology, Marxism-Leninism. They all encountered problems and began to respond, sometimes in similar ways and sometimes quite differently. We remain interested in their stories. We want to know what comes next.

Therefore, when we refer in this book to Second World systems, we mean the sixteen states that were once internationally recognized as Marxist-Leninist and were governed by leaders who purported to be actively engaged in the building of communism.[2] The leaders did not contend that they had achieved communism

1

(this remained a goal related to Marx's utopian future) but that they were dedicated to working toward it. A salient feature of these systems was the dominant role of a single political party, the Communist Party, a feature that has changed fundamentally in many of the states we are studying. Listed alphabetically, the states of the Second World are Albania, Bulgaria, Cambodia (Kampuchea), China, Cuba, Czechoslovakia, East Germany, Hungary, Laos, Mongolia, North Korea, Poland, Romania, the Soviet Union, Vietnam, and Yugoslavia.[3]

How to refer to these states today is indeed a problem and should be clarified as much as possible as we begin this book. The following guidelines may be useful. The terms *Marxist* and *Marxist-Leninist* will refer to the original efforts of these states to apply the thoughts of Karl Marx and Vladimir Ilyich Lenin. The term *Stalinist* will refer to those states that later pursued Joseph Stalin's highly centralized, coercive model of communism. The term *communist* will be used to refer to those states that contended that they were engaged in the building of communism. The term *traditional communist* will be used to refer to the Marxist-Leninist-Stalinist model of communism that evolved and was applied in the many states that aspired to communism through the 1950s, '60s, and '70s. *Reform communist* will refer to those states and leaders that are trying to save communism but are pursuing new, non-Stalinist approaches to communist development. Finally, the term *Second World* is the most general term that refers to the broad grouping of countries we are covering in this book.

One should be careful and critical about the use and misuse of these and related terms. They are often used in confusing and unfortunate ways. In the December 6, 1989 issue of the *New York Times*, Flora Lewis quoted the former dissident, playwright, and new President of Czechoslovakia, Vaclav Havel, about misuses of the term socialism and the "saving of socialism":

> Gorbachev wants to save socialism with the market and free speech. Li Peng [the Chinese leader] saves socialism by massacring students and Ceausescu [the ousted Romanian leader] by rolling a bulldozer across his country. It is always worthwhile to mistrust words. . . . You spoil less by mistrusting words than by giving them excessive confidence.

This is good advice to all students of politics and particularly to those of us who are studying the rapidly changing states of the Second World.

How should we study these states? Over the years, both area studies and comparative approaches have been used to study these political systems. Area studies focus on single countries, such as the Soviet Union, and seldom compare one system with another. Most books on communism utilize the area approach and concentrate on single countries and explain in considerable detail their historical and contemporary features. Although this is a valid and useful way to study Second World systems, it does not adequately address some of the interesting questions of our ages, namely, how have these different states fared under the communist experiment? How has the imposition of a similar founding ideology and political system affected the different states? How did the ideology, political culture, and other important features of these systems evolve? Furthermore, what went wrong, and how did the problems that they experienced vary from one state to another? The reasons for these experiences, their similarities and differences, and their consequences can best be determined and examined by the *comparative* study of Second World systems.

Comparison is an integral part of intellectual activity and one in which we are constantly engaged. To compare means to look for similarities and differences so that we can more fully understand what we are studying. Genuine understanding requires careful, systematic comparison. To understand and evaluate universities requires examining different universities. To understand diseases requires examining and comparing different diseases. And so it is with political systems. This book will attempt to compare critical features of the sixteen Second World states to better understand the evolution and experience of communism. Why did some systems attempt to reform whereas others resisted it? Why did revolutions come to some systems but not to others? Comparison will aid in answering such questions.

Our study and comparison of political life in Second World states will be a difficult and challenging task. One reason for the difficulty relates to the rapid changes that continue to take place. It is difficult to examine and compare systems that are being transformed as we study them. We will try to do so, however, because of the need to better understand the communist experience. What were the original goals? How were these political systems organized? Where did they succeed, and where did they fail?

Although comparative study of these states and the communist experience is a great challenge, greater access to information is making our study much easier than it once was. Increased news reporting and scholarly exchanges have added substantially to what we know about the Second World states. Literally thousands of Western journalists are reporting daily from these countries. And many American and other scholars from the West are spending considerable time conducting research in these countries and are publishing numerous books and articles about what they have found. During the last few decades, thousands of college professors and graduate students have travelled annually to the Soviet Union and other Second World countries for extended periods for research and study.

An important development determining what we can today study, compare, and know results from the extraordinary opening of communist societies in the 1980s. Led by Mikhail Gorbachev in the Soviet Union, most leaders have become less secretive about developments in their societies. As a result, the Second World shares much more information today than it ever did in the past. We are provided with revealing reports of high-level Party and governmental meetings; with scholarly studies that investigate public opinion, social and economic programs and problems, and other important aspects of these societies; and, with hard-hitting investigative accounts of the seamier side of life (e.g., alcoholism, prostitution, drugs) by native journalists reporting on issues that were covered up until the recent past. Although there is still a great deal we do not know, the information available and the research compiled put us in a much better position today to study and compare these states than was the case ten or twenty years ago.

Politics and Values

When a liberal friend of mine returned from a trip to the People's Republic of China during the period of radical Maoist rule in the 1960s, I asked him to evaluate the impact of communism on Chinese society. In his words, communist governments in general and the Chinese communists in particular had done more to destroy the human dignity of their populations than any other government in modern political history. At about the same time, another friend of mine, a Marxist, made a starkly different appraisal. The Chinese communists, he noted, had restored human dignity to the Chinese people; they were making the people proud to be Chinese once again. These two observers, both intelligent and informed scholars who have studied society and politics across the globe, disagreed because they held different value systems and contrasting conceptions of the meaning of "human dignity."

The first scholar approached the Chinese Maoist experience from a liberal, democratic tradition that considers the promotion and preservation of individualism the primary attribute of human dignity. According to this value system, the individual is viewed as an end in him- or herself and is served by—and placed above—the group. Individual liberties and private conscience are considered inviolate rights and conditions necessary for the realization of human dignity. When evaluating the Maoist experience, this scholar saw little evidence of the individual rights and conditions that he considered vital to the enhancement and protection of his conception of human dignity.

The second scholar, a Marxist, attempted to view human dignity in China in somewhat the same manner as the Maoists viewed it and as a result came away with a starkly different evaluation. Where the first scholar saw repression of individual rights, the second observed a collective spirit that placed the public good before private interests. Where the first perceived a lack of individualism, the second saw greater cooperation and some semblance of brotherhood and sisterhood.

In traditional communist ideology, the term *individual* was typically used in a negative, pejorative sense. The self-centered individual was encouraged to restrain his or her greed and, under communism, to serve the common good. Through their identification with and contri-

bution to the collectivity, individuals were expected to realize human dignity within a more cooperative social environment. Although Marxist and communist values are in a state of considerable flux today, we should note that they still contrast considerably with those of the liberal, democratic tradition predominant in the West.

The liberal, democratic conception of human dignity tends to be based on individualism, private rights including freedom of religion, and the principle that both the personal and public good can be best served under a pluralist system of private rights and opportunities. The communist conception has traditionally stressed collective action and the duties and responsibilities of the individual for promoting the public good. In the West, personal liberties are given a higher priority than social and economic equalities; in traditional Communist Party states, these priorities were reversed. Such differing concepts resulted in the two appraisals of China noted above, and such concepts are likely to affect our study of Second World systems. For that reason, it is necessary to confront these contrasting value systems and determine how we should utilize them in a study of our sixteen states.

When we study, compare, and evaluate these systems, including their policies and performance, should we try to view political life as communists have traditionally done, or should we utilize our own democratic values and standards of performance? Unfortunately, an excessive dose of ethnocentrism has characterized many American studies of foreign countries, particularly those with ideologies and value systems different from our own. Although we neither can nor should ignore our own values when we study and appraise political life in other countries, if we want to understand these countries better, we must pay close attention

4

to *their* value systems and how the people who hold them view the world. We must ask ourselves, for example, what was it that communist revolutionaries fought for? What is it that contemporary leaders and their people are trying to accomplish?

To the true believer, communism is an ideal state of being in which genuine human dignity will be realized.[4] Basing their ideas on the writings of Karl Marx (1818–83), Marxists have asserted that communism is the ultimate stage in societal development, the final form of socialism, and that it is to be achieved only after the destruction of the remnants of capitalist institutions and ideas. (Marx and his ideas will be discussed in more detail in the next chapter.) Believing that this change may take a rather long time, Marxist leaders have claimed not to have succeeded in attaining genuine communism, but only to have worked toward that end. As they see it, the closer a society comes to being communist, the greater the opportunities for human dignity.

This book will devote a good deal of attention to the concept of human dignity and to four values related to it. Theoretically speaking, what is the Marxist conception of human dignity and how is it related to communism? To Marx (but not necessarily to the traditional or Stalinist communist), human dignity was a state of being in which: (1) political *power* was to be shared under a system of participatory democracy; (2) *respect* was to be given to all individuals on the basis of universalistic norms; (3) *well-being* was to be provided equally to all people on the basis of need; and (4) *enlightenment* was to be granted to all so that everyone would have the opportunity to become a well-rounded, productive citizen. The ideal society called communism, therefore, has been considered by Marxists as one in which these four values are equally available to all members of society. The extent

to which such a distribution of values is achieved determines the level of human dignity.

It should be clear to all today that traditional communist states historically did a very poor job in distributing these values in a way which promoted human dignity. Allocations of the four values in traditional Second World states have shown little correspondence to the Marxist ideal. Political power was not shared in a democratic fashion; respect was not provided to all; the level of well-being was generally low and was not always distributed equally among all individuals and groups; and the average communist citizen was not well informed about his or her society and world. In the chapters ahead, we will look at the way in which these important values have been distributed in the past and then make some assessments concerning the problems in and prospects for enhancing human dignity in the Second World states today and in the future.

Politics as the Allocation of Values

A good deal of political science research has been conducted through the years to determine what people value in life and how political systems go about providing these values to their people. In this book we will examine and compare how the four basic values mentioned above have been allocated in Second World systems and then determine how these allocations and the forces that affect them influence the question of human dignity. Although politics can be viewed and defined in many ways, in this book it refers to the process by which the values of *power, respect, well-being,* and *enlightenment* are authoritatively allocated.[5] Because these four values are so central to attempts to construct the new social and political orders associated with communism, they are of central concern throughout this book.

The first value, power, is the ability to influence public policy and concerns the distribution of policy-making rights and responsibilities in a political system. Struggling to wrest political power from the old elitist governments, the communist revolutionaries originally fought for a proletarian dictatorship where the workers would rule. This dictatorship was viewed by Vladimir Ilyich Lenin and other early communist leaders as a temporary stage that would eventually evolve into communism and democracy, where all individuals would participate in the administration of society.

Power is the most significant of the four values because it is very important in determining how the other values will be allocated. In the words of Karl Deutsch, a leading American political scientist:

> Power can be thought of as the instrument by which all other values are obtained, much as a net is used in the catching of fish. . . . Since power functions both as means and end, as net and fish, it is a key value in politics.[6]

The question of power may be the most important question in any society. Power in Second World states, as in all political systems, is the ability to effect political outcomes and influence the allocation of other basic values. Joseph Stalin held dictatorial power and made many personal choices that determined the distribution of power, respect, well-being, and enlightenment in Soviet society during the quarter century of his rule. Because he had so much power, he was able to monopolize the allocation of values in Soviet society and to dictate who could share this power with him. Some Communist Party officials were advanced under Stalin and allowed to share his power at the top of the Party hierarchy; others who were not so fortunate were executed, banished to Siberia, or coercively removed from political life. During Stalin's years, the ideal of worker rule was substantially revised and the idea of one-man, or totalitarian, rule became the guiding principle.

Another value all people desire is respect. Respect refers to the desire of most people to enjoy secure and supportive relationships with others, including political authorities. Respect concerns the status, honor, and prestige given to different individuals and groups, and it also involves the feelings of affection and loyalty afforded to such people. Marxist-Leninist doctrine posited that the workers' revolution and the establishment of socialism would halt the historical exploitation of class over class. In their famous *Communist Manifesto*, Karl Marx and Friedrich Engels argued that the history of all preexisting societies (i.e., slavery, feudalism, capitalism) was the history of class struggle. One class was pitted against another, which resulted in a condition leading to exploitation. In the eyes of Marx and Engels, previous societal forms such as feudalism and capitalism were incapable of promoting the value of respect because of their economic structures and resultant class divisions.

Under socialism and communism, economic classes were supposed to be abolished and the basis for socialist equality established. With no classes, there would be no exploitation, and the people would relate to one another as comrades. As truly human social relations developed in this conflict-free atmosphere, the new consciousness was supposed to facilitate the evolution of the ideal political community called communism and a society devoid of oppression and exploitation. This was theoretically the scenario for communist development; a review of

6

what has really happened in Second World states will provide us the opportunity to compare utopian ideals with realities.

The third value is what we might call social and material well-being. Marx and Engels expected proletarian revolutions to occur and communism to take root in capitalist countries that had already completed the difficult process of industrialization. Accordingly, they expected fairly developed socioeconomic settings in which there would be plenty of food, clothing, and basic material goods. This material abundance would be accompanied by guaranteed social services such as health, welfare, and comfort. The basic principle guiding social relationships in the new communist society was to be "from each according to his abilities, to each according to his needs"; people were to produce what they could and consume what they needed. To Marxists, socialism and communism were expected to contribute more to the general well-being of entire societies than did feudalism and capitalism.

Contrary to Marx and Engels's expectations, however, communist takeovers came in countries with rather backward economies and less-developed socioeconomic systems. With a few exceptions, the states were largely peasant and agrarian rather than industrialized societies, and they were marked by economic backwardness and deprivation. In most of the new Communist Party states, the top priority became one of rapid industrialization, often at the expense of other economic sectors. The backward socioeconomic settings made the task of promoting the social and material good of the people much more difficult than anticipated.

The final value, enlightenment, involves the process by which individuals learn about themselves and the world. Enlightenment is a multifaceted concept and includes psychological, social, and behavioral components. Enlightened citizens, from the traditional communist viewpoint, were considered to be individuals who had cast off the bourgeois mentality of the past, those who had been educated in the principles of Marxism-Leninism and trained to contribute to the building of communism.

We should remind ourselves that Marxist preferences, and Stalinist or reformist communist preferences for that matter, concerning the nature and ideal distribution of these four values—that is, who should get what in terms of *power*, *respect*, *well-being*, and *enlightenment*— are likely to be quite different than our own. Although we may disagree with their preferences, we must recognize them as we set out to study the political process and the leaders' allocation of these values in Second World states.

The Political Process: Goals, Actions, and Outcomes

As in all political systems, political processes in Second World states are marked by a series of *goals*, *actions*, and *outcomes*. Policy makers in the Soviet Union today, for example, are guided (and increasingly divided) by certain *goals* concerning the way political power ought to be distributed; they carry out policy *actions* to accomplish these goals; and, finally, these actions result in political *outcomes* or consequences that may or may not fulfill the desired goals. The political process in the Soviet Union has produced a certain distribution of power and well-being among the populace, but in China, a different set of goals, actions, and outcomes has resulted in a far different distribution of values.

Such a policy approach—examining the relationships among goals, actions, and outcomes—will provide the framework of this book. Many different approaches have been used to examine Second World systems. We will use a policy approach because it emphasizes and sheds light on the critical human and institutional features of politics that influence the allocation of values.

One important factor affecting the allocation of values is the extent of agreement on their proper distribution. No society is blessed with total agreement on how such values as power and well-being ought to be allocated. At one time, many observers believed Marxist-Leninist ideology was a widely accepted blueprint for communist policy makers and that the proper distribution of values was directly deduced from the ideology. Actually, Marxist-Leninist ideology is a blueprint in only the most general sense, and communist decision makers have disagreed violently over conflicting interpretations of the values deduced from their ideology. Although in the past, most people interpreted communist ideology to prohibit private property, a considerable portion of the agricultural land in certain Second World states has always been owned by private farmers. Furthermore, most of the East European states have now legalized private property, and fierce debates are being waged in other Second World states about the need to expand private holding throughout the economies in order to promote economic development.

It should be emphasized that it is not only the general, abstract nature of Marxism-Leninism that has led to varying interpretations of its social and political values but also the personal preferences of the policy makers themselves. Considerable evidence suggests that Vladimir Ilyich Lenin, Joseph Stalin, Mao Zedong, and others preferred the flexibility that the abstract ideology provided; it enabled them to adopt and carry out policies to suit their own purposes or the needs they perceived as their countries'. The same is true for leaders in Second World

societies today. Thus, the differing interpretations of Marxist-Leninist ideology have resulted in surprisingly different value priorities and allocations among the various Second World states.

There are also different interpretations and considerable disagreement among common, everyday citizens of Second World societies about the proper distribution of values—that is, who should get what. Some more democratically inclined citizens feel that policy making is the right of all citizens, but others prefer to leave political power in the hands of a small number of political elites. Indeed, some researchers believe that the latter preference is still widely held in the Soviet Union, where centralized leadership and security are apparently more highly valued by many Soviet citizens than democracy and personal freedom. Although differences of opinion will always exist, political leaders would like to develop among the populace a common set of political attitudes about value distributions. Communist elites traditionally were active in this respect and utilized the Communist Party, schools, the mass media, and a variety of different organizations to try to mold common values among their peoples. Overall, these efforts at political socialization had surprisingly little effect; substantial differences of opinion still exist within each of the countries we will be studying as well as among the different countries. The differences are being accentuated during the present period of change, restructuring, and revolution. Such differences are the basis of political conflict and competition, the very substance of politics.

In the 1917 Bolshevik Revolution, the Russian Marxists espoused and fought for a new distribution of values. These revolutionaries—Vladimir Ilyich Lenin, Joseph Stalin, Leon Trotsky, and others—felt that too many values to which humans aspire, including power, respect, well-being, and enlightenment, were being monopolized by the exploiting class, which they referred to as the bourgeoisie. They waged a revolution to change the old values of the autocratic tsarist system and to reorder the list of priorities to the benefit of the working class.

Recently, many Second World leaders have raised pointed questions about how poorly their states have done in achieving the goals put forth by the original Marxist revolutionaries. We, too, should be raising such questions. For example, why didn't revolutionary and traditional communists improve well-being, broadly distribute power, provide for social equality, and encourage enlightenment within their societies? Are the original goals of the Marxist revolutionaries still being pursued by today's reformist leaders? Are their reforms helping to advance, by new means, the original goals of the revolutionaries, or are they advancing an entirely new set of values independent of Marxism-Leninism?

This book will make the argument that communist states have encountered great difficulties

in the past because they failed to provide the values—particularly, power, respect, well-being, and enlightenment—that they promised to their people. The resulting allocation of values did not promote human dignity in an optimal fashion. As more and more of the people and many of the leaders of these states began to recognize this basic shortcoming in the 1980s, they tried to correct it by seeking alternative policies and institutions. Their discontent brought and continues to bring considerable change to the countries we will be studying in the pages ahead.

Outline of the Book

We will use a plan, or what social scientists call an analytical model, to guide our policy approach to the study of politics in Second World states. The basic features of the model are diagrammed in Figure I.1. Briefly, the plan is to examine the impact of aspects of the environment (e.g., history, economics, political culture)

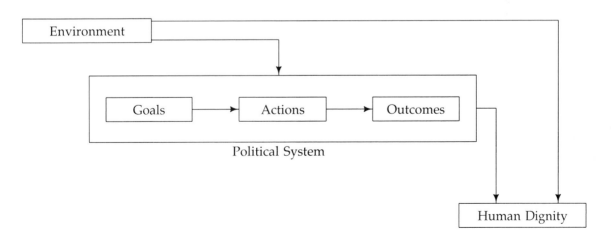

Figure I.1 Diagram of the analytical model.

on the political system. Probing into the political system, we will determine how the policy process—the relationship among goals, actions, and outcomes—and the environment interact to influence the course of human dignity in communist societies today.

The first three chapters of the book focus on the environment. Chapter 1 examines the historical background of the establishment of communism in the sixteen Second World states we will be studying. Chapter 2 reviews the social and economic features of the different states, and Chapter 3 examines political culture—that is, the ideas and values of the people—and the ways political culture is affected by political socialization. These three chapters provide some basis for understanding the impact of what might be called environmental forces on the political process and human dignity.

Chapters 4 to 6 probe into the political system to examine the ways in which political actors and institutions have been involved in the al-location of values. Chapter 4 examines the nature, structure, and roles of Communist Parties as well as recent changes in the traditional one-party system. Chapter 5 concentrates on the nature and structure of the governments and bureaucracies. In Chapter 6, we examine the way in which policies have been made by focusing on policy making and the relationships among goals, actions, and outcomes. By examining some case studies of policy making, we get a clearer idea of the practical aspects of how decisions have been made in Second World systems.

Chapter 7 addresses the issue of political performance by examining how the values of power, respect, well-being, and enlightenment have been allocated and how this affects the human dignity of the people. By examining the relationships between environmental and political forces, we intend to develop a fuller understanding of the determinants of human dignity in the states we are studying.

Notes

1. Richard C. Gripp, *The Political System of Communism* (New York: Dodd, Mead, 1973), pp. 13–14.

2. Because these states in the past thought of themselves as socialist and not yet communist, our reference to them as communist political systems has always been somewhat of a misnomer. Because it is widely done, however, we sometimes use these designations along with such other terms as *socialist*, *Marxist-Leninist*, and *Second World* to describe the states noted above. Referring to these countries as Second World states corresponds with the use of the terms *First World* for the more developed states of North America and Western Eu-rope and *Third World* for the less-developed states of Asia, Africa, and Latin America.

3. Some possible inclusions, such as Afghanistan, Angola, and Mozambique, are not listed here because of the many uncertainties surrounding their strategies of development, or the fact that they disclaim being communist. For an annual review of the established, aspiring, and changing communist states, see Richard Starr, ed., *Yearbook on International Communist Affairs*, 1989 (Stanford, Calif.: Hoover Institution Press, 1989).

4. We should note, however, that communism has always meant different things to different people.

For a consideration of its many conceptions, see Alfred G. Meyer, *Communism*, 4th ed. (New York: Random House, 1984).

5. These values are derived from the eight-value scheme of Harold Lasswell. See *The Future of Policy Science* (New York: Atherton, 1963) and *A Preview of Policy Sciences* (New York: Elsevier, 1971).

6. Karl W. Deutsch, *Politics and Government* (Boston: Houghton Mifflin, 1970), pp. 23–24.

C H A P T E R 1

HISTORICAL SETTING

Karl Marx and the Nineteenth Century

Communist history cannot be understood without studying the man one American journalist called the least funny of the Marx brothers.[1] The philosophy of Karl Marx has had a greater impact on twentieth-century life than any other political philosophy or creed. The son of a Jewish lawyer who later became a Christian, Karl Marx was born in Germany in 1818. During his education at the universities of Bonn and Berlin, he became attracted to the philosophies of Georg Hegel and Ludwig Feuerbach. On graduation, Marx became a political writer and joined the staff of the liberal newspaper *Rheinische Zeitung*. After he was named editor, he became involved in various revolutionary causes and, in protest against the Prussian government, moved to Paris in 1843. In France, Marx undertook the serious study of what he called scientific socialism and met many prominent socialist thinkers. One not so prominent at that particular time but who later became one of the era's great radical philosophers was another German, Friedrich Engels.

Engels, the son of a wealthy German manufacturer, had been sent abroad by his father to oversee the family's business interests. While earning his livelihood from the system he so vigorously condemned, Engels came to France where he became involved in socialist thinking and writing. When he met Marx, they formed a deep bond that lasted through Marx's lifetime.

In 1848 Marx and Engels wrote one of the most important political documents of modern history. This document was a short but stirring call to arms for the working class and became the creed of the Communist Party. Known as the *Communist Manifesto*, it contains the immortal words: *"Workers of the world unite! The proletarians have nothing to lose but their chains."* In concise, ringing language, the *Communist Manifesto* sets forth the basic tenets of Marxist philosophy. Telling of the bourgeoisie's (the owners') exploitation of the proletariat (the workers), Marx predicted a proletarian uprising and an end to capitalism and exploitation.

Marx returned to Germany for a short time following publication of the *Manifesto* but was tried for sedition and expelled from the country in 1849. He then went to England, where he remained for the rest of his life. During his years in Great Britain, Marx worked long hours in the reading room of the British Museum on his chief endeavor, *Das Kapital*. Although the first volume appeared in 1867, the second and third volumes did not appear until after his death in 1883. In contrast to the *Communist Manifesto*, which is a rousing declaration, *Das Kapital* is a mammoth, plodding, scientific study of capitalism that describes its origins and its predicted demise. Because his writings and theories were based on observed facts, Marx wanted to distinguish himself from the utopian socialists. He believed he had developed a scientific theory of socialism. The utopians hoped for socialism; his theory predicted that it was inevitable.[2]

Marx's lifelong endeavor was to discover the laws of human and social development and to provide evidence of their scientific validity. Believing that the world was governed by predictable forces, he spent most of his life trying to understand them. He had a voracious appetite for reading and his typical day in the British Museum began early and ended late. During this exhaustive research he reached several important conclusions.

According to Marx, all traditional societies— for example, feudal or capitalist—were divided into two main classes. Because the interests of these two classes were constantly at odds, they were involved in class struggle. The *Manifesto* notes:

The history of all hitherto existing society is the history of class struggles. Freeman and slave, patrician and plebeian, lord and serf, guildmaster and journeyman, in a word, op-

pressor and oppressed, stood in constant competition to one another.[3]

In nineteenth-century Europe, the class struggle between the bourgeoisie (those in control of the means of production) and proletariat (the working class) was generated by the Industrial Revolution. Capitalism had developed in Europe and although economic development soared, great human costs were incurred. Those in control of the means of production were exploiting the working class in the production process. According to Marx, the proletariat had no means of production and were forced to sell their labor to live. Marx predicted that the exploited working class would develop a political consciousness and throw off the ruling bourgeoisie. This revolution would result in a new form of society—a form called socialist— in which the working class would rule. Because classes would be dissolved, exploitation and class struggle would disappear. This societal form would finally evolve into communism, a perfect state free of classes, exploitation, material scarcity, and government coercion.

Marx was a man of his times. He lived in nineteenth-century Europe and observed some of the worst features of industrialization. Attracted from the countryside to the cities, the new working class was subjected to treatment incomprehensible by today's standards. Because labor unions and collective bargaining had not developed, the proletarian class had no voice against the powerful bourgeoisie, was paid subsistence wages, and lived in deprivation and poverty.

As a humanitarian and social scientist, Marx was forced to rebel against the injustices he saw. Not a man of the sword, although he believed in violence, he utilized the written word to call attention to the degraded state of mankind. Marx wanted the quality of life to be im-

Karl Marx (1818–83), seen here with his eldest daughter, Jenny, was described by some as a warmly affectionate family man. Because of his radical political views, Marx was forced to leave his native Germany. After meeting his collaborator Friedrich Engels (1820–95), Marx settled in England, where he prepared his major works.

proved for the impoverished masses and he wished to develop a theory that demonstrated improvement was not only possible but inevitable and scientifically predictable.

Before his death in London in 1883, Marx experienced constant hardship and frustration. He and his family lived near the poverty level and suffered from poor housing, lack of nutrition, and inadequate medical care. His two sons and a daughter may have died as a result of these conditions. He was often without any means of subsistence and had to rely on the financial support of his friend and collaborator, Engels.[4]

But to Marx, the physical suffering was minor compared with his broken dream of proletarian revolution. Marx hoped and predicted that workers' uprisings would occur in nineteenth-century Europe. By his death, however, there had been no major proletarian revolution and no founding of a Marxist state. Although we must acknowledge Marx's contribution to the beginning of modern social science analysis, we must also recognize that he was a product of the period in which he lived and was limited by it. It is obvious that he did not predict many of the developmental nuances of the twentieth century.

By the end of the nineteenth century, socialism and revolution were discussed by students, workers, revolutionaries, and other interested observers across the continent. Throughout the coffeehouses of Europe, revolutionaries of different viewpoints and motives plotted to end the injustices they perceived around them. Many were without direction, lacking either political theory or power; others found inspiration and guidance in the writings of Marx and had firm ideas on how power could be obtained. One such individual was the Russian, Vladimir Ilyich Ulyanov, later to become known by the pseudonym Lenin.[5] Born in Simbirsk (renamed Ulyanovsk), Russia, in 1870, Lenin was the son of a school inspector and a teacher. Although the Ulyanov family was of an apparently conservative and religious background, the children were radical and became involved in a plot to overthrow the tsarist autocracy. Lenin's sister, Anna, and brother, Alexander, were arrested

14

on charges of belonging to a revolutionary organization conspiring to kill the tsar. Alexander
was hanged in 1887 along with four fellow con-
spirators for his complicity in the abortive plot.

One year later, in 1888, Lenin was introduced
to Marxism and before long began writing revolutionary materials that plotted the overthrow
of the tsarist government. Traveling between
St. Petersburg, the capital of tsarist Russia, and
the nations of Europe, Lenin established his
credentials as a Marxist and a revolutionary.
On his return to Russia in 1897, he was arrested
and sent to Siberia, where he was incarcerated
until 1900.

By the spring of 1900, Lenin was a free man
in the city of St. Petersburg (renamed Leningrad

Vladimir Ilyich Lenin (seated, third from left) with fellow revolutionaries prior to 1917.

in 1924). Dedicated to the overthrow of the autocracy that had imprisoned him and had executed his brother, Lenin plotted with other Russian Marxists. When he returned to exile in Switzerland and Germany, he published the article "What Is to Be Done?" in the party journal, *Iskra* (The Spark). In that article, he argued for a small, centralized, revolutionary organization to lead the uprising, as opposed to a broad-based, mass movement. The plan was accepted by a faction of the Russian Marxists, who adopted the name Bolsheviks, and Marxism was soon put to the test.

The Bolshevik Insurrection

At the beginning of the twentieth century, the autocracy of Russia under Tsar Nicholas II was in serious trouble. Europe was industrializing and generally prospering, but Russia, always comparatively backward, was falling further and further behind. Economic difficulties, including a scarcity of food and consumer goods, declining services, and poor wages, were worsened by ill-advised military ventures. The Russo-Japanese War of 1904–05 proved an embarrassing defeat to Imperialist Russia and a great drain on her available resources. Then, Russia became involved in World War I at enormous cost, and the human and physical resources of the state were further depleted.[6]

During the 1907–17 period, Russian Marxists were a disorganized, faction-ridden organization, unprepared to assume political power or even to apply pressure to the failing tsarist regime. Many were in exile (Lenin) or imprisoned (Stalin); most of the remainder were involved in ideological disputes and intraparty fighting. One major conflict among the Marxists was between the Bolsheviks and the Mensheviks. Whereas the Mensheviks favored a broad-based

movement and a more evolutionary path to power, the Bolsheviks were inclined toward a small, conspiratorial movement that could assume power quickly and decisively. Led by Lenin, the Bolsheviks prevailed over all other revolutionary and opposition movements and brought about the communist takeover.

The stage was set for a Bolshevik victory with the abdication of Tsar Nicholas II in February 1917 and the political vacuum that followed. Power was assumed by the noncommunist but democratic-liberal and socialist Provisional Government under Alexander Kerensky's leadership. By November 1917, however, it too had proved incapable of quickly resolving Russia's difficulties. Returning from Switzerland to St. Petersburg in April 1917, Lenin organized the insurrection. Under his leadership, the Bolsheviks prepared for their takeover by appealing to the masses with such slogans as "Bread, Peace, Land" and by organizing a conspiratorial military organization. Careful planning, utilization of a new organizational weapon (the Communist Party), the use of armed force and propaganda, and the revolutionary leadership all aided in the successful seizure of the Winter Palace on the night of November 7, 1917. The initial Bolshevik victory in St. Petersburg was incredibly easy: The provisional government had few answers and little support; the Russian army had been so consumed by World War I that it had no energy or inclination to try to keep power from the revolutionaries; and other opposition and revolutionary groups were largely ineffective. Suddenly in power, Lenin was confronted with almost insurmountable economic and social problems as he began the construction of the first Marxist state.

It may appear surprising that the tsarist regime and the traditional political structure could be toppled by such a small band of untested revolutionaries. But the victory was neither as difficult nor as easy as it may seem. Imperial Russia was a sick and dying state; even if it had been able to cope with the challenges of modernization, its entanglement in World War I proved costly. This situation left the Bolsheviks with a vulnerable opponent, and when the political vacuum developed in 1917, the organized, determined, and politically astute communists grasped power. The revolution was not easy in the sense that major difficulties for the Bolsheviks came after they had seized power, not from the defeated tsarist autocracy, but rather from other groups (Mensheviks, Socialist Revolutionaries, many anticommunist groups) that challenged the Marxist leaders. Although the Bolsheviks had grasped power, a struggle for the rule of Russia would continue for many years.

To the Bolsheviks' dismay, the writings of Marx were of little help in the ensuing years. Although Marx went to great lengths to explain the impending fall of capitalism and the victory of socialism, he wrote little *about the nature and construction of socialism* and, therefore, was of minimal help to the new Russian leaders as they began their difficult task. As a result, Lenin and the communist leaders had to set out largely on their own. Their problem was worsened because Russia was not "prepared" for the socialist victory, in the sense that it had not gone through, although it definitely had begun, the capitalist stage of industrialization and development. According to Marx, socialism would triumph after capitalism had outlived its usefulness. But the Bolsheviks' seizure of power came before Russia had completed that important stage of development. As a result, Lenin and his fellow leaders had to complete Russia's industrialization before they could devote their attention to the construction of communism.

Other pressing problems also confronted the Bolsheviks in the immediate postrevolutionary period. World War I continued to drain Russian resources. In addition, Bolshevik rule was not readily accepted throughout the Russian state, and a bloody civil war broke out (1918–21) that saw Western intervention (including the United States) on the side of the anticommunist forces. Subsequently, Western hostility and suspicion of the Bolsheviks and communism precluded the possibility of assistance from abroad. So, although the Bolshevik victory of 1917 placed the Marxists in power, it in no way guaranteed the future success of communism.

Lenin's first objective was to get Russia out of World War I. On March 3, 1918, Russia signed the Treaty of Brest-Litovsk, obtaining peace with the Central Powers in return for yielding valuable land and resources. The communist leaders then began consolidating the homeland. During the Civil War, opposition movements were eliminated as the Communist Party moved to assert dictatorial control. Then, to facilitate economic recovery, the leaders adopted the New Economic Policy (NEP) (1921–28) that permitted a partial return to private enterprise and eventually got the economy back on its feet.

During the postrevolutionary construction years, the communist leaders were concerned with survival, both of the state and of their regime. The Communist Party became a leading organizational tool for consolidating power and organizing political rule. In these building years, the ideals of proletarian rule and democracy were lost among the pressing needs for survival. According to most Western observers, the ideal of a dictatorship of the proletariat in which the workers were supposed to rule became in reality a dictatorship of the Party.[7]

After the death of Lenin in 1924, this dictatorship invested increasing power in the hands of one man, Joseph Stalin. Although a dying Lenin warned the Party against Stalin's ascendancy to power, a struggle ensued and Stalin

Joseph Stalin (1879–1953) delivers an order to his foreign minister, Vyacheslav M. Molotov, at Yalta in 1945. Stalin placed the USSR on the road to becoming an industrial and military power, but his oppressive rule cost greatly in terms of social welfare, democracy, and human rights and took Soviet ideology far afield from classic Marxism.

soon achieved dominance. During his rule (1926–53), Stalin revised Marxism in many ways. Differences in degree grew into differences of kind. The combination of environmental forces (for example, the need to industrialize) and Stalin's pathological character resulted in a highly centralized, totalitarian state. Most observers agree that Stalin's imprint on Marxism during these formative years of development took communism far afield of the more humanitarian theories of Marx, and this Stalinist brand of communism was exported to Eastern Europe and China at the end of World War II.[8]

At the time of the Bolshevik victory, the Russian leaders expected victorious revolutions elsewhere in Europe.[9] During the early 1920s, optimism about this possibility began to fade. The recognition that these victories would not occur quickly or easily was made official by Stalin in 1924 when he formulated his famous "socialism in one country" doctrine. According to this doctrine, attempts to promote world revolution would be abandoned.[10] Because capitalism had temporarily stabilized itself, it was better to turn inward and concentrate efforts on building Russia into a bastion of socialism.

Closely tied to the Bolshevik victory was the establishment in 1921 of the second Communist Party state, Mongolia. Dominated through history by both Imperial Russia and Imperial China because of its unfortunate location between the two more powerful countries, Mongolia finally gained statehood in 1911. Shortly thereafter, the Russian Civil War brought Red Army troops to Mongolian soil. Using Mongolia as a base of operations, renegade White Russian bands were tracked down and destroyed by the Red Army and the partisan Mongols. In 1921, the victors established the Provisional Revolutionary Mongol People's Republic. Since that time, the Soviet and Mongolian states have had close ties and relations.

Although Marxist states were established in Russia and Mongolia early in the century, no other revolutions were successfully carried out until after World War II. But the absence of new Marxist states did not mean the absence of communist revolutionary activity. The most violent, intense, and significant activity occurred behind the Great Wall of China.

Revolution in China

A powerful determinant of present-day diversity in communist states is the past. Examining this point, one scholar argues that the remarkable differences between Chinese and Russian revolutionary outcomes can be attributed in large part to the influence of distinct prerevolutionary sociopolitical structures and patterns of economic development. According to Theda Skocpol, old regime structures helped to shape specific variations in the revolutionary outcomes not merely by surviving but also by influencing the communists' consolidation and use of state power.[11] China's prerevolutionary experience was certainly of great importance.

China's ruling tradition was one of upper-class government, the city ruled over the countryside through a network of local gentry and warlords, and the few ruled over the many. To the peasant, the central government seemed remote and unconcerned with the problems of the masses. A Chinese folk poem expresses what must have been the feelings of the masses.

We work when the sun rises,
We rest when the sun sets.
We dig wells for drink,
We plow the land for food.
What has the Emperor to do with us?

The institutions of family, gentry, and government perpetuated ancient Confucian traditions and provided the mortar that gave China its long, stable history.[12] But the events of the nineteenth century drastically changed the course of Chinese history. Conceived of by its leaders and the masses as the Central Kingdom, China was now battered by Western imperialism, resulting in intense national humiliation. This was intensified in the latter part of the century by unequal treaties imposed on China by the European powers and by her defeat to Japan in the Sino-Japanese War (1894–95). During this period, parts of China, such as Hong Kong and Shanghai, became Western colonies, where the local populace was subject to foreign law. Evidence of this is the now-famous photograph of a sign in a city park of Shanghai: NO CHINESE OR DOGS ALLOWED!

The twentieth century presented not only the dawn of a new Chinese culture but, more importantly, the birth of Chinese nationalism. One of the leaders of this movement was Dr. Sun Yat-sen, a radical but compassionate politician, educated in the Chinese classics and Western medicine. In 1911, the Manchu dynasty was toppled. Sun assumed leadership and established a Chinese republic based on democracy, socialism, and nationalism. The revolutionary's accomplishment brought about the end of more than 2,000 years of dynastic rule in China, but even he was unable to cope with the political, social, and economic problems that contributed to the fall of the Manchus. One major problem was posed by the warlords. From 1916 to 1926, China was torn by strife among provincial dictators, who pitted Chinese against Chinese in their greed for increased power and wealth. Combined with the humiliation at the hands of the imperialist European powers, this internal conflict made it difficult for Sun and his supporters to unite the Chinese and promote social and political development.

By the second decade of the twentieth century, China found a more interested and active sector of the Chinese population committed to speak out against foreign and domestic exploitation. In the spring of 1919, large groups took to the streets to protest foreign domination and imperialism. Known as the May Fourth Movement, a wave of patriotism touched off street demonstrations and political harangues that motivated the Chinese delegation to refuse to sign the Treaty of Versailles at the 1919 Paris Peace Conference, an agreement that would have legitimated and prolonged foreign imperialism in China.

In the early part of the century, several Chinese scholars became acquainted with Marxism and other varieties of socialism, and interest grew when the antiquated Russian autocracy was overthrown in 1917. Many Chinese intellectuals followed the events in Russia closely and began to study the Russian experiment with Marxism; one was Li Dazhao[13] (1888–1927), a history professor and chief librarian at Beijing University. While studying Marxism, Li met with students in his office, which became known as the Red Chamber. One of the young intellectuals attending these meetings was Mao Zedong, a man soon to take a leading role in the growing Chinese drama.

A major reason for the growing appeal of Marxism-Leninism in China resulted from the Soviet position in imperialism. To many Chinese intellectuals, Marxism-Leninism represented the key to Chinese development. It told them how to be scientific and "modern" in dealing with the problems of development and how to be uncompromisingly anti-imperialist and nationalist in being Chinese. Soon Russian agents from the Communist International (Comintern) arrived in China to aid Chinese Marxist-Leninists in promoting communism. In July 1921, the Chinese Communist Party (CCP) was established and a new actor joined the revolutionary cast.

The Russian Comintern agents advised the Chinese communists to form a united front with the Nationalists [Kuomintang (KMT)], which was under the leadership of Dr. Sun Yat-sen.

Mao Zedong (1893–1976) on the reviewing stand at a mass political rally in Beijing. After establishing communism in China in 1949 by ousting Chiang Kai-shek and the Nationalists, Mao developed a more radical brand of communism, and split with the Soviets in the early 1960s.

Although the native communists found this a bitter pill to swallow because they preferred to organize for revolution on their own, it was sweetened somewhat by the fact that the Nationalists were also committed anti-imperialists. The alliance, although often shaky, lasted through Sun's death in 1925 and the rise of his successor, Chiang Kai-shek. However, in April 1927, Chiang turned on the communists in Shanghai, slaughtered them by the thousands, and established himself as the head of the new Chinese government. Stalin then ordered the Chinese communists to seize power, but this only resulted in the killing of more communists. After Stalin's disastrous plans led to the eviction of all Soviet advisers and a new annihilation of the Chinese communists, the CCP grew more estranged from the Russian communists.

It was during this period that Mao advanced to power. Through a trial-and-error process, Mao groomed the CCP into a political force that would redirect the course of Chinese history. In 1934, Nationalist military pressure forced the CCP troops to take an epic trek—the Long March—across 6,000 miles of difficult terrain. One-hundred-thousand Chinese began the march; only 20,000 survived. The conclusion of the Long March, in the northern city of Yanan in the province of Shaanxi, began an important stage of CCP development, commonly called the Yanan period. During these years, Mao consolidated his power within the Party and formulated the ideological and military plans that would carry the communists to victory. Building on the power of human will, Mao engaged the CCP in a "proletarian revolution" in a peasant society which lacked any semblance of capitalist infrastructure. Mao and the CCP called on the power of the Chinese peasantry to accomplish what was theoretically impossible: the founding of a Marxist state in China.

Chinese involvement in World War II aided the communists' ascendancy to power. When Japan brutally invaded China beginning in 1937, Chiang Kai-shek was faced with an important decision—whether to concentrate his forces and efforts against the Japanese, which he referred to as a disease of the skin and body, or against Mao and the communists, which he considered a disease of the heart and spirit. Considering the latter the more pressing evil, Chiang set out once again to destroy the CCP forces. While the Nationalist and communist forces were engaged in a civil war, Japan launched a relentless attack on the Chinese mainland that destroyed Chinese industrial capabilities and caused widespread suffering. Under such conditions, the Nationalist government had limited capabilities, few answers, and even less success at resolving the pressing social and economic difficulties facing the Chinese people. The government and KMT Party under Chiang were marked by corruption and were out of touch with the Chinese masses. At the same time, the war gave Mao and the CCP time to consolidate their forces, to appeal to the Chinese intellectuals and masses, to fight the Japanese, and, ultimately, to build up their strength to challenge and defeat the Nationalists. Just as World War I encouraged the downfall of tsarist Russia, World War II did the same to Nationalist China.

With the Japanese surrender in 1945, the communists and the Nationalists tried to negotiate an agreement to end their conflict. Although the United States attempted to mediate the dispute, the negotiations failed and the two factions reverted to a state of civil war. Although the Nationalists had superior equipment and support, the communists were able to draw on the vast Chinese populace to defeat Chiang's forces. The Nationalists retreated to the Chinese island of Taiwan (Formosa) and in 1949 the communists controlled the entire Chinese mainland. It was at this time that the People's Republic of China (PRC) was formed.

The Russian and Chinese revolutionary experiences were quite different. Whereas the Bolshevik takeover occurred quickly and the real test of the new leaders came after the revolution, the Chinese takeover took several decades.[14] This meant that when Mao and his comrades finally took office in 1949, they had been tested under fire. They were a united, cohesive, militarized group. Because they had won power on their own, they were loath to have someone else dictate to them concerning their postrevolutionary development. As we will see, who wins power is of considerable importance in determining who gives orders after power is won.

Following World War II, China's neighbor, Korea, also became communist. Similar to the division and occupation of Germany after World War I, Korea was divided at the 38th parallel into northern and southern zones with the USSR and the United States serving as occupational powers. During the three-year Soviet occupation of the North (1945–48), the Red Army installed communist-oriented leaders to manage the affairs of the occupied zone. The head of the communist government was Kim Il Sung, a military figure who had fought along with the USSR in World War II. The Soviets initially set up a coalition government—the North Korean Provisional People's Committee—before establishing a more monolithic communist regime. Although the Korean communists were not initially in a particularly strong position, Soviet assistance and the fusion of the socialists and communists into the Workers' Party provided the necessary power base to ensure a communist government in North Korea. In 1950, the communist regime of North Korea attempted to take over South Korea; this brought about U.S.

and U.N. military involvement on the side of South Korea and Chinese involvement on the side of North Korea. When the Korean armistice was signed on July 27, 1953, the division of Korea into a communist North and noncommunist South was perpetuated.

Communists Come to Power in Eastern Europe

Perhaps more so than in Asia, World War II markedly altered the political setting of Eastern Europe. Before the war, none of the Eastern states were communist; within a few years of the war's conclusion, all eight countries were governed by communist regimes.[15] What had happened in this short span to prepare the way for communism? We can identify two distinct patterns: (1) Communist Parties winning power during World War II, principally through their own internal efforts (Yugoslavia and Albania); and (2) Parties obtaining power through the occupation, pressure, and assistance of the Soviet Union (Czechoslovakia, Poland, Romania, East Germany, Bulgaria, and Hungary).

Communist Victory from Within

Yugoslavia is a state of recent political origin. Prior to World War I, the South Slavic peoples—who comprise contemporary Yugoslavia—were subjects of larger European empires or lived in independent states. Most of the southern part of the land area was under the administration of the Ottoman Empire, whereas the north was part of the Austro-Hungarian Empire. From the ashes of World War I came a new state, the Kingdom of Serbs, Croats, and Slovenes, later—in 1929—to be called Yugoslavia.

The South Slavic ethnic groups of this new state represented different cultures, languages, religions, and traditions. The northern part of the country used the Latin alphabet, was Catholic, and was mostly Western in culture and tradition; the southern part was inhabited by nationalities who used the Cyrillic alphabet, were Orthodox or Moslem in religious faith, and held more to Eastern cultures and traditions. This complex mix of nationalities and ethnic groups generated intense conflict in Yugoslavia between the two world wars. To quell such conflict, unite the country, and move the state toward its goals, autocratic King Alexander established a dictatorship in 1929. This centralized form of government only exacerbated the existing problems and undermined still further the regime's fading support.

Through the 1920s and 1930s, a small group of Yugoslavs were attracted to Marxist philosophy and what it might do for Yugoslavia. One such individual was Josip Broz, later known as Tito, a young man who had been wounded fighting for the Austrians in World War I and had been taken to Russia as a prisoner of war. On his release in Russia, he became interested in the Bolshevik cause and later returned to Yugoslavia to promote the ideals of socialism and communism. Although King Alexander outlawed the Communist Party, Tito and the Yugoslav communists were able to organize a secret Party that relied on Moscow for guidance and direction.

On March 25, 1941, the government under Prince Paul, who replaced the King after his assassination in Marseilles, signed the Tripartite Pact guaranteeing collaboration with the Nazis. In the national uproar that followed, the army revolted, deposed the government, and repudiated the pact. Yugoslavia virtually was without a government until the end of the war. In its place, various movements organized, including the Chetnik movement representing the Serbs and the Ustashi, which was pro-Nazi and primarily Croatian. But the most successful was the communist movement led by Josip Broz Tito.[16]

Tito and the communist partisans, gaining considerable support from all the South Slavic groups of Yugoslavia, waged a courageous battle against the Nazis as well as against such other anticommunist Yugoslav forces as the Chetniks. Because Tito and the communists were perceived by the West as the most effective force against the Nazis, they ultimately won the backing of the Allied Powers. After years of guerrilla warfare in the mountains of central Yugoslavia, the victorious partisans recaptured the land from the Nazis and quickly established a Communist Party state. This was all accomplished with little aid or advice from the hardpressed Soviets, a fact significantly affecting the Yugoslav experience as a socialist state.

The communists' advent to power in Albania was closely tied to the Yugoslav movement. During World War II, Albania was occupied by Italy and later Germany. As in Yugoslavia, various resistance groups arose, one communist-inspired. This movement received both aid and advice from Yugoslav emissaries and, under the leadership of Enver Hoxha, seized power in 1941 and has held it to the present day. The fraternal ties that originally characterized Albanian and Yugoslavian relations, however, soon deteriorated into fear and suspicion. Today, Albania is a small, undeveloped enclave on the southern boundary of Yugoslavia.

Communist Victory from Without

During and following World War II, the Soviet Union was instrumental in uniting antifascist groups and, subsequently, for eliminating noncommunist alternatives and placing Communist

Party regimes in power in the remaining six East European states. In view of Soviet military predominance in the area at the end of the war, the USSR was in a strong position to determine the character of the postwar governments in these liberated states. The Teheran Conference of 1943 and the Yalta and Potsdam conferences of 1945 gave the Soviet Union great freedom in determining the political character of postwar Eastern Europe. Some contend that it could have gone so far as to incorporate the liberated areas into the USSR.[17]

The Soviets chose not to adopt the more radical policy of incorporating these European states into the Soviet Union; instead, they opted for the more gradual policy of national fronts. This meant that the governments in the liberated states were to be reconstituted into coalition governments with the communists sharing power; at the proper moment, the communists were to seize complete control. Although there are certain similarities in all cases, there are sufficient differences to warrant brief discussion of each.

The communists' advent to power in Czechoslovakia occurred under unique circumstances. In the prewar Czechoslovak state, the communists were an influential and respected political party. Liquidated by Adolph Hitler in 1939, the Czechoslovak government under the noncommunist President, Eduard Beneš, went into exile in London for the duration of the war. But back at home, the Czech and particularly the Slovak communists formed underground resistance movements to fight against the Nazis. While in London, the Czechoslovak government maintained good relations with both the Soviet and the home communists and, with the liberation of the country, President Beneš returned to preside over a coalition government with strong communist representation. Although the coalition appeared to be working well, the communists staged a coup in 1948 (strong Soviet involvement was suspected) and occupied broadcasting stations, government buildings, and other key power organs. Quickly and decisively the coalition was transformed into a solid Communist Party regime under the leadership of Klement Gottwald.

Like Czechoslovakia, the prewar Polish government went into exile in London during World War II. Resisting the Nazis at home under terrible odds were the Home Army and underground government. These resistance forces recognized, and were recognized by, the Polish government in exile. Although this noncommunist government initially maintained reasonably good relations with the Soviet Union, a series of disputes ensued, resulting in full Soviet support of the Polish communists. In 1942, a group of Polish communists traveled from Moscow to occupied Poland to join the native communists who had stayed at home. One of these who came from Moscow was Wladyslaw Gomulka, who was to become the head of the postwar Soviet-oriented regime. As the Nazis were driven from the country, a predominantly communist Committee of National Liberation was formed to administer the liberated areas. Following the full liberation of the country, the Committee acted as a provisional government and assumed control of the Polish state. Although the Western powers intervened at the 1945 Yalta Conference and succeeded in having representatives of the London government included, the communists retained predominant influence. With the help of the Soviet Union, local communists were eventually successful in eliminating political opposition and in placing Gomulka and his associates in full control.

As in the Polish case, the takeover in Romania was a relatively protracted process occurring at the end of World War II. The takeover began with the Soviet Red Army's "liberation" of the

country from Nazi occupation and Soviet diplomatic pressures based on the national-front
policy. This included disarming the Romanian
army, prohibiting noncommunist political parties, and severely restricting political suffrage.
Western pressure in 1945 again added noncommunists to the coalition government but dominant power remained in the hands of the communists under the leadership of Peter Groza.
Elections held in an atmosphere of communist
intimidation, the arrest of opposition leaders,
and the abdication of King Michael placed communists in a position of power under the Sec-
retary-General of their Party, Gheorghe
Gheorghiu-Dej.

In East Germany, the Soviet Red Army was
the sole occupying power following the war
and automatically was placed in a position of
exclusive control. Walter Ulbricht, a German
who had returned from Moscow to Berlin with
the Red Army, assumed the key ruling position
in the new government. Although political parties continued to exist and performed certain
political and administrative functions, the occupying Soviet officials and German communists
assumed total control. In October 1949, the
German Democratic Republic (East Germany)
was formed and the dedicated communist, Ulbricht, and his monolithic Socialist Unity Party
were firmly in command.

The Soviet Red Army entered Bulgaria on
September 8, 1944, and departed late in 1947.
During that three-year period, domestic anticommunist opposition was crushed and dominant political control of the Bulgarian Communist Party was assured. The day after the
Red Army's intervention in 1944, a Soviet-
backed coup brought power to a socialist movement called the Fatherland Front. Under the
leadership of General Kimon Georgiev, a government was formed that placed communists
in key leadership positions. After a series of

political purges and pressure tactics, the communist-dominated Fatherland Front won 78
percent of the vote in the 1946 elections. This
new Bulgarian government was headed by a
former General-Secretary of the Comintern, a
longtime communist and friend of the Soviets,
Georgi Dimitrov.

As in Bulgaria, Soviet intervention in Hungary
placed native communists on the inside track
to power. Because Hungary had taken an active
part in military operations against the Soviet
Union, the Red Army took an aggressive position concerning postwar political developments. The occupying Soviet Army purged
noncommunist leaders, accused many of collaboration with the Nazis, and, by 1947, had
moved Hungarian Marxists into power, including the leader of the Hungarian communists, Mátyás Rákosi. Having spent 16 years in
Hungarian prisons for being a communist, Rákosi was now intent on achieving absolute power
in the postwar Hungarian state. Although noncommunist parties initially had considerable
influence (in the open election of 1945 the
Smallholders Party's victory led to the formation
of a noncommunist coalition), Rákosi and the
Soviets soon achieved a dominant position
through the controlled 1947 elections.

Suddenly and somewhat unexpectedly, the
political character of Eastern Europe was radically transformed. The proud young states of
pre–World War II Europe were now cast behind
what became known as the Iron Curtain. The
Soviet Union's strategy had succeeded remarkably well in establishing communist regimes in its neighboring states of Europe. It
had established a buffer zone, which helped
calm Soviet fears of German invasion and of
American aid to a resurgent Europe. Caught
up in their own concerns of postwar reconstruction, the Western powers were slow to
react. Soviet involvement in and control of

Eastern Europe was so complete and so successful that by the time the West fully recognized what had been done, diplomatic action was hopeless. A military response from the Western powers would have undoubtedly brought another violent military conflict. In its place, the Cold War developed—a period of extreme ideological hostility and enmity between the West and the Communist Party states of Europe.

The Special Cases of Cuba and Southeast Asia

Given its proximity to the United States and the continuing acrimony in United States–Cuban relations, the establishment of a communist government in Cuba takes on special interest and meaning. Closely tied to and highly dependent on the United States, pre-Castro Cuba was run by an unpopular and corrupt dictator named Fulgencio Batista. Fidel Castro, a gifted revolutionary who had apparently not yet become a Marxist or communist in the 1950s, plotted and then fought against the dictatorship in an effort to promote representative democracy. As a result of growing Cuban sympathy and the support of other groups and sectors in Latin America and even in the United States, Castro was able to stage a successful revolution against Batista's corrupt and inefficient army.

Castro and his minuscule force of less than 100 persons (subsequently reduced to around a tenth of that) began their takeover with an invasion from Mexico in 1956. Basing their guerrilla warfare in the Cuban mountainous region of the Sierra Maestra, Castro and his forces attacked depots, cities, bases, and other key targets throughout the country. With growing popular support and revolutionary power, Castro forced the Batista regime to surrender in January 1959 and took over the reins of government. Unlike so many of the other countries discussed, the Cuban countryside was not in a state of total revolution and disorder. Rather, Castro was able to take over a country with a flourishing economy and a relatively healthy populace.

Contrary to considerable opinion, available evidence suggests that the Cuban revolution was not initially directed by a Communist Party or by any political or ideological organization other than Castro's nationalistic, revolutionary band. Apparently, at that time, Castro did not consider himself a Marxist-Leninist.[18] Although there was a Cuban communist group, known as the Popular Socialist Party, the first contact between it and Castro's forces did not take place until 1958. The communists were extremely skeptical of Castro's movement and placed their faith in a popular-front strategy that would unite all anti-Batista forces.

At what point Castro, or Castro's Cuba, became communist is still debatable. Castro was and is a radical with a deep desire for the social transformation of Cuba, but he is not a disciplined communist in the sense of being a strict adherent to Marxism-Leninism or the Soviet Union. Although communist ideology played a minor role in the revolution and the initial period of Cuban transformation, that soon changed. It seems clear in retrospect that Castro felt Cuban socialism was threatened by the United States in such challenges as the U.S.-supported invasion in 1961, known as the Bay of Pigs, which prompted him to turn to Soviet patronage and, thus, eventually to Soviet-style communism.

The territory today known as Vietnam had been under French control since the late nineteenth century. During World War II, the rather larger area of Indochina was the scene of warfare between national troops under Ho Chi Minh and the Japanese occupational forces. With the defeat of the Japanese and the withdrawal of the Chinese Nationalist troops from the northern part of the Indochinese peninsula, Ho established the Democratic Republic of Vietnam (North Vietnam). At first, the French accorded it provisional recognition; then, negotiations broke down and the Ho regime initiated military action against French forces and the South Vietnamese (September 2, 1945). Carrying on a people's war, Ho and the Vietnamese communists were involved in almost constant struggle for the next quarter of a century, first against France (1946–54) and later against the United States. The United States had come to the aid of the South Vietnamese in the 1960s. On April 30, 1975, the American forces were withdrawn from Vietnam. Under the party leadership of First Secretary Le Duan (Ho Chi Minh had died in 1969), the North Vietnamese entered Saigon and brought an end to the partition of Vietnam.

Generally refused an enclave on Cambodian soil by the royalist government under Prince Norodom Sihanouk, Ho Chi Minh's Cambodian communist allies spent most of their time exiled in North Vietnam. With Lon Nol's successful right-wing coup against Sihanouk in 1970, about 1,000 Cambodian communists returned home to wage war against the new republic under Nol. The bloody war that had been raging in Vietnam during the 1960s and had spread to Laos now engulfed Cambodia as well. Old and new revolutionaries, known as the Khmer Rouge resistance movement, waged a relentless guerrilla war against the new and weak Cambodian Republic supported by the United States. The revolutionaries, under Pol Pot, won the conflict and ousted Lon Nol in 1975 and adopted a new constitution the next year that established an independent state called Democratic Kampuchea. The Pol Pot regime used extreme bru-

tality, killing millions, to impose terror and a rigid ideology in this once peaceful land. Finally, in December 1978, the Vietnamese communists invaded and occupied Kampuchea and installed a puppet regime headed by President Heng Samrin. Talks took place and agreements were signed in 1989, intended to end Vietnam's occupation of Cambodia.

During the Vietnamese conflict, the Laotian communist movement, known as the Pathet Lao, controlled the northeastern section of Laos bordering on North Vietnam. Advised and supplied by the North Vietnamese, the Pathet Lao exploited the ineptitude and weakness of the royalist government and spread its control over an expanding portion of the country. Finally, in December 1975, the Lao People's Revolutionary Party emerged from the coalition government to abolish the monarchy and establish the Lao People's Democratic Republic.

It should be apparent by now that the establishment of communist regimes in Vietnam, Cambodia (Kampuchea), and Laos did not bring immediate peace and prosperity to the area of Southeast Asia. Conflict continues to rage at staggering costs to the people of that troubled region.

A Comparative Overview

It is clear that communism came to many different countries under a variety of circumstances and for many different reasons. We will now try to identify the most significant similarities and differences by considering the following questions. Generally speaking, *how* did communist movements come to power? *When* and *where* did they come to power? *Who* led these successful movements? And, perhaps the most interesting and important question, *why* did they come to power? As students of comparative politics, our guiding purpose is to establish some general patterns that explain the advent of communism throughout the world.[19]

How Did Communist Movements Come to Power?

Most observers of Communist Party states agree that the way in which a Party comes to power is important in determining how it uses power and makes policy in subsequent years. Communist Parties that come to power through independent revolutionary movements—for example, the USSR, China, Yugoslavia, Cuba—have had more freedom in planning and carrying out policy than states—for example, Mongolia, Bulgaria, East Germany—in which the Party came to power through the outside influence of the Soviet Union.

Communist Parties have come to power as a result of independent internal movements, through the imposition of a Communist Party regime by an outside force, or as a result of some combination of the two. The first column in Table 1.1 summarizes the experiences of each country. The two major powers within the communist world, the Soviet Union and China, came to power primarily as a result of internal movements. In addition, two countries in Eastern Europe, Albania and Yugoslavia, as well as Cuba and Vietnam had independent movements and became communist largely as a result of their own actions.

In the remaining countries of Eastern Europe, the Soviet Occupation at the end of World War II led to the imposition of communist-dominated regimes. Although the conditions, timing, and exact strategies varied somewhat from case to case, the idea of a national front served as the guiding policy. Coalition-type governments were initially installed but were soon transformed into communist-controlled govern-

ments. Although it occurred in a different part of the world, the communist ascendancy to power in North Korea was initially similar to the East European experience, particularly to that of East Germany and Poland. North Korea escaped Soviet domination after 1950, however, when China's influence increased and growing Sino-Soviet competition in North Korea allowed the Koreans to follow a more independent road.

The Vietnamese and Cuban revolutions were quite different from the East European examples where the Soviet Union played a dominant role. Ho Chi Minh and Fidel Castro were both nationalists and revolutionaries intent on ending exploitation and imperialism and bringing democratic socialism to their governments. Unlike the East European cases, they were successful in doing so without major assistance from or the occupation of an outside power. With few exceptions, those regimes that established communism on their own exhibited greater independence and autonomy in the international arena. On the other hand, with the notable exceptions of Romania and North Korea, those coming to power as the result of an outside occupation showed less independence of action, particularly in relation to the USSR. In addition, those leaders coming to power by means of the independent route (e.g., Mao, Tito, Castro) enjoyed relatively cohesive, stable reigns. Although there are exceptions, such as North Korea, those placed in power by outsiders tended to be less popular among their own people and more susceptible to Soviet interference, power struggles, or other developments resulting in abbreviated tenure.

In summary, communist movements can be and have been generated by internal and external forces. Thus, we can conclude that both domestic and international factors determine the manner in which communism develops in various nations.[20]

Table 1.1 Chronological Listing of Successful Communist Movements

	Attributes for Comparison			
State	*How*	*When*	*Where*	*Who*
Soviet Union	Independent movement	1917	Europe	Vladimir Ilyich Lenin
Mongolia	Armed occupation (USSR)	1921	Asia	Sukhe-Bator and Khorloin Choibalsan
Albania	Independent and outside (Yugoslavia)	1944	Europe	Enver Hoxha
Yugoslavia	Independent movement	1945	Europe	Josip Broz Tito
Vietnam	Independent movement (unification)	1945 (1975)	Asia	Ho Chi Minh (Le Duan)
North Korea	Armed occupation (USSR)	1945	Asia	Kim Il Sung
Romania	Armed occupation (USSR)	1945	Europe	Gheorghiu-Dej
Bulgaria	Independent and outside (USSR)	1946	Europe	Georgi Dimitrov
Hungary	Armed occupation (USSR)	1947	Europe	Mátyás Rákosi
Poland	Armed occupation (USSR)	1947	Europe	Wladyslaw Gomulka
Czechoslovakia	Independent and outside (USSR)	1948	Europe	Klement Gottwald
East Germany	Armed occupation (USSR)	1949	Europe	Walter Ulbricht
China	Independent movement	1949	Asia	Mao Zedong
Cuba	Independent movement	1959	Latin America	Fidel Castro
Laos	Independent and outside (Vietnam)	1975	Asia	Kaysone Phomvihan
Cambodia	Independent (Outside—Vietnam)*	1975 (1978)	Asia	Pol Pot (Heng Samrin)

* Vietnam invaded Cambodia in 1978 and installed the puppet regime headed by Heng Samrin.

When and Where Did Communist Movements Occur?

The chronological listing in Table 1.1 shows that most successful movements occurred at the end of World War II. With the exceptions of the Russian (1917) and Mongolian (1921) takeovers at the end of World War I and the relatively recent Cuban and Southeast Asian experiences, most successful movements followed the serious disorders of World War II. Wars and other major destabilizing forces establish the conditions for revolutionary change. In one way or another, communist victories tended to come in the wake of international or civil war.

Geographically speaking, communist movements have been victorious in both East and West. Although most occurred in Eastern Europe, movements in Asia and Latin America illustrate that communism was not bound to any one part of the world.

Past communist movements and takeovers also show no particular bounds in terms of culture. When communism first took hold in Russia, some experts attributed its success to the nature of Russian culture. Their Slavic culture, "soul," and general spiritual characteristics (according to these theorists) made them well suited to an ideology emphasizing collectivism and socialism. Because of these spiritual and cultural requisites, scholars noted, communism was unlikely to go to other parts of the world. Subsequent movements and the spread of communism to the different cultures in Asia and Latin America seemed to invalidate this idea of cultural requirements.

Communism also came to power in countries at different levels of economic development. Most had been agricultural societies at the early stages of economic growth. Some, such as Czechoslovakia and East Germany, had rather advanced economic systems; others had been at intermediate stages of development; still others, in Asia, had very primitive economic systems. Overall, it is fair to say that communist movements and takeovers have occurred under many different geographical, cultural, and socioeconomic conditions.

Who Led These Victorious Movements?

Were Lenin, Mao, Tito, Ho Chi Minh, Castro, and others indispensable elements in the revolutionary process or could victory have been achieved without them? Perhaps more important: Which came first—the revolution or the revolutionary? To evaluate an individual's impact on a process as complex as revolution is difficult and risky. What can be said is that most had extremely capable leaders, men who well understood their countries and the military and organizational dynamics of the revolutionary process. Leaders like Mao and Tito were able to seize on international forces (e.g., World War II) and to combine them with domestic needs to build successful resistance and revolutionary forces. Although they were "great" leaders in many respects, we can probably observe that the social and economic forces were larger than the men. If a Tito, Mao, Lenin, or Castro had not existed, it is likely that some other individual would have come to the fore and directed the revolutionary movement. "Great" men cannot necessarily make history, but they can influence it by recognizing and exploiting emergent social forces. At the very least, the individuals listed in Table 1.1 were the right men in the right place with the foresight and ideas to bring revolutionary visions to fruition.

Why Were the Communist Movements Successful?

Table 1.1 contains no entry with the heading *Why?*. Although the why of successful movements is far too complex to summarize in a brief word or two, we can make some broad generalizations about the trends leading to the demise of the old state systems and to the establishment of communism.

All the regimes that preceded the establishment of communism suffered from a number of severe shortcomings. Most had lost the confidence of the broader society, and their leaders were unable to inspire and gain the support of the mass populace. Often there was government corruption and inefficiency that resulted in disillusionment and disappointment with the old autocracy. The difficulties of the times were further exacerbated by forces of international and civil war, conflicts in which the armies were either unable or unwilling to protect incumbent regimes. In every case, either internal or international wars (and often both) contributed to the final collapse of the old regime. What followed was disorder, economic stagnation, and a political vacuum.

But why were the successor states communist rather than some other political doctrine or creed? One reason for the success of communist movements concerns the use of a new organizational weapon, the Communist Party. Centralized, conspiratorial, and militant, the Party became the organizational agent for effecting revolutionary change. Operating in a period of political disorganization and general social disorder, the organized Communist Parties of the revolutionaries capitalized on the unstable setting to grasp the reins of power. It is in this respect that the leaders often showed the attributes of the great-men syndrome. Understanding the use of organizations and the domestic and international contexts in which they were operating, the leaders assumed and consolidated political power.

The revolutionary leaders and the Parties they represented also understood the meaning and role of military power. "Power grows out of the barrel of a gun," proclaimed Mao Zedong. Use of the Communist Party as a military as well as a political organization was a major factor in most takeovers. In some states, armed force meant the intervention of the Soviet Army and a period of military occupation. This factor represented a key element in the communists' ability to assume and retain political power, especially in those states often referred to as being in the Soviet bloc.

Although comparison is difficult because of the many differences among the communist movements, we can identify some general patterns concerning the advent to power. Authoritarianism, misrule, mass discontent, and alienation, when combined with international warfare and foreign imperialism, are the factors that have led to a toppling of old state systems. Then, organized resistance and revolutionary movements, led by astute leaders operating within centralized Communist Party organizations, often with the armed assistance of the USSR, helped establish new communist systems. Because there are obviously other states that have experienced such conditions and have not gone communist, we should not consider these patterns universal laws. At the same time, there are enough similar conditions and forces to point up general patterns that involve the establishment of communist rule.

A Review of the Communist Experience

Before we move into our examination of contemporary issues, it will be useful to put the historical experience of communism in broader perspective. First, we should note the significance of the application of Marxism-Leninism in Russia and the deep impact that the Soviet experience has had on subsequent communist

31

development. It was in the authoritarian Russian setting that communist rule took on its oppressive, centralized features. Power was consolidated under the heavy hand of dictatorial Soviet rulers, not the least of which was Joseph Stalin.

Stalin did much to pervert the original, Marxist goals of communism. Stalin had a pathological personality and mistrusted the people he ruled and those he ruled with. He imposed great human costs on Soviet society as he ruthlessly and coercively pursued his conception of building a Soviet, communist state. Terror, repression, and the centralization and arbitrary uses of power became key elements of Marxism-Leninism-Stalinism, or what has often been referred to as the Stalinist model of communism.

It was this Stalinist model of communist rule that was subsequently exported to and imposed on China and Eastern Europe. Although it may not be entirely accurate to call Mao a Stalinist, it is fair to say that he was willing to use terror, coercion, and centralization of political power in his quest to build communism in China. Stalin himself, the Communist Party of the Soviet Union, and the Soviet Red Army did much to impose the Stalinist model of communism in the East European countries after World War II. Although there were indigenous communist movements in most of these states, it was Soviet power that determined the postwar character of communist rule in Eastern Europe.

This was a scenario for disaster. The proud nationalities of Eastern Europe stagnated under Soviet dominance. The imposition of the centralized political system generated frustration, discontent, cynicism, dissidence, and apathy among the people. The centralized, command-type economic system impeded the development of these states' economies. There were numerous uprisings in Eastern Europe over the postwar period—in East Berlin in 1953, Poland and Hungary in 1956, Czechoslovakia in 1968—which suggested that there were problems and cleavages in what we generally referred to as the Soviet bloc. The national aspirations of these countries were in conflict with Soviet goals of a Soviet-led, international communist movement.

The first major crack in the facade of communist internationalism came with the dispute between Stalin and Tito and Yugoslavia's expulsion from the Soviet bloc in 1948. When Stalin sensed that Tito was failing to toe the Soviet line, he excommunicated the Yugoslavs from the communist camp. Yugoslavia moved to develop what it called its own "road to socialism" outside of the Soviet bloc.

Other East European countries would have liked to have done the same but were not permitted to do so until Gorbachev brought about his changes in the late 1980s. In Hungary in 1956 the Hungarian leadership and people sought to gain sovereignty over the building of socialism in their country. After the Yugoslav experience, the Soviet leadership was unwilling to see their hopes of Soviet-directed internationalism suffer another setback. When Hungary declared its neutrality and attempted to withdraw from the Warsaw Pact in 1956, the Soviet Army suppressed the national uprising. Before Soviet control was forcibly reasserted, some 7,000 Soviet soldiers and 20,000 Hungarians were killed.

The next great setback to a united movement of socialist states came with the growing disaffection between the Chinese and the Soviets in the late 1950s. Resulting in an open split in 1960, the Sino-Soviet dispute buried all illusions concerning the possibility of socialist harmony.[21] Chinese and Soviet animosities reached unprecedented heights in the late 1960s as both sides prepared for war. The Sino-Soviet border became the site of encampments of huge armies

Gorbachev and other communist leaders at the 1989 celebration of forty years of communism in East Germany, just prior to the collapse of communist rule throughout Eastern Europe.

and occasional military skirmishes. The Soviet communists' ideal of a united communist movement under their leadership dissolved as ideological and national differences came to divide the Second World.

There were other significant problems in the communist movement as well. A critical one involved economics. As the years passed, it became increasingly clear that the centralized system of state socialism could not compete with capitalism and the various hybrid forms of socialism and capitalism that existed in Western Europe, the Far East, and North America.

It is believed by many that the stagnation of the socialist economies was one of the most powerful forces leading to the demise of the Stalinist form of communism as the world had come to know it.

There are other factors that contributed to the demise of Stalinism. The repression of the people, lack of human rights, growing human costs, and other such forces led to tremendous disaffection with the Stalinist model in Second World societies. This in turn led to a significant decline in the legitimacy of the communist rulers, particularly those of a Stalinist bent. By the

1980s, it had become increasingly clear that traditional communist leaders had not provided the values that they long promised their people.

With the passing of the ideological Mao and conservative Brezhnev regimes, China and the Soviet Union had an opportunity to engage in new thinking and reform. Deng Xiaoping engineered an opening and reforming of China in the 1980s, and Mikhail Gorbachev began the process in the Soviet Union after his assumption of power in 1985. Although both developments were significant, it was the glasnost, perestroika, and reform movements under Gorbachev that had the greatest impact on what happened elsewhere in the Second World. When Gorbachev began to emphasize the themes of openness, democracy, and sovereignty within the communist movement, he unleashed a powerful dynamic of great significance. Where it will lead is difficult to tell, but by 1990 it had ushered in a tumultuous period of reform and revolution in the Second World.

Suggestions for Further Reading

Billington, James H., *Fire in the Minds of Men: Origins of the Revolutionary Faith* (New York: Basic Books, 1980).

Brzezinski, Zbigniew K., *The Soviet Bloc: Unity and Conflict,* rev. ed. (New York: Praeger, 1961).

Burks, R. V., *The Dynamics of Communism in Eastern Europe* (Princeton, N.J.: Princeton University Press, 1961).

Carr, Edward H., *The Bolshevik Revolution, 1917–1923,* 3 Vols. (New York: Norton, 1985).

Dallin, Alexander, *Diversity in International Communism: A Documentary Record, 1961–1963* (New York: Columbia University Press, 1963).

Drachkovitch, Milorad M., ed., *Marxism in the Modern World* (Stanford, Calif.: Stanford University Press, 1965).

Drachkovitch, Milorad M., and **Branko M. Lazic,** *The Comintern: Historical Highlights, Essays, Recollections, Documents* (New York: Praeger, 1966).

Fairbank, John K., *The Great Chinese Revolution, 1800–1985* (New York: Harper & Row, 1986).

Fejto, Francois, *A History of the People's Democracies* (New York: Praeger, 1971).

Gasster, Michael, *China's Struggle to Modernize* (New York: Knopf, 1972).

Goodrich, L. Carrington, *A Short History of the Chinese People,* 3rd ed. (New York: Harper & Row, 1959).

Hammond, Thomas T., ed., *The Anatomy of Communist Takeovers* (New Haven, Conn.: Yale University Press, 1975).

Hunt, R. N. Carew, *The Theory and Practice of Communism,* 5th ed. (Baltimore: Penguin, 1963).

Johnson, Chalmers, *Peasant Nationalism and Communist Power* (Stanford, Calif.: Stanford University Press, 1962).

Kennan, George F., *Russia and the West Under Lenin and Stalin* (New York: New American Library, 1961).

Laqueur, Walter, and **Leopold Labedz,** *Polycentrism: The New Factor in International Communism* (New York: Praeger, 1962).

Lichtheim, George, *Marxism: An Historical and Critical Study,* 2nd ed. (New York: Praeger, 1965).

McCrea, Barbara P., et al., *The Soviet and East European Political Dictionary* (Santa Barbara, Calif.: ABC-Clio, 1984).

Meisner, Maurice, *Mao's China: A History of the People's Republic* (New York: Free Press, 1977).

Pares, Bernard, *A History of Russia,* 5th ed. (New York: Knopf, 1949).

Schapiro, Leonard, *The Origins of Communist Autocracy* (Cambridge: Harvard University Press, 1955).

Seton-Watson, Hugh, *From Lenin to Khrushchev: The History of World Communism* (New York: Praeger, 1960).

———, *The East European Revolution,* 3rd ed. (New York: Praeger, 1956).

Selden, Mark, ed., *The People's Republic of China:* *A Documentary History of Revolutionary Change* (New York: Monthly Review Press, 1979).

Snow, Edgar, *Red Star over China* (New York: Random House, 1938).

Trotsky, Leon, *A History of the Russian Revolution,* trans. Max Eastman (3 vols.) (New York: Simon & Schuster, 1932).

Ulam, Adam B., *Expansion and Coexistence: Soviet Foreign Policy, 1917–1973* (New York: Praeger, 1974).

———, *Titoism and the Cominform* (New York: Praeger, 1971).

Volgyes, Ivan, *Politics in Eastern Europe* (Chicago: Dorsey Press, 1986).

Zagoria, Donald S., *The Sino-Soviet Conflict, 1956–1961* (Princeton, N.J.: Princeton University Press, 1962).

Zinner, Paul E., *Revolution in Hungary* (New York: Columbia University Press, 1962).

Notes

1. The adjectives *communist, Marxist-Leninist,* and *Second World* are used interchangeably to refer to the states we will be addressing in the chapters that follow. Because some of these states are moving away from communism and Marxism-Leninism as we enter the 1990s, these first two terms will not always be useful and accurate descriptions in the future.

2. For a useful collection of the basic writings of Marx and Engels, see Robert C. Tucker, *The Marx-Engels Reader,* 2nd ed. (New York: Norton, 1978).

3. Ibid., pp. 335–336.

4. Isaiah Berlin has written a splendid book about Marx's life: *Karl Marx: His Life and Environment,* 3rd ed. (London: Oxford University Press, 1963);

also see David McLellan, *Karl Marx: His Life and Thought* (New York: Harper & Row, 1974).

5. David Shub, *Lenin, a Biography* (New York: Penguin, 1976); Rolf Theen, *Lenin: Genesis and Development of a Revolutionary* (Princeton, N.J.: Princeton University Press, 1980).

6. Several books analyze the decline of tsarist Russia. Among the best are Hugh Seton-Watson, *The Decline of Imperial Russia, 1855–1914* (New York: Praeger, 1952); and M. T. Florinsky, *The End of the Russian Empire* (New Haven: Yale University Press, 1931).

7. Solzhenitsyn argues that the roots of the dictatorship of the Party are to be found in the nature of the ideology itself.

8. Two excellent accounts of Stalin and his rule are Robert C. Tucker, *Stalin as a Revolutionary, 1879–1929* (New York: Norton, 1973); and Adam B. Ulam, *Stalin: The Man and His Era* (New York: Viking, 1973).

9. At the Third International Party Congress (First Congress of the Comintern) held in 1919, Lenin told the delegates that conflict between the capitalist and socialist worlds was inevitable and that socialism would soon result from proletarian uprisings throughout Europe.

10. Stalin's policy conflicted with Leon Trotsky's theory of permanent revolution (formulated in 1905). The fiery Trotsky was expelled from the country in 1929 for his views and was assassinated by a Stalinist agent in Mexico in 1940. Trotsky's book, *The Revolution Betrayed* (New York: Pathfinder Press, 1972), provides an interesting personal account of this and related issues.

11. Theda Skocpol, "Old Regime Legacies and Communist Revolutions in Russia and China," *Social Forces* 55 (2) (1976), 284–315.

12. The ancient traditions are deeply embedded in China and represent conservative forces even today. For an excellent analysis of the past, see Mark Elvin, *The Pattern of the Chinese Past* (London: Eyre Methuen, 1973); for a contrast of the past with the present, see Lucian W. Pye, *China* (Boston: Little, Brown, 1972); also see John K. Fairbank, *The United States and China*, 4th ed. (Cambridge: Harvard University Press, 1979).

13. Chinese names are transliterated in the Pinyin system now standard in China. Familiar names, like Confucius, Kuomintang, Chiang Kai-shek, and Sun Yat-sen are not rendered in Pinyin but follow the Wade-Giles system used in the past.

14. For an analysis of the Chinese approach, see Chalmers Johnson, *Peasant Nationalism and Communist Power* (Stanford, Calif.: Stanford University Press, 1962).

15. For an excellent account, see Hugh Seton-Watson, *The East European Revolution*, 3rd ed. (New York: Praeger, 1956).

16. For an interesting account of the life of Josip Broz Tito, see Milovan Djilas, *Tito: The Story from the Inside*, trans. Vasilije Kojbic and Richard Hayes (London: Weidenfeld: Nicholson, 1981).

17. In fact, it did so in the case of Latvia, Lithuania, Estonia, and the eastern sections of Czechoslovakia, Romania, Poland, and Germany.

18. For an account of Castro's ideological philosophy prior to and during the Cuban revolution, see Hugh Thomas's monumental work, *Cuba: The Pursuit of Freedom* (New York: Harper & Row, 1971).

19. The advent of communism in Communist Party states is analyzed in Thomas T. Hammond, ed., *The Anatomy of Communist Takeovers* (New Haven: Yale University Press, 1975). Also see Hugh Seton-Watson, *From Lenin to Khrushchev: The History of World Communism* (New York: Praeger, 1960).

20. It should be noted that Marxist rule was brought to Chile in 1970 through the ballot box. Although elected, the communist-oriented government of Salvador Allende Gossens was subsequently overthrown by military leaders in 1973.

21. See Donald Zagoria, *The Sino-Soviet Conflict, 1956–61* (New York: Atheneum, 1964).

C H A P T E R 2

THE SOCIAL
AND ECONOMIC
SETTINGS

By the end of the 1980s, everyone knew that the Marxist-Leninist experiments were in trouble. Communist systems had neither achieved the progress their leaders promised nor had they established conditions conducive to achieving their goals in the future. No less a figure than Mikhail Gorbachev admitted that the Soviet Union and other communist states had failed to create the conditions necessary for the building of communism. Because such conditions tell us much about the communist experiments of the past and prospects for the future, it is worthwhile to examine the environmental settings characterizing the Second World states.

This chapter will focus on economic and social conditions. When addressing the economic settings, we will note that the centralized, Stalinist-type economic systems failed in the Second World countries and required their leaders to search for better models and methods for promoting economic development. When examining the social settings, we will find that the Second World systems have provided neither the living standards (what we refer to as the level of well-being) nor the equality that was promised under socialism. We will also see that ethnic and national differences remain in these countries and, in many cases, have intensified and resulted in deep cleavages that do not allow relations based on the "brotherhood and unity" promised by the Marxist-Leninist leaders.

These economic, social, and ethnic (or nationality) problems represent important elements of the setting in which politics takes place. These conditions were not in correspondence with or conducive to promoting the ideals of communism. Therefore, the challenges confronting communist leaders and their peoples in the 1990s are formidable. Although we will consider in the pages ahead many of the sixteen Second World states discussed in the previous chapter, we will concentrate our attention on the Soviet, Chinese, and some selected East European cases.

The Economic Setting

Economics is at the heart of Marxist ideology and the current Second World predicament. Marx predicted that the socialist revolution would occur in capitalist countries that had undergone the Industrial Revolution. In point of fact, communism arose in agriculture-based societies where the industrial sector was a very small percentage of the working population. In East European societies, the industrial sector of the societies ranged between 5 and 40 percent (see Table 2.1). The societies of Asia—China, Cambodia (Kampuchea), Laos, and Vietnam— were less industrially and more agriculturally oriented than their European counterparts. The United Nations estimates that nearly 80 percent of China's present-day labor force still works in agriculture. Therefore, although Marx predicted that industrial development would precede and economic abundance and equality would come with the victory of socialism, the social and economic conditions of most aspiring Marxist states did not correspond with these ideals.

In the Soviet Union, the initial challenge facing Lenin and the communist leaders after the Bolshevik victory was Russia's reconstruction. After removing the country from World War I, the Bolsheviks went about the task of consolidating power and building socialism within their country. In 1918, Lenin's decree nationalized

heavy industries, land, and the means of production; private ownership of land and industry was strictly forbidden. During the ensuing period of civil war and foreign intervention (1918–21), however, little could be done to set up a rational system of economic administration. It was during this period of "war communism" that Soviet economic output fell to 20 percent of what it had been before the outbreak of World War I.

To get the economy going again, the Soviet leaders adopted the New Economic Policy (NEP) in 1921. Although large industries remained nationalized, this new policy called for a mixed economic strategy that denationalized small industries and agriculture. Representing a temporary return to capitalism, the NEP saved the Bolshevik government from bankruptcy and got the Soviet economy back on its feet again. By 1926, economic output had reached its prewar levels.

With Lenin's death in 1924 and Stalin's assumption of power, Russia's leadership embraced the monumental task of rapid industrialization. With the first Five-Year Plan of 1928–33 (a centralized plan coordinating economic goals and policies for the entire country),

Table 2.1 Working Population (%) before Socialism, by Sector of Economy

	Czechoslovakia (1934)	Hungary (1930)	Poland (1931)	Romania (1930)	Bulgaria (1935)	Yugoslavia (1936)
Industry	38.3	24.1	19.4	7.7	8.0	9.9
Agriculture	25.6	53.0	60.6	76.9	80.0	76.3
Trade	9.2	5.9	6.1	3.3	2.4	4.2
Other	26.9	17.0	13.9	12.1	9.6	9.3
Total	100.0	100.0	100.0	100.0	100.0	99.7

(Source) Walter D. Connor, *Socialism, Politics, and Equality: Hierarchy and Change in Eastern Europe and the USSR* (New York: Columbia University Press, 1979), p. 31.

the Stalinist strategy of economic development began to materialize. Because there was no real possibility of bringing foreign capital into the country (the socialist leaders did not want to become dependent on the capitalist West and the West was suspicious of, and unwilling to support, Russian development) Soviet economic policy had to devise a method of generating capital internally. By adopting a policy that exacted high costs from the peasantry and that funneled nearly all economic surpluses back into the industrial sector, the Soviets attempted to accumulate funds on their own. To achieve the Communist Party's economic goals, Stalin established a centralized administrative structure and readopted the policies of nationalization of industry and collectivization of agriculture. Designed to mobilize the population to attain unreasonably high economic goals, this developmental policy incurred great human costs. Individuals or groups who disagreed with nationalization or the collectivization of agriculture were sent off to Siberia or annihilated.[1] The human costs surrounding Stalin's programs were high—millions were killed or died—but the economic benefits were substantial. Even in view of the devastation and economic setbacks caused by World War II, the Soviet economic strategy propelled the USSR to the stature of a world power by the end of the Stalinist era in 1953. Utilizing a command-type economic system based on government control of the means of production, central planning, and a high rate of capital investment, production in the Soviet Union drew close to and even surpassed that of some of the Western powers.

The Soviet Union's economy continued to grow in the post-Stalin era. In 1950, the Soviet GNP was estimated at less than one third that of the United States. By 1965, Soviet GNP had grown to approximately half that of the United

States and three times that of Great Britain. The general economic goal through the first 70 years of Soviet development was that of basic capital investment. Stated simply, the Soviets opted for the development of heavy industry—hydroelectric plants, steel mills, and so forth—at the expense of the consumer sector. As we will see later, however, the Soviet strategy was not nearly as successful as it might earlier have appeared. With the benefit of hindsight, most observers in the Soviet Union and abroad now consider the strategy a tragic mistake.

Assuming power in 1949, Mao Zedong and the Chinese communists faced a far less developed economy, more devastated country, and a more chaotic economic system than the Bolsheviks confronted. The economy was in such a deteriorated state that it did not even have the capacity to manufacture the primary vehicle for Chinese transportation, the bicycle. Unlike the Bolsheviks, Mao and his compatriots did not rush to nationalize industry and collectivize agriculture. To stimulate economic recovery, they attempted to use capitalist industry and redistribute agricultural land among the peasants; nationalization and collectivization would occur gradually over the span of several years. This policy of gradual transformation was carefully followed during the 1949–52 period and resulted in political consolidation, economic growth, and improved internal and international prestige. Slowly, the leadership began to transform privately owned enterprises into a cooperative form of state/private management. At the outset of the first Five-Year Plan in 1953, these joint enterprises accounted for approximately half of China's economic output; by 1956, practically all private enterprises had been changed to the cooperative operation. The first Five-Year Plan (1953–57), based on a general conception of Stalin's model but benefiting from the hindsight of Soviet mistakes, resulted in substantial material growth and economic progress. Utilizing aid and advice from the USSR and East European states, China appeared well on the way to economic recovery.

Soon after the second Five-Year Plan was proclaimed (1958–62), however, the recovery encountered a number of serious setbacks, the first of which was the Great Leap Forward campaign beginning in 1958. Based on the Maoist line of "going all out and aiming high to achieve greater, quicker, better, and more economical results in building socialism," this radical program was intended to make China a world economic power in a matter of decades. With expectations of surpassing Great Britain in industrial output in fifteen years, the strategy called on both modern and traditional methods of development (what the Chinese refer to as "walking on two legs"). Among other naive strategies and policies, Chinese citizens were encouraged to build smelter furnaces in their backyards to increase the output of steel. Sacrificing quality for quantity and suffering from poor planning and execution, the Great Leap Forward resulted in a large step backward. Planning became difficult, product quality declined, economic imbalances were experienced, and the idealistic but misguided campaign ended in disgrace.

The period of 1959–61 also brought a series of problems, including natural calamities such as droughts and floods, that further reduced Chinese economic capabilities, diminished agricultural production, and hindered development. In their midst came the Soviet Union's withdrawal of material aid and technical assistance in the summer of 1960. Precipitated by a growing ideological dispute, the Soviet Union's withdrawal interrupted many developmental programs that relied on foreign assistance.[2] At this point in Chinese reconstruction, the economic future looked bleak indeed.

In the early 1960s, the Chinese brought an end to the Great Leap Forward program and began to reevaluate their economic policies. This period ushered in an emphasis on greater self-reliance and a search for policies uniquely suited to Chinese needs and capabilities. The reappraisal changed the general strategy from one emphasizing heavy industry (the Soviet Union's approach) to one emphasizing agriculture. The new order of priorities became agriculture first, light industry second, and heavy industry third. As recovery proceeded and the third Five-Year Plan entered its second year in 1967, however, the economic system encountered another destabilizing campaign. Intended to "take firm hold of the revolution and stimulate production," the Great Proletarian Cultural Revolution (GPCR) of 1966–69 once again set the economic system into a state of disarray. Young revolutionaries, the Red Guards, were dispatched to the factories and other social and economic organizations to stimulate production through revolutionary and ideological means; their political intrusion incurred great economic costs. Such policies that were intended to rejuvenate the revolutionary spirit of the populace continued to disrupt the Chinese economy until Mao's death in 1976.

The East European economic settings were also contrary to the building of communism. Always economically behind their West European counterparts, the East European economies were further damaged by the devastations wrought by World War II. For example, during their evacuation of Yugoslavia at the end of World War II, the Nazis destroyed much of the country's transportation system and industrial facilities. The Yugoslavs began the task of reconstruction by nationalizing and collectivizing private holdings according to the Stalinist mode of development. However, growing friction between Joseph Stalin and the Yugoslav leaders culminated in a decision that shocked the communist world. Unexpectedly, in 1948, Stalin expelled the Yugoslavs from the international communist organization, Cominform, and initiated a sudden freeze in Soviet-Yugoslav relations.[3]

A few years after the expulsion, the Yugoslavs began considering alternatives to the Soviet command-type economic system. Slowly experimenting with and implementing a number of reforms, the Yugoslavs moved to a decentralized form of market socialism that based production more on the laws of supply and demand and less on the commands of a central economic plan. Movement to a market-based economy was in part motivated and certainly hastened by the Soviet's economic blockade of Yugoslavia that followed the expulsion from the Cominform. Weathering this blockade and several natural catastrophes with economic assistance from the United States, the Yugoslavs began a steady period of economic growth. Through the 1950s and 1960s, the Yugoslav economic growth rates were among the highest in the world. The good news resulting from economic experimentation was not to last, however. In the 1970s and 1980s there was clear evidence that the Yugoslav economy was in serious decline.

Although some countries fared worse than others, World War II also unleashed destructive forces on the economies of the other East European states. The extent of these damages and the amount of reparation required by the region's victor, the Soviet Union, largely determined the initial pace and extent of postwar recovery.[4] In many cases, the Soviets stripped factories of machinery or dismantled entire plants for shipment to the USSR to help pay for war damages. By the early 1950s, however, all the states were back to their prewar levels of production. East Germany was the last to

reach this level because of its unusually high reparations to the USSR.

Following Stalinist policies of Soviet economic development, the economies of the East European states were virtually all nationalized by 1950. Forced to emulate the Soviet economic model and working within the supranational Council for Mutual Economic Assistance (CMEA or COMECON) established in 1949, the different states adopted rather similar economic policies and procedures.[5] Attempting to expand the industrial base (particularly mining, machine building, ironworks, and steelworks) while simultaneously retarding personal consumption, the states hoped to increase the margin for capital investment. The resultant economic systems were inefficient and unable to promote the well-being of their societies. Economic recovery from the ravages of war was achieved at high costs, including poor working conditions, low salaries, and a scarcity of basic consumer goods.

Economic Forms and Reforms

The ideal of communism described by Karl Marx envisioned an economic system based on the principle "from each according to his abilities, to each according to his needs." This principle presupposed an economic system in which there were no shortages and where the members of society did not have to pay for food, goods, or services. Individuals were to work and produce according to their abilities and consume only what they needed.

To move toward the ideals of communism, the Second World states all established some sort of socialist economic system. Under socialism, workers produce according to their ability and are paid according to their contribution. In this economic system, theoretically speaking, the factors of production are owned collectively and controlled by the public. Marx believed that this system was a lower stage than communism, unjust because more important work would be more highly rewarded than less important work; however, it would accomplish certain necessary benefits. Basically, socialism would produce a system of material abundance in which the state would "wither away," and the "oppressive government of men" would be replaced by the "administration of things." For Marx, socialism would provide the necessary socioeconomic prerequisites for the emergence of true or pure communism.

The Second World states have displayed a variety of socialist institutional arrangements and policy preferences, each officially designed to facilitate the evolution from socialism to communism. Because the state rather than the public owned the factors of production, the Soviet Union's traditional economic system was often referred to, especially by its various detractors, as one of state socialism. In such a system, state ministries and government bodies at different levels invest in, own, and manage the factors of production. Because industries and enterprises receive their directives from central planning agencies, the term command-type system also has been used to describe this type of economic system. Although the market and the idea of supply and demand have some effect on production, the planning agencies assume primary power and responsibility for determining the type and level of economic output. Under such a system, profits and losses accrue to the state, not to the enterprise or to the workers.

Although a basic purpose and desired benefit of the centralized, administered system of state socialism were economic efficiency, many economists have called attention to considerable waste and inefficiency in the Soviet and East European systems. The administered system was expected to be useful in tackling high-priority tasks, such as the development of heavy industry or the decision to promote intensive capital investment. However, vesting ownership in the state and control in the government ministries ruled out important economic dynamics that promote efficiency and development. A key example involves the attitude and commitment of the average worker. Marx contended that under capitalism, workers had become alienated from their work, but under socialism they were to regain control of their work because the work enterprise was to be publicly owned. But under a centralized system of state socialism, workers once again were exploited and given little control over or incentives in their work.

There were a number of reactions to this development in the form of experimentation with alternative forms of socialism. The first was the Yugoslav experiment, with their self-managing form of socialism. Referred to by a variety of terms, including decentralized socialism, laissez-faire socialism, or a mixed free enterprise/public ownership system, the Yugoslav experiment represented an attempt to resolve some of the problems of state socialism. Hoping to eliminate excessive bureaucracy, low productivity and efficiency, and a relative absence of motivation and initiative, the Yugoslavs developed a hybrid economic system that combined elements of both socialism and capitalism.

Beginning in the 1950s, Yugoslavia began to abandon many features of the Stalinist command-type system. In a series of reforms, Yugoslav leaders deemphasized centralized planning, provided economic enterprises with more decision-making autonomy, and made competition and profit a central motivating feature of the economy. All these and additional policies came under the movement toward self-managing, market-oriented socialism.

Although accounts of the motivating forces behind self-management vary, some say it included Yugoslavia's desire to put power in the hands of the worker, where, according to Marx, it rightly belongs. This involved the establishment of workers' councils in economic enterprises. These councils of elected workers were to assume major responsibility for running the affairs of the firm. Under this system, central government planning was deemphasized while the autonomy of the enterprise was increased. Considerable authority was transferred from central planning ministries to the enterprises themselves, and the enterprises began to base their decisions more on the market and less on the government's commands. However, as we will see later when we examine the economic crisis of contemporary Yugoslavia, these attempts at reform were no panacea. They did not bring about Yugoslav prosperity.

Early Yugoslav reform efforts came under hostile attack from both the Chinese and Soviet leaders. A pamphlet published in Beijing in 1964 noted:

Although the Tito clique still displays the banner of "socialism," a bureaucrat bourgeoisie opposed to the Yugoslav people has gradually come into being since the Tito clique took the road of revisionism, transforming the Yugoslav state from a dictatorship of the proletariat into a dictatorship of the bureaucrat bourgeoisie and its socialist public economy into state capitalism.[6]

During the 1960s and 1970s the Soviet leaders also looked critically on the economic revisionism being followed in Yugoslavia and warned leaders in the other European socialist states to stay clear of the Yugoslav heresy.

Taking the advice of the Soviet leaders, the East European states adopted more orthodox (i.e., Soviet-styled) economic strategies and systems. In these states, an initial mixed-economy (i.e., capitalist and socialist) period after World War II was followed by the adoption of a command-type system emulating the Soviet model. Launching Five-Year Plans that emphasized industrial development, nationalizing trade and industry, and subordinating labor unions to the Communist Party, the economic models of the other East European states looked much like that of the Soviet system.

Increasingly, however, many of the East European states began to experiment with reforms. Some observed with keen interest the economic experimentation and reform in Yugoslavia. Many felt that the planned economies established in their countries at Soviet insistence after World War II were impeding optimal development. Having experienced prewar histories of rather successful economic growth and possessing definite economic potential, some economic planners in these states blamed their difficulties on the Soviet-style administered system. Although the responses in the 1960s and 1970s differed from country to country, many were eager to experiment with new economic forms. As a result, policy changes intended to bring about economic liberalization and reform were initiated at different times in a number of the countries, particularly Czechoslovakia, Hungary, and Poland. However, because the USSR perceived these policies as endangering the preservation of the command system, the Soviets intervened and forced these countries back into more orthodox positions. One such example was the Czechoslovak experiment in the late 1960s when they attempted to undertake far-reaching social and economic reforms. One dimension of this experiment was economic liberalization designed to take some of the planning and policy-making functions away from the Party and central ministries. Although significant economic progress was being made and other social and political reforms were gathering momentum during the spring of 1968 (the so-called Prague Spring), Soviet reservations about these reforms resulted in military intervention that brought an end to Czechoslovak economic and political liberalization.[7] Organizing a joint intervention by the Warsaw Treaty Organization (WTO) states, troops and tanks from Bulgaria, East Germany, Poland, Hungary, and the Soviet Union marched onto Czechoslovakian soil on August 20, 1968, and brought an end to Czechoslovakia's attempt to develop socialism with a "human face."[8] Many Czechoslovak leaders, including the Communist Party leader, Alexander Dubcek, were ousted as the country returned to the more orthodox position that characterized the economic systems of the other WTO and COMECON states.

In January 1968, the Hungarian communists began implementation of their own program of economic liberalization, the New Economic Mechanism (NEM).[9] By carefully depoliticizing the program and by proceeding cautiously, the Hungarians gradually decentralized and strengthened the Hungarian economy without provoking the sort of Soviet intervention that occurred in Czechoslovakia. Under the NEM, centrally determined quotas and prices were slowly replaced by general national guidelines, the introduction of profit incentives, and the privatization of many sectors of the Hungarian economy. Hungarian economic reforms really picked up steam in the late 1980s. For example, revolutionary laws were introduced in 1989 that included a number of provisions intended to promote private enterprise. For example, one law allowed the transformation of state enterprises into joint stock companies giving Hungarian citizens full involvement in these enterprises. It permitted Hungarians to buy and sell shares in such companies and even

allowed foreign investors to buy Hungarian companies.

The appointment of the reform-minded Mikhail Gorbachev as the Soviet Party leader in 1985 finally brought significant economic experimentation and change to the Soviet Union. Under the general concept of *perestroika* (restructuring), the Soviet leaders hoped to reform the overly centralized, stagnant economy by introducing what officials then referred to as more "intensive development policies." These policies emphasized greater entrepreneurship, initiative, efficiency, decentralization, and accountability. The early Gorbachev years stressed *uskoreniye*, or acceleration, which involved greater discipline, improved effort, and increased conservation. Later, in 1987, Gorbachev and his associates began to talk about more radical reforms.

Gorbachev emphasized repeatedly in the late 1980s that economic restructuring and domestic development were the highest priorities of his rule. His economic reforms were in response to the fact that the Soviet economy had stagnated and had generated little hope for economic progress in the future. The 1981–85 average annual growth rates of 2 percent in the USSR were simply too low to fulfill Soviet hopes and expectations. Using terms like "radical reform" and "profound transformation," Gorbachev began to encourage fundamental change in the economic management of the Soviet economy.

Although many of the specifics were lacking, the broad outlines of radical change, intensive development, and accelerated economic growth were made clear early in Gorbachev's tenure. The 1986–89 Five Year Plan and the economic guidelines to the year 2000 proposed that the economy grow at 4.5 percent a year, considerably above the 1981–85 levels. How was this to be brought about? Perestroika was Gorbachev's plan. Soviet workers were to become more efficient and productive. There were to be organizational changes intended to decrease the central government's micromanagement of the economy and to increase the roles of enterprises and the territorial units of the Soviet state. There was to be technological progress and new machinery, better managers, and improved methods. These and other proposals were part of the Soviet strategy of perestroika.

The strategy was outlined in 1987 in an official document entitled "Basic Provisions for Radical Restructuring of Economic Management." Gorbachev referred to this document in his book *Perestroika* in the following way: "Perhaps this is the most important and the most radical program for economic reform our country has had since Lenin introduced his New Economic Policy in 1921."[10] The proposals in the 1987 Basic Provisions were intended to change the highly centralized, command-type Soviet system to one where local units were given greater power and central government authorities were relegated to a planning role.

Among other things, the 1987 Basic Provisions established the Soviet enterprises (i.e., the firms)—rather than the central government and its planning bodies—as the primary actors in the Soviet economy. This principle was embodied in considerable detail in the 1987 Law of the USSR on State Enterprises. The 1987 law promised enterprises more independence and required them to be economically self-sustaining. They had to be self-financing and self-accounting, that is, responsible for their own profits and losses. The provisions also acknowledged that worker-incentive systems (meaning significant wage differentials) were important and made worker organizations (enterprise work collectives) responsible for electing the enterprise leaders.

The 1987 provisions were intended to reduce the role of the central government so that enterprises could operate more efficiently. In the past, GOSPLAN (the State Planning Committee) and other high level bodies attempted to control all economic activity, that is, to micromanage the Soviet economy. The new provisions called for central-planning organs to be relieved of the day-to-day management of the economy and to refocus their efforts on broader guidance and implementation of the country's economic activity. By removing themselves from micromanagement of the economy, they were to allow enterprises and local territorial units within the Soviet Union to assume more decision-making authority and accountability.

The 1987 Basic Provisions also dealt with other important issues, such as wages and social well-being. The provisions rejected the idea of wage leveling (i.e., equality) and argued that wage differentials can act as important incentives to workers. The provisions also called attention to the human factors of development and for an increase in the level of the nation's prosperity and the standard of living.

By the end of the 1980s, it was apparent to all that perestroika and the Gorbachev reforms would not quickly and easily revive the failing Soviet economy. In 1989, Leonid Abalkin, a leading Soviet economist and deputy prime minister of the government, drew attention to a colossal budget deficit of $165 billion and called it the most important economic problem facing the country. The $165 billion would put the USSR's deficit at approximately 11 percent of the Soviet GNP, much higher than the worrisome U.S. deficit, which during the same period stayed at about 4 percent of the American GNP. To deal with the deficit, Abalkin said the Soviet government would have to slash military and civilian spending and shift many government projects to private financing.

Other official reports were calling attention to Soviet economic problems. A bleak report published in the government newspaper *Izvestia* in January 1989 concluded that the country's economic situation was precarious. According to the report, agricultural output grew only 0.7 percent in 1988, far short of the 6.3 percent target in the government's economic plan. National income grew 4.4 percent in 1988 instead of the targeted 6.6 percent goal. Gorbachev attempted to buoy the spirits of the Soviet people, indicating that there were a number of reasons for the continuing Soviet economic difficulties in the late 1980s. He cited such causes as the investments required by the war in Afghanistan, the tragic 1988 earthquake in Armenia, the nuclear accident in Chernobyl, and the drop in oil export prices. Although these and other reasons no doubt helped explain the continuing economic difficulties in the Soviet Union, it was also apparent that the changes Gorbachev referred to as perestroika were not working well and were unable to bring quick relief to the Soviet economy.

Following the Soviet lead and in response to serious economic decline in their own country, Polish leaders introduced an important economic reform program of their own in the late 1980s. Among other things new Polish laws removed all limits on the size of a private business, which meant that Polish capitalists were to be allowed to own factories with thousands of employees. The new laws also said that any business activity not legally prohibited may be freely undertaken. This reversed the previous principle of state control, under which no private business activity could be undertaken without official authorization. A new Polish law on foreign investment allowed foreign companies to set up operations with an unlimited number of employees. That meant that Americans could go to Poland (and increasingly to the Soviet Union and other communist countries as well) and establish pri-

vate businesses that were under the total ownership of American capitalists.

In early 1990, the Polish leaders adopted a series of radical economic reforms designed to greatly accelerate the transformation of their economy from one based on socialist principles to one based on principles of the free market. Some of the economic shock measures undertaken in Poland included decontrol of almost all prices; the abolition of most consumer subsidies; widespread privatization of state enterprises; and the devaluation of the Polish currency, the zloty, in an effort to make it convertible on international exchanges.

After Mao's death in 1976, the Chinese also realized their economic stagnation and began to consider reform. In 1984, the leaders announced sweeping economic reforms, what Deng Xiaoping referred to as a "revolution." The reforms called for greater decentralization of industrial management and more competition among factories. At the core of the reforms was an attempt to invigorate the state enterprises by granting them more autonomy. The reforms were intended to introduce more market forces in industry and make businesses compete so that, in the Chinese communists' words, "only the best survive." Another key component of the reforms was the drastic modification of centralized planning. The reforms reduced the scope of mandatory planning to include only items that were vital to the national interest and people's livelihood, such as the production of energy and raw materials. Service industries and the production of small commodities, on the other hand, were to be left to market forces.

There was further evidence of dramatic change in China in the 1980s. In 1984, the Chinese Communist Party newspaper, *People's Daily*, said that although the works of Marx and Lenin should be studied, they were not necessarily applicable to the contemporary problems and challenges confronting China. In a front-page commentary, *People's Daily* noted that "Marx died one hundred and one years ago. . . . We cannot depend on the works of Marx and Lenin to solve our modern day questions." This dramatic statement was qualified somewhat the next day when the newspaper ran an inconspicuous three-line "supplementary correction" that said the last part of the commentary should have read: "We cannot depend on Marx and Lenin to solve *all* our modern day questions." (Italics added.) A few days later, a senior Chinese Communist Party ideologist told foreign journalists that although Marx was a great revolutionary whose ideas still underpinned Chinese theory, he did not provide practical answers and advice on how to build a socialist economy. The ideologist noted that some of Marx's theories were far from enough to resolve the contemporary problems of socialist economic construction. These and related developments underscored the fact that the 1980s were a time of economic challenge and change in much of the Second World.

The Social Setting: Well-Being and Equality

The Marxist-Leninist experiments brought neither well-being nor equality to their societies. This is not to say that people are living in these states in utter poverty or that the gap between the "haves" and "haves nots" has not been reduced under socialism. Rather it is to say that observers both within Second World systems (including the highest level leaders) and from abroad agree that socioeconomic progress has not been impressive and certainly not as great as was promised by past communist leaders.

Let us begin by observing, first, general indicators of economic and social standing, and second, how equally these economic and social resources have been shared within the societies.

Economic and Social Well-Being

We can begin by looking at the Gross National Product (GNP) figures for each of the countries; GNP tells us something about the size of the national economies (see Table 2.2). Although the Second World countries vary considerably in economic size and strength, the GNPs tend to be considerably smaller (with the exception of the USSR) than those of the more developed economies of the First World. When examining GNP per capita figures, which tell us how this overall, national economic strength looks when spread among the entire population, we see that the Second World societies are far behind the United States and much of the highly industrialized countries of the First World. The 1986 GNP per capita figure for Americans ($17,478) was about double that of the Soviet Union ($8,442) and most of the East European states. However, the real standard of living for Americans is even more than double, as we will see later, because of the high level of Soviet spending for defense and investment. That is to say that although there have been considerable economic resources in many Second World states, an extraordinarily large portion of them has been invested in capital and military development and an unusually small portion in the consumer realm. Therefore, the GNP per capita figures for these states are inflated, overstating the amount of economic resources that have been available for social and consumer investment.

There are also important differences within the Second World. Although the Soviet GNP

Table 2.2 Socioeconomic Indicators, 1986

Country	GNP (billion US $)	GNP per capita (US $)	Global Economic-Social Standing*
Albania	4.2	1,391	55
Bulgaria	44.4	4,955	33
Cambodia	1.1	147	130
China	314.9	299	94
Cuba	20.0	1,999	40
Czechoslovakia	103.8	6,688	29
East Germany	146.5	8,808	16
Hungary	66.0	6,212	28
Laos	0.8	227	120
Mongolia	1.7	880	67
North Korea	25.7	1,231	55
Poland	188.6	5,034	37
Romania	91.8	4,024	46
Soviet Union	2,357.0	8,442	25
Vietnam	14.0	229	101
Yugoslavia	85.1	3,659	43
USA†	4,219.2	17,478	4

* Represents average rankings of 142 countries, based on GNP per capita and education and health indicators.
† The USA is included for comparative purposes.
(*Source*) Adapted from Ruth Leger Sivard, *World Military and Social Expenditures, 1989* (Washington, D.C.: World Priorities, 1989), pp. 47–55.

per capita of $8,442 is far below that of the United States, Yugoslavia ($3,659) is far below that of the USSR, and China ($299) far below that of Yugoslavia. Perhaps the two most important observations we should make when examining the figures in Table 2.2 are, first, that the economies of the Second World lag far behind those of the United States and other industrialized countries of the First World, and second, there is a great range of socioeconomic resources within the Second World.

The differences in the GNP, GNP per capita, and Economic-Social Standing figures among the states listed in Table 2.2 have a direct impact on the standards of living found in the various countries. Economic development is of course a major factor determining the physical or material quality of life. Because the economic indicators describing the U.S. economy are much stronger than those for the Soviet Union, we can infer that much more money is available for investing in the American people. And because the indicators of economic development are much higher in the Soviet Union and East European countries than in their Asian counterparts, so too is the standard of living. That means that the amount and quality of housing, the availability of food and social services, and so forth are much better in the Soviet Union—no matter how bad they may be—than in places like Vietnam, Cambodia, and China.

Most Second World countries have done fairly well in providing the basic necessities of life such as food, housing, and health care; very few people are starving in these states and few are without some form of housing and health care. The caloric intake and protein consumption of Soviet citizens, as a matter of fact, compare well with the highly industrialized countries of the West. And social services such as pension systems, worker benefits, health care, and urban transportation are not bad and, in fact, sometimes better than those found in the West.

These and some other indicators of the quality of life in communist systems look good on paper. For example, the number of Soviet physicians and hospital beds per capita is far higher than that found in the United States. However, the quality of health care, food, and social services tends to be very poor in communist systems. Medical doctors are poorly trained and often inattentive. Hospital beds are available but often cramped in overcrowded and unsanitary facilities. The difficulties encountered by the Soviet government when responding to the great tragedy of the 1988 earthquake in Armenia called attention to some of the Soviet shortcomings in the provision of medical and emergency social services.

Additionally, although the caloric and protein intake in the Soviet Union and East European countries is high, the quality of the diet is very poor. Meat and fresh produce are often unavailable, and long lines in front of meat markets and produce and department stores continue to be seen throughout much of the Second World. Their dietary and consumption standards are far below those of their neighbors in Western Europe.

Although housing is cheap in Second World states, it is often of poor quality and space is very cramped. The average living space for families in the Soviet Union is estimated to be less than half of what it is in the United States. Twenty percent of Soviet urban families in the mid-1980s lived in communal apartments, where they shared kitchens and bathroom facilities. During the same period, 25 percent of the state-controlled urban residences contained no running water, and 10 percent had no sewerage or central heat.

The availability of housing has also been a major problem in most of these states. Because there is a severe shortage of housing units, many who desperately need living quarters have to wait long periods of time before receiving any housing. This shortage has many social consequences; for example, it deters many people from marrying at a young age. Moreover, because marriage often means living with one's in-laws for years waiting for cramped apartment space to become available, the housing shortage also contributes to divorce. Clearly, the Soviet and other Second World systems are still struggling with the challenge of improving the availability and quality of housing for their people.

There is also a shortage of consumer items throughout much of the Second World. People generally have plenty of money but very little to buy. In the 1980s, the number of televisions per capita in the Soviet Union was one half that in the United States, the number of radios one fourth, and the number of automobiles less than one tenth. Before recent changes, East Germans had to wait fifteen years for a little Trabant, the underpowered, smoke-belching car of the GDR.

Consumers in Second World systems have lived in environments of general deprivation when compared with the standards of the West. Although well-being is much more than food, housing, and the ability to buy consumer goods,

These empty shelves in a Warsaw meat market in 1989 were representative of the food shortages throughout Eastern Europe and the Soviet Union in recent years.

these conditions do tell us about what communist systems have been able to do to promote the physical quality of life. The material deprivation existing in these states had a great deal to do with the growing expression of discontent and resulting political changes that swept over Eastern Europe in the late 1980s. The East European standard of living was considerably below what was found in counterpart states in the West. When the East Germans streamed through the Berlin Wall in 1989, their expressions of amazement with the West's material abundance were a clear indication of the different standards between East and West. Other Eastern societies, like Romania, lived in even more deprived environments than the East Germans. Due to the malaise in the Romanian economy and the dictator Ceausescu's austerity programs, the average Romanian citizen lived a life of extreme material deprivation in the 1980s. Many homes were allowed to burn only one light bulb and to turn on the heat for only a few hours a day in the dead of winter.

The material deprivation so prevalent in the Second World is likely to grow in the short term as many Second World states undertake economic reform programs. Many in the Second World are learning that the transformation from a command to a market economy can be painful; that there is no quick fix. The economic shock treatment applied to Poland in early 1990 initially resulted in even greater shortages of goods and longer lines than what had existed under the traditional Polish command economic system.

The inflationary pressures, unemployment, currency devaluations, disruptions of supply, and shortages that accompany the tearing down of a communist economic system are making life very frustrating for many in the Second World today. Their standard of living is being destabilized and threatened by the reform processes that many expected to be a cure-all. They are being told by political leaders and economists at home and in the West that in the long run they will be better off under a market system. They are asked to be patient and accept uncertainty. For people who for years have lived in a highly stable and predictable, if not prosperous, economic environment, the present uprooting and change in their lives must be very unsettling. Just how long their patience and tolerance for economic reform will last remains an unanswered question.

If communist systems have not done so well in providing a reasonable level of physical well-being, how have they done in promoting equality, that is, an equal distribution of available resources among their people? Before trying to answer this question, let us see what Marxist-Leninists think about equality.

Equality

In the *Communist Manifesto*, Karl Marx and Friedrich Engels wrote, "The history of all hitherto existing society is the history of class struggles." According to Marxist theory, modern industrial society had given birth to the proletariat and bourgeoisie, the two antagonistic classes of the capitalist stage of development. With the establishment of communism, a new historical epoch was to occur. This socioeconomic system was to be free of classes and exploitation and based on the principles of social and material equality.

The avenue leading to communism, said Marx and Engels, leads through the socioeconomic stage of socialism, in which property is made public and private ownership abolished. According to Marxist theory, private property is the force that divides people during the capitalist stage of development. If you forbid private property, you dissolve the basis for class antagonism.

During the early period of their rule, the Communist Parties moved to nationalize—sometimes quickly, at other times more gradually—private property and place power, at least theoretically, in the hands of a proletarian dictatorship. Although the dissolution of private property was gradual in some states, such as in China where Mao wanted to use the capitalists and avoid class warfare, or incomplete, as in some East European societies where small private farms and businesses continued to exist, large holdings of private property were outlawed and transferred to collective social or state ownership. Under socialism, the proletarian dictatorship was to be a temporary arrangement preceding communism, the idealized classless society. The basic question concerning this theory and the hypothesized developments involves their validity. Would socialism necessarily lead to equality? Would class boundaries and distinctions dissolve under Communist Party rule? Would this lead to the development of the classless community of peoples envisioned under communism?

The experience of the Second World states suggests that, although some inequalities were radically reduced, development of a classless society under socialism was not, at least in the short run, an easy task. There were a number of forces making the transition difficult if not impossible, and these involve some central features of an industrializing society. Most social theorists maintain that a division of labor is a necessary prerequisite to or at least a component of industrialization. Division of labor refers to the structure of jobs and the specialization of occupational skills needed to achieve industrial development. For example, an industrializing society requires engineers, planners, and workers; these occupations vary in terms of training and skills. As we have noted, the guiding principle of socialism is "from each according to his abilities, to each according to his contribution"; therefore, those occupations that contribute more important skills receive greater rewards. All the countries we are studying adopted this philosophy of a differentiated reward system during their socialist phases of development. The communist ideal of "from each according to his abilities, to each according to his *needs*" remains an unachieved ideal today.

Although Vladimir Ilyich Lenin and the Bolsheviks initially instituted a policy of wage leveling, they soon opted for a system providing incentives in the form of sizable wage differentials. Through the 1930s and 1940s, Stalin was willing to rationalize inequality in wages as a necessary incentive to attract workers into desired occupations. Soviet industrialization during this phase of development required skilled workers, planners, and engineers as well as clerical and administrative personnel. These and other occupations provided crucial functions required of an industrializing society, and they represented the division of labor that characterizes all modernizing societies. Although Nikita Khrushchev launched a campaign in the 1950s to reduce these wage differentials, they were never eliminated. Table 2.3 indicates the differentials among some selected occupations in the USSR and four East European countries after the Khrushchev period. Using worker salaries as a base unit (100), the data indicate that although pay generally became more egalitarian between 1960 and 1973, particularly in the USSR, significant differences according to occupation remained. Such differences remain through the present.[11]

It is easy to see why a growing specialization and division of labor had made the establishment of a classless society difficult. When you have considerable differences between the highest- and lowest-paid workers, you encounter strong forces encouraging the formation of classes. Some communists would attempt to refute this argument by noting that although Second World societies do exhibit occupational wage differences among individuals and groups, they do not represent the traditional classes of earlier forms of society. In a capitalist society, they would argue, the *bourgeoisie* control and exploit the working class. In earlier societies (primitive, slave, feudal, and capitalist), the nature of class differences led to an inevitable class struggle—"the history of all hitherto existing society." Therefore, Marxists contend that although wage and status differences may exist in socialist societies and may lead to a system of social stratification, they will not result in the social classes and resultant conflict of old. Although the issue is debatable, we can at least conclude that social divisions are present in Second World societies and that they do have some of the characteristics of social classes under capitalism.

Occupational and income differences are among the primary elements associated with social stratification in contemporary Second World societies. A top-ranking engineer or a dean in a university is much more likely to have a disproportionate share of respect, well-being, enlightenment, and power than a blue-collar worker. The official ideology maintains that all occupational roles contribute equally to the building of socialism, but some are considerably more valued than others. A nuclear physicist at Moscow State University, an engineer in Beijing, and a director of an economic enterprise in Yugoslavia command a higher income and status than rank-and-file workers. In addition, their opportunities for attaining the values associated with enlightenment are greater, as are their opportunities for achieving a preferred state of well-being and political power.

The gap between the highest- and lowest-paid occupations tends to be smaller in Second World than in First World states. In many First World states such as the United States, salary differences can be more than 300 to 1, meaning that the highest-paid people earn more than 300 times what the lowest-paid people earn. A considerable body of research supports these points. The distinguished American sociologist Gerhard Lenski has noted that the range of salaries and incomes generally seems to have been reduced in Marxist societies to a level well below that in most comparable non-Marxist societies.[12] His research indicated a ratio of 50 to 1 between top salaries and the minimum wage in the USSR in the 1970s, 40 to 1 in China before Mao's death, and 7.3 to 1 in Cuba. (Again, the corresponding ratio in the United States in recent years has been approximately 300 to 1.) As Lenski cautioned, these figures should not be taken at face value, and they do not provide a direct

Table 2.3 Average Pay by Occupational Category*

	1960	1973
Bulgaria		
Intelligentsia	142.1	132.1
Routine nonmanual	93.8	95.5
Worker	100.0	100.0
Peasant	92.1	91.5
Czechoslovakia		
Intelligentsia	116.8	120.4
Routine nonmanual	77.0	81.3
Worker	100.0	100.0
Peasant	79.2	98.1
Hungary		
Intelligentsia	157.2	142.4
Routine nonmanual	94.8	92.4
Worker	100.0	100.0
Peasant	na[†]	94.1
Poland		
Intelligentsia	156.7	144.3
Routine nonmanual	105.1	100.1
Worker	100.0	100.0
Peasant	na[†]	77.5
USSR		
Intelligentsia	150.9	134.1
Routine nonmanual	82.1	84.5
Worker	100.0	100.0
Peasant	57.7	76.5

* Intelligentsia, routine nonmanuals, workers (all in state industry), and peasants (workers in state/socialist agriculture).
† Not available.
(*Source*) Adapted from Walter D. Connor, *Socialism, Politics, and Equality: Hierarchy and Change in Eastern Europe and the USSR* (New York: Columbia University Press, 1979), p. 231.

measure of differentials in living standards. However, Lenski concluded that the Marxist experiments have, in fact, resulted in a reduction of inequality in income and living standards in Second World societies. At the same time, he called attention to a number of Marxist failures, including: (1) the persistence of very high levels of political inequality, (2) the persistence of worker alienation, (3) the persistence of gender inequality, (4) the persistence of urban-rural inequality, and (5) the failure of Marxist societies to give birth to the new socialist man.[13]

Urban and rural distinctions also contribute to a stratified society. The differences between life in Moscow, Warsaw, or Belgrade and the backward peasant life of the villages is extreme. Urbanization has been a major agent of social change and, in some respects, has had a leveling effect on a host of social differences. The common experiences of city life have softened some occupational and cultural differences, whereas life in the agricultural areas often remains parochial and provincial. The social differences between a typical college student in New York City and one in Moscow are considerable but tend to be less significant than those between a Russian student in Moscow and his counterpart in a remote Siberian village.

Communists stood and fought for the emancipation of sexes as well as of workers. In some respects, however, gender tends to stratify societies within the Second World because women predominate in many of the unskilled, "physical" professions (e.g., construction workers, machine operators, bus drivers). Unlike the situation in some First and Third World societies, in socialist states women represent an extremely large and important sector of the total work force. In addition to their predomination in many of the unskilled occupations, women also represent an important sector of the work force in many professional occupations. For example,

Soviet women outnumber men in such occupations as economic planner, doctor, and dentist.

The greatest gender discrimination in the Soviet Union, and traditionally in other Second World states as well, has been in the area of politics. Although there is a relatively high proportion of women in ceremonial political roles, there is a very small percentage in positions of real power in either the Party or the government. Underrepresentation of women is also evident in some nonpolitical directing posts, such as those in hospitals, factories, and in the field of higher education. Another interesting and more subtle form of discrimination seems to take place in the home. After putting in a full day as a machine builder, bus driver, or economic planner, a woman typically returns home to assume the major household responsibilities. Perhaps to a greater extent than in the West, Soviet and East European men do little to share in the burdens of housework. Social discrimination against women, deeply embedded in the traditional value structures of Second World cultures, will have to be eradicated before a genuine equality of sexes can be achieved in these societies.

We should now be aware that standards of living and their associated systems of social stratification vary considerably among the socialist states comprising the Second World. Although some of these differences can be attributed to political choices, environmental factors such as socioeconomic development help determine who gets what in the socialist states. Nobody gets very much in China simply because there is not very much to go around. The average citizen gets a little more in the Soviet Union, primarily because the state is at a somewhat more advanced economic level. Furthermore, the average citizen in Leningrad or Moscow enjoys a higher standard of living than his or her counterpart in the less developed republic of Kazakhstan, largely owing to the fact that the socioeconomic capabilities of the Russian region are higher than those of Kazakhstan.

However, there are political choices that account for some of the differences in the values people enjoy. For example, Communist Party officials have traditionally enjoyed a better standard of living than the average citizen in Second World states. Until recently at least, these officials have been given top priority in the distribution of state goods and property. They have allowed themselves to bypass the numerous lines and waiting lists the average citizen has had to endure to acquire everything from cars to shoes. They have had the nicest homes and eaten the best food. They have shopped in special stores, open only to them, where they have bought imported consumer goods unavailable anywhere else in their country. Their children have gone to the best schools and been given the most attractive jobs the state has had to offer. Some communist leaders have used their position in the Communist Party to amass huge personal wealth. The Swiss bank accounts, elaborate homes, and luxurious lifestyle of the late Romanian communist dictator Nicolae Ceausescu, for example, have proved to be the equal of any personal fortune built by a monarch or successful capitalist.

In addition to the benefits that have been granted to Communist Party officials in the past, other social groups within Second World states have also received economic and social advantages that run contrary to Marxist principles of social equality. One of these groups has been the star athletes of most Second World states. Communist leaders have long viewed international sports competitions like the Olympic Games as opportunities to enhance the reputation of their states and a means to add legitimacy to their own rule. Their rationale was

that if communist athletes were judged to be best in the world, the system they lived in and were governed by could more easily be promoted as also being the best in the world. To guarantee that their athletes would be the best in the world, communist leaders had to make sure that their sports stars were catered to in all aspects of their personal and professional lives. East Germany was perhaps the best example of this. By offering many of the material advantages to star athletes that they themselves enjoyed, communist leaders provided the necessary incentives to ensure that their athletes worked hard and strove to do their best in international competitions. Judging by the resounding success communist athletes have typically enjoyed in these competitions over the last two decades, it is safe to say that the athletes did what was expected of them by their leaders—they brought medals home to their motherland. It will be interesting to see how well the athletes of Eastern Europe compete in the future in their changing environments.

Ethnicity and Socialism

The Second World settings are also very much affected by the sociocultural features of nationality and ethnicity. In the *Communist Manifesto*, Marx and Engels predicted that nationality was a dying force in the contemporary world. They believed that with the increasing freedom of commerce in the international market and with the growing uniformity of production and conditions of life, national differences would dissolve. Furthermore, as exploitation and antagonism between classes began to cease under socialism, so too would hostility among nations and nationalities. As national differences began to disappear (again, according to Marx and Engels), we would witness the development of internationalism within the socialist world. In this phase of historical development, workers of the world would be united by the bonds of socialist or proletarian internationalism and the forces of nationalism and ethnocentrism would cease to exist.

As we witness events in the contemporary world, we can see that Marx and Engels underestimated the power of nationalism. Nationality, or nationhood, is a strong and enduring sociocultural force that grows out of the history, geography, language, and culture of groups of people. As we approach the twenty-first century, we seem to be witnessing a growth rather than a decline in nationalism in the Second World.

Although we usually refer to the "nations" of the communist world, strictly speaking, this is misleading. Some of the Second World "nations" are composed of many distinct nations or nationalities, each with its own language, customs, and sense of the past. For example, the Soviet Union is a multinational state and includes such nationalities as Russians, Ukrainians, Armenians, Georgians, Lithuanians, Tatars, a variety of Asian nationalities, and many, many others. There are more than 100 national and ethnic groups in the Soviet Union. And although Russian, the official language of the state, tends to be spoken by most members of all groups, the Soviet Union still displays a rich mix of languages that represents many distant points in Europe and Asia.

The largest Soviet nationality by far is the Russians, who comprise just over half of the total population (see Table 2.4). The bulk of these Russians resides in the Russian Republic (RSFSR), which stretches from Moscow and Leningrad eastward to the Pacific (see the map of the USSR), although many Russians live in other republics as well. The Russian Republic in the Soviet Union is huge, almost twice the size of the United States. The Russian Republic contains sixteen autonomous republics, five autonomous regions, and ten national areas, representing a heterogeneous multinational mosaic of groups. The next largest Soviet nationalities are the Ukrainians, who reside primarily in the Ukrainian Soviet Socialist Republic, and the Uzbeks, who inhabit the Uzbek Soviet Socialist Republic. The fourth largest is the Byelorussians, or White Russians, and they too have a republic within which they predominate.

Administratively and constitutionally, the early Soviet leaders designed a federal political arrangement to reflect the extreme diversity in the society. This federal structure divided the Soviet state into the fifteen union republics and the autonomous republics indicated on the map. The units coincide with the complex array of national and ethnic groups in the state and vary in status according to the size and strength of the groups. Although the constitution guaranteed these federal units important rights and privileges, past Soviet leaders did not honor them. This all began to change, however, during the Gorbachev period.

Growing nationalism is one of today's pressing challenges, if not the most critical challenge, that will affect the future of the Soviet Union. After decades of repression, national differences began rising to the surface, often violently, with the appearance of glasnost in the late 1980s. A brief review of a few important cases will help convey how critical an issue today's ethnic and national relations is to the Soviet future.

One case involves the growing unrest in Central Asia, the area in the Soviet Union that is populated by most of the USSR's 45 million Moslems. Because the Soviet Union has the fifth largest Islamic population of any country in the world, and because of the growth of Islamic nationalism and the fear of Islamic fundamentalism in the USSR, the Soviet authorities

Table 2.4   Major Nationalities of the USSR, 1979 (with populations >1 million)

Nationality	Population	Percent of Total	Linguistic Group	Traditional Religion
Russian	137,397,089	52.4	Slavic	Orthodox
Ukrainian	42,347,387	16.2	Slavic	Orthodox
Uzbek	12,455,978	3.6	Turkic	Islam
Belorussian	9,462,715	3.6	Slavic	Orthodox
Kazakh	6,556,442	2.5	Turkic	Islam
Tatar	6,317,468	2.4	Turkic	Islam
Azeri	5,477,330	2.1	Turkic	Islam
Armenian	4,151,241	1.6	Indo-European	National Christian
Georgian	3,570,504	1.4	Iberian	Orthodox
Moldavian	2,968,224	1.1	Romance	Orthodox
Tadjik	2,897,697	1.1	Iranian	Islam
Lithuanian	2,850,905	1.1	Baltic	Roman Catholic
Turkmen	2,027,913	0.8	Turkic	Islam
German	1,936,214	0.7	Germanic	Lutheran
Kirgiz	1,906,271	0.7	Turkic	Islam
Jewish	1,810,875	0.7	Yiddish	Judaism
Chuvash	1,751,366	0.7	Turkic	Orthodox
Latvian	1,439,037	0.5	Baltic	Lutheran
Bashkir	1,371,452	0.5	Turkic	Islam
Mordvinian	1,191,765	0.5	Finnic	Orthodox
Polish	1,150,991	0.4	Slavic	Roman Catholic
Estonian	1,019,851	0.4	Finnic	Lutheran

(*Source*) Tsentral'noe statisticheskoe upravlenie, *Chislennost' i sostav naseleniia SSSR po dannym vsesoiuznoi perepisi naseleniia 1979 goda* (Moscow: Finansy i Statistika, 1985), 71–73; Barbara A. Anderson and Brian D. Silver, "Estimating Russification of Ethnic Identity Among Non-Russians in the USSR," *Demography* 20 (November 1983), 466; Philip G. Roeder, *Soviet Political Dynamics* (New York: Harper & Row, 1988), p. 372.

are deeply concerned about the increasing discontent in that part of the country. Our case begins in 1986 with the removal of First Secretary Dinmukhammed Kunaev, the powerful leader of the Kazakh Republic since 1964, and the appointment of a nonresident Russian as his successor. The leaders in Moscow considered Kunaev, the Kazakh leadership, and many of their supporters as corrupt and felt that they had to bring in an outsider to manage a far-reaching purge. However, the appointment of an ethnic Russian with no experience in Kazakhstan showed extraordinary insensitivity to Kazakh national sentiments and set off violent rioting in Alma-Ata, the capital of the Kazakh Republic. Thousands stormed through the capital city, looted stores, burned cars, waved Kazakh-language banners, and attacked Russians and their

The proclamation of Lithuanian independence shown here is a clear indication of the continuing presence and power of national identity in the Soviet Union.

property. Although early reports referred to these disturbances as being the result of "hooligans," subsequent dispatches suggested that Kazakh officials also were involved and bore some responsibility for the rampage. A resolution of the central Community Party authorities in Moscow charged that the former Kazakh leadership had committed serious mistakes in implementing the country's nationalities policies. Although the Kazakh movement was largely repressed, the 1986 uprising and ensuing events were among the many signals that the Soviet Islamic minorities would no longer tolerate in the age of glasnost what they perceived to be Russian domination of their political and economic affairs. Ethnic tensions and disturbances in Islamic areas such as Uzbekistan and Tadzhikistan in the late 1980s indicated that other Central Asian nationalities also had strong feelings about their situations. As we will see later in this book, nationality in the Soviet Union raises complex questions and concerns about proper allocation of the values of power, respect, well-being, and enlightenment. The Islamic minorities, along with many others, do not think they are receiving their fair share.

Another case took place in the late 1980s in the southern area of the USSR, but west across the Caspian Sea in the region known as the Caucasus. This case involves a virulent dispute between the Christian Armenians and the Moslem Azerbaijanis and the relationship of both to the Soviet state and centralized Communist Party rule. Both nationalities have long been concerned with what they consider Russian discrimination and their less-than-ideal situations in the Soviet Union. But it was Armenian concern over an enclave of Armenians who reside in Nagorno-Karabakh, an autonomous region close to the Armenian republic but officially under the jurisdiction of the Azerbaijan republic that precipitated violence and bloodshed in 1988. Armenian concerns were extensive and elaborate, but basically they felt the Azerbaijanis were repressing the social and cultural development of their fellow Armenians who were living on Azerbaijan soil in Nagorno-Karabakh. Accordingly, they demanded that the Armenian enclave in Azerbaijan be united with Armenia. Simultaneously, they raised broader Armenian concerns, including expanded Armenian autonomy vis-à-vis the central government in Moscow; increased teaching of the Armenian language; the creation of Armenian military units where Armenians could serve on their own soil rather than in the far reaches of the Soviet state; and the elimination of hazardous industrial sites on Armenian soil. This final demand took on further significance in the aftermath of the tragic earthquake that destroyed whole cities and killed approximately 50,000 Armenians in December 1988.

Although Gorbachev and Communist Party leaders in Moscow considered and acceded to some of the Armenian demands in the late 1980s, they were unwilling to put Nagorno-Karabakh under Armenian control. This brought about a further deterioration in relations among the concerned parties and an outbreak in violence in which many were killed. Demonstrators defied government bans on public rallies, and hundreds of thousands flocked to air their grievances in Yerevan and Baku, the respective capitals of the republics of Armenia and Azerbaijan. By the close of 1988, more than 100,000 people had fled their homes, and military forces were brought in to preserve the peace. In an attempt to defuse the violent ethnic dispute that had brought virtual martial law to the two republics, the Soviet government decided in 1989 to put the disputed territory of Nagorno-Karabakh under the direct rule of the central government in Moscow, thereby ending sixty-five years of Azerbaijani control over the contested region.

The tragic earthquake that struck Armenia made the situation even more serious. This natural disaster provided further evidence to Armenians of their disadvantaged situation and Soviet discrimination. Armenians criticized the Soviet government for their inadequate rescue and reconstruction efforts. When Armenian nationalists tied these criticisms to the larger issue of what they perceived to be a cavalier and callous Soviet disposition toward Armenian concerns, they were arrested, which further heightened Armenian nationalist sentiments. The Azerbaijan-Armenian conflict subsequently exploded on numerous occasions and resulted in the imposition of Soviet troops and martial law on Azerbaijan soil in early 1990. Although much is uncertain as this book goes to press, we can expect the Armenians and Azerbaijanis to continue to press their demands for power, respect, well-being, and other values to which they feel entitled.

Another proud nation in the Caucasus, the southwestern part of the Soviet Union, is the

Georgians, who also are deeply concerned about the values to which they feel entitled. The Georgians are a fiercely nationalistic nation, and many are pressing for independence from the Soviet Union. In April 1989, twenty independence demonstrators were killed in the Georgian capital of Tbilisi as they pressed their demands in a clash with Soviet authorities. Georgian concerns continue to fester in this nationalistic region of the Caucasus.

Our final Soviet case involves the Baltic nationalities—the Estonians, Latvians, and Lithuanians—and their efforts to expand their power, well-being, and respect vis-à-vis the central Soviet government in Moscow. Like the Armenians, the small Baltic nationalities have suffered much throughout history. Their cherished independence between WWI and WWII was ended as a result of Soviet annexation of their territories in 1940. The Stalinist government accused and arrested many Baltic nationals as class enemies, moved Russian authorities into key positions, unleashed a frontal assault on private farming and enterprise, and did great damage to the thriving economies in this proud region. The experience of the Baltic nationalities under Soviet rule has not been a pleasant one. The Estonian, Latvian, and Lithuanian nationalities do not feel they have received the values they deserve.

In the context of increasing openness and growing discussion about the relationships between the central and republic governments in the late 1980s, Baltic nationalism underwent a powerful resurgence. A significant event that triggered the reactions of the Baltic peoples involved discussions in Moscow about Gorbachev's reform program and the future of republic-federal government relations. Whereas the Baltic groups desired more political and economic freedom, some in the central government in Moscow wanted to maintain the

central government's traditional domination of the republics and local governments.

The reactions of the Estonians convey the concerns of the Baltic nationalities, so let us focus for a moment on the Estonians. Feeling spiritually closer to the West (and particularly to Finland) than to the Soviet Union, the Estonians were keen to take advantage of glasnost and perestroika to bring about changes promoting their national interests. Accordingly, as a first step in reaction to the discussion in Moscow, the Estonian parliament adopted by unanimous vote in 1988 a resolution giving Estonian authorities the right to refuse to apply Soviet laws. This declaration of Estonian sovereignty was a clear and dramatic statement intended to increase the republic's power in relation to the central Soviet authorities. It proclaimed Estonian sovereignty and power in all matters except defense and foreign policy. An estimated 900,000 of the 1.5 million Estonian populace signed petitions protesting Soviet policy and favoring the Estonian declaration. The other Baltic nationalities—the Latvians and Lithuanians—shared the Estonian point of view. An estimated 1.5 million of 3.6 million Lithuanians and 300,000 of 2.6 million Latvians signed similar petitions.

The Lithuanians took even more serious actions in the late 1980s to push for their interests. The Lithuanian parliament passed proposals to create a commission to rewrite the Lithuanian constitution and to make Lithuanian rather than Russian the official language and the traditional, independent Lithuanian flag the official flag of the republic. In 1990 the Lithuanian government declared its independence from the Soviet Union, provoking a dramatic showdown with Secretary Gorbachev and the Soviet authorities. As this book goes to press, resurgent Baltic nationalism continues to challenge Soviet authorities as Estonian, Latvian, and Lithuanian leaders attempt to promote the interests and values of their proud peoples. If Soviet authorities cannot convince these and the other constituent nationalities that their best interests are served by belonging to the Soviet Union, they will be confronted with growing secessionist movements. Because of this, most observers believe that the Soviet Union will lose substantial territory by the end of this decade.

Yugoslavia is also a multinational state that continues to be confronted with nationalist movements that challenge the unity and future of Yugoslav communism. Comprised of five South Slavic nationalities—the Croats, Macedonians, Montenegrins, Serbs, and Slovenes—as well as sizable non-Slavic nationalities like the Albanians, the federal Yugoslav system has traditionally given these constituent nationalities a higher level of independence and autonomy than counterpart groups have received in the Soviet Union. This has not brought an end to nationalist tensions, however, as many groups continue to be unhappy with their situations and roles in the Yugoslav union. The largest nationality, the Serbs (comprising 40 percent of the total population of the country), feel that they should have more power in view of their size and importance within the country. Smaller nationalities from more developed regions like Slovenia feel they should have more autonomy to allow them to pursue a more independent course of economic development. The major minority from the most deprived part of the country, the Albanians, feel they should have more aid and autonomy. These and other conflicting demands, along with increasing economic problems, brought Yugoslavia to the brink of ethnonationalistic conflict in the late 1980s. In 1990 the Slovenian communists walked out and aborted the National Party Congress, leading Yugoslav newspapers to write about the end of the Communist Party (or League of Communists) as it is known in Yugoslavia. Ethnonationalism con-

tinues to be a troublesome impediment to the idealistic Yugoslav visions of brotherhood and unity that were held in earlier days.

China is another example of a heterogeneous multiethnic state in the Second World. Although 93 percent of the population is of the basic Chinese nationality (the Han), it is divided into groups characterized by many social, cultural, and linguistic differences. Among the Hans, the spoken language in one region, such as in Canton, may be unintelligible to people from other regions. The Chinese do, however, share a unified written language. In addition to the Han people, China has over 50 million members of minority groups, more than double the total population of Yugoslavia. Of these, more than fifty groups have been designated as minorities and have been given ninety-eight autonomous areas at the provincial, intermediate, and county levels. These autonomous areas, usually named after the group or groups who predominate, provide the minorities greater freedom and government rights—although all these rights are subordinate to national programs, laws, regulations, and organizations. The map of China outlines the twenty-one provinces and five autonomous regions. Autonomous regions are areas heavily populated by non-Chinese minorities. Some of these minorities, like the Tibetans, continue to challenge the authority of the central leaders. Poor relations between the central authorities and Tibet resulted in a major Tibetan rebellion in 1959 and difficulties that continue to the present time.

The economic, social, and ethnic conditions surveyed in this chapter are important when considering the context in which politics takes place. When conditions are bad—when economic resources are limited, when social needs are going unmet, when national unity is strained by ethnic conflict—the challenges of governing are much greater. And that is where many of the Second World states find themselves as we enter the 1990s. Before moving on to our analysis of government and politics, we will consider in the next chapter political cultures, another part of the setting in which politics takes place.

Suggestions for Further Reading

Banac, Ivo, *The National Question in Yugoslavia: Origins, History and Politics* (Ithaca, N.Y.: Cornell University Press, 1984).

Barnett, A. Doak, *China Economy in Global Perspective* (Washington, D.C.: Brookings Institution, 1981).

Bennigsen, Alexandre, and **Marie Broxup,** *The Islamic Threat to the Soviet State* (New York: St. Martin's Press, 1983).

Bergson, Abram, *Soviet Post-War Economic Development* (Stockholm: Almqvist & Wiksell, 1975).

Bialer, Seweryn, *Politics, Society, and Nationality Inside Gorbachev's Russia* (Boulder: Westview Press, 1989).

Conner, Walker, *The National Question in Marxist-Leninist Theory and Strategy* (Princeton, N.J.: Princeton University Press, 1984).

Conner, Walker D., *Socialism, Politics, and Equality: Hierarchy and Change in Eastern Europe and the USSR* (New York: Columbia University Press, 1979).

Eckstein, Alexander, *China's Economic Revolution* (Cambridge: Cambridge University Press, 1977).

Fischer-Galati, Stephen A., *Twentieth Century Rumania* (New York: Columbia University Press, 1970).

Griffith, William E., *Albania and the Sino-Soviet Rift* (Cambridge, Mass.: MIT Press, 1963).

Hewett, Edward A., *Reforming the Soviet Economy* (Washington, D.C.: Brookings Institution, 1988).

Jancar, Barbara Wolfe, *Women under Communism* (Baltimore: Johns Hopkins University Press, 1978).

Matthews, Mervyn, *Poverty in the Soviet Union: Lifestyles of the Underprivileged in Recent Years* (New York: Cambridge University Press, 1986).

Moore, Barrington, Jr., *Authority and Inequality under Capitalism and Socialism* (Oxford: Clarendon Press, 1987).

Nelson, Daniel N., ed., *Communism and the Politics of Inequalities* (Lexington, Mass.: Lexington Books, 1983).

Sirc, Ljubo, *The Yugoslav Economy under Self-Management* (New York: St. Martin's Press, 1979).

Tyson, Laura D'andrea, *The Yugoslav Economic System and Its Performance in the 1970s* (Berkeley: University of California, Institute of International Studies, 1980).

U.S. Congress, Joint Economic Committee. *China's Economy Looks Toward the Year 2000,* Vols. 1 and 2 (Washington, D.C.: U.S. Government Printing Office, 1986).

U.S. Congress, Joint Economic Committee. *Gorbachev's Economic Plans,* Vols. 1 and 2 (Washington, D.C.: U.S. Government Printing Office, 1987).

Notes

1. Stalin's collectivization drive of 1929–36 was a radical program to transfer the private ownership of land to collective farms under state administration. The drive ended with the abolition of 90 percent of private farming and the deportation of over 1 million peasant households. For a detailed history of Stalin's collectivization drive, see Robert Conquest, *Harvest of Sorrow: Soviet Collectivization and the Terror Famine* (Oxford, Oxford University Press, 1986).

2. These and other events resulted in the so-called Sino-Soviet conflict, a dispute characterized by hostile interstate relations between the two communist powers. See Donald Zagoria, *The Sino-Soviet Conflict, 1955–1961* (Princeton, N.J.: Princeton University Press, 1962).

3. The Communist Information Bureau (Cominform) was established in 1947 to bind the East European socialist states more closely to the USSR. In a letter of March 27, 1948, addressed to the Yugoslav communists, Stalin and the Soviet Central Committee castigated the Yugoslav leaders and excommunicated them from the socialist camp. Because they considered themselves loyal to the Soviet Union, this was initially a bitter blow to the Yugoslav communists. For a firsthand account of their reactions and subsequent search for alternative economic and social policies, see Vladimir Dedijer, *The Battle Stalin Lost* (New York: Universal Library, 1972).

4. For a discussion of Soviet demands for reparation payments from the new Communist Party regimes to cover war damages inflicted by the Axis Powers, as well as other forms of Soviet involvement in the postwar economic setting of Eastern Europe, see Nicholas Spulber, *The Economies of Communist Eastern Europe* (Cambridge: MIT Press, 1957).

5. COMECON was established as a response to the Western Marshall Plan and was intended to coordinate reconstruction, planning, production, and foreign trade within Eastern Europe. It originally included Bulgaria, Czechoslovakia, Hungary, Poland, Romania, and the USSR. Subsequently, it was broadened to include Albania, Cuba, East Germany, and Mongolia.

6. *On Khrushchev's Phoney Communism and Its Historical Lessons to the World* (Beijing: Foreign Languages Press, 1964), p. 47.

7. The Soviet leaders were worried by factors other than economic liberalization. There were fears, for example, concerning Western influence and involvement in Czechoslovakia and the possibility that the reforms would result in a Czechoslovak withdrawal from the Warsaw Treaty Organization (WTO) and COMECON pacts.

8. The Warsaw Treaty was signed in 1955 by Albania, Bulgaria, the German Democratic Republic (GDR [East Germany]), Hungary, Poland, Romania, and the USSR as a response to the establishment of the North Atlantic Treaty Organization (NATO). Like NATO, the treaty pledged mutual military assistance in the event of an attack on one of the signatories. The so-called Brezhnev Doctrine that grew out of the 1968 intervention in Czechoslovakia broadened the assistance to include perceived domestic threats to socialism.

9. For details on the Hungarian NEM, see Ivan Volgyes, *Hungary: A Nation of Contradictions* (Boulder, Colo.: Westview, 1982).

10. Mikhail Gorbachev, *Perestroika: New Thinking for Our Country and the World* (New York: Harper & Row, 1987), p. 33.

11. Wage differentials remain a characteristic of all socialist societies, even the most egalitarian, the Chinese.

12. Gerhard Lenski, "Marxist Experiments in Destratification: An Appraisal," *Social Forces* 57(2) (1978): 370–371.

13. Ibid.: 371–376.

OCEAN

Boundaries of Soviet Socialist Republics (S.S.R.)

Boundaries of Autonomous Soviet
Socialist Republics (A.S.S.R.)

Wrangel I.

BERING
SEA

SEVERNAYA
ZEMLYA

NEW SIBERIAN
ISLANDS

LAPTEV

SEA

S O C I A L I S T   R E P U B L I C S

YAKUT A.S.S.R.

REPUBLIC

SEA

OF

OKHOTSK

S O C I A L I S T

Sakhalin I.

Kuril Islands

BURYAT-MONGOL
A.S.S.R.

TUVA
A.S.S.R.

MONGOLIAN

REPUBLIC

CHINA

SEA

OF

JAPAN

JAPAN

NORTH
KOREA

SOUTH
KOREA

EASTERN EUROPE

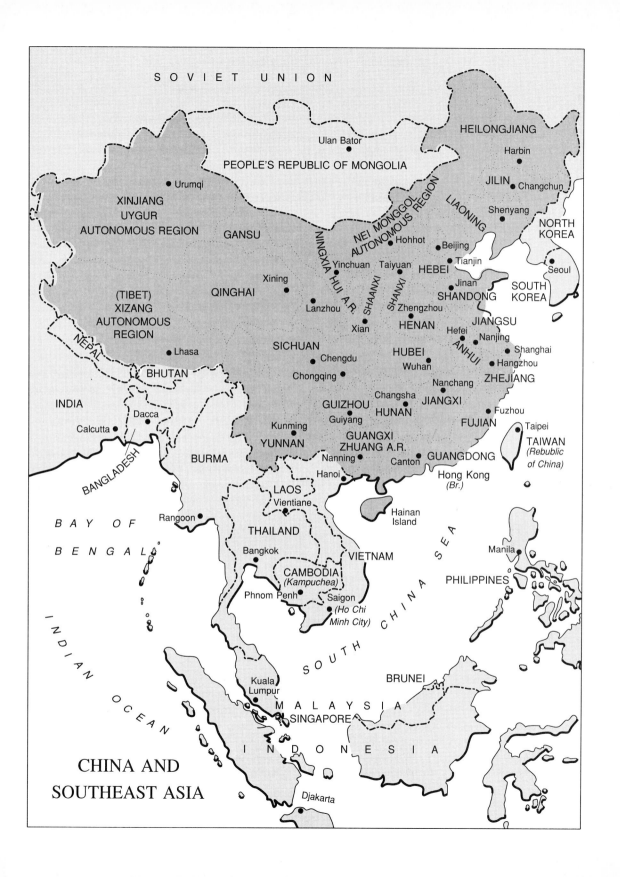

SOVIET UNION

PEOPLE'S REPUBLIC OF MONGOLIA

Ulan Bator

HEILONGJIANG

Harbin

JILIN

Changchun

Urumqi

XINJIANG
UYGUR
AUTONOMOUS REGION

GANSU

NEI MONGGOL
AUTONOMOUS REGION

Hohhot

LIAONING

Shenyang

NORTH
KOREA

NINGXIA HUI A.R.

Yinchuan

Taiyuan

Beijing

Tianjin

HEBEI

Seoul

(TIBET)
XIZANG
AUTONOMOUS
REGION

QINGHAI

Xining

Lanzhou

SHAANXI

SHANXI

Zhengzhou

Jinan

SHANDONG

SOUTH
KOREA

NEPAL

Xian

HENAN

Hefei

Nanjing

JIANGSU

Shanghai

Lhasa

SICHUAN

Chengdu

HUBEI

Wuhan

ANHUI

Hangzhou

ZHEJIANG

BHUTAN

Chongqing

Nanchang

INDIA

Dacca

Changsha

JIANGXI

Calcutta

BANGLADESH

GUIZHOU

Guiyang

HUNAN

Fuzhou

Kunming

GUANGXI
ZHUANG A.R.

FUJIAN

YUNNAN

Nanning

Canton

GUANGDONG

Taipei

TAIWAN
(Rebulic
of China)

BURMA

Hanoi

Hong Kong
(Br.)

BAY OF

BENGAL

Rangoon

LAOS

Vientiane

Hainan
Island

SOUTH CHINA SEA

Manila

THAILAND

VIETNAM

PHILIPPINES

Bangkok

CAMBODIA
(Kampuchea)

INDIAN OCEAN

Phnom Penh

Saigon
(Ho Chi
Minh City)

Kuala
Lumpur

BRUNEI

MALAYSIA

SINGAPORE

INDONESIA

CHINA AND
SOUTHEAST ASIA

Djakarta

CHAPTER 3

POLITICAL CULTURE AND POLITICAL SOCIALIZATION

What do we know about the political attitudes and ideas of the millions upon millions of people who live in Second World societies? What do they want? Do they support their leaders? Are there signs of psychological and attitudinal change in these societies? How are they responding to the experiences of reform and revolution? These important questions take us to the topics of political culture and political socialization.

Because of the past leaders' commitments to build communism, and because of the importance of the human dimension in the process of political change, the concepts of political culture and political socialization are of special significance in our study. Gabriel Almond, the distinguished American political scientist, has noted, "Every political system is embedded in a particular pattern of orientations of political action."[1] This pattern of attitudes and beliefs that people hold toward their system is referred to as political culture; it represents the orientations that define the setting in which politics takes place. The political culture of the Soviet Union is the total composite of that society's ideas about political life. Orientations about

glasnost and perestroika, justice and democracy, welfare and equality, and reform and revolution represent dimensions of the larger Soviet political culture. As in all other states, these orientations have an influence on power, politics, and policy in Second World political systems.

Although we may refer to a Chinese political culture, a Soviet political culture, and so forth, we should realize that it is a simplification to speak of the total set of attitudes and values of the populace and to consider it a homogeneous whole. Obviously, like other societies, those of the Second World are heterogeneous in their beliefs and values, just as they are in social and economic characteristics. However, when we discuss and compare societies, it is useful to have a concept to refer to the general attitudinal and psychological setting within political systems. Political culture is the term for such a concept.

How can one study something as abstract as political culture? What does one try to observe? Some researchers have conducted massive opinion surveys of large samples of national populations. For example, in their book *The Civic Culture*, Almond and Verba surveyed attitudes and values of over 5,000 citizens from the United States, Great Britain, West Germany, Italy, and Mexico to better understand the political cultures of these states.[2] Although some Second World states are beginning to allow such studies, this quantitative approach to the study of political culture was generally not possible in Communist Party states in the past because their governments were unwilling to allow Western scholars to study issues that they considered so sensitive. In this book, we take an inductive approach and base our study on a growing body of research conducted by native and foreign scholars. Although this research is not always based on scientific surveys, it draws on the personal contacts and research of scholars who know these countries well.

Political culture has certain things in common with—but is quite distinct from—a state's ideology. Although the term has been conceptualized in many ways, ideology commonly refers to the set of arguments and beliefs used to justify an existing or desired social order. Although there is bound to be considerable overlap, the ideologies of the Second World states deviate in certain important respects from their political cultures. Whereas in the past, Marxist-Leninist ideology traditionally represented the official arguments and beliefs put forth by Communist Parties to explain and justify their social order, the political cultures of Second World countries have always represented many personal values opposed to Marxism-Leninism. Ideology and political culture differ. There is much ideological and cultural change taking place in Second World states, which makes it even more challenging for authorities who hope to mold attitudes among their citizens that correspond with the changing ideology.

This issue and attempts to mold political culture introduce us to the concept of political socialization. Most political scientists conceive of political socialization as the process by which official or prevailing attitudes and beliefs are transmitted to a society, particularly to newcomers, such as children or immigrants. When the Communist Party states suddenly adopted the ideology of Marxism-Leninism in their political past, in a sense all of their citizens were newcomers and great efforts had to be made to inculcate political orientations conducive to the building of socialism. Because the prerevolutionary societies in these countries had distinctive, noncommunist traditions and political cultures of their own, the transmission of new political orientations to the populace was exceedingly difficult. The leaders of the new Marxist-Leninist states realized that if their political and economic policies were to be carried out successfully, traditional political beliefs had to be replaced. In their place, the leaders hoped to develop a new set of attitudes and values, ones that corresponded with and supported their interpretations of Marxist-Leninist doctrine and their drives for modernization and rapid industrialization. As we will see in the pages that follow, this task was more challenging than anyone imagined.

Changing the Traditional Political Cultures

When Vladimir Ilyich Lenin, Mao Zedong, Fidel Castro, and others assumed power in their states, the traditional political cultures were not conducive to, and in many respects were even hostile toward, changes the leaders felt were necessary for building socialism. The political orientations of the people in these countries had been molded over hundreds, even thousands, of years. Centuries of tsarist rule in Russia and imperial rule in China resulted in undemocratic, elitist political cultures. We must remember that most of the Second World societies that became communist were primarily composed of peasants, with the bulk of the population working the land. These people generally accepted the prevailing social hierarchy: the strong ruled, the weak were ruled. In most Second World countries, the traditional belief was that those who governed had been chosen by divine mandate. The coronations and the ritualistic ceremonies such as those accorded the Russian tsars, Chinese emperors, and East European kings and ruling families made the rulers and masses acutely aware of the divine significance of the rulers' power. The masses were expected to remain passively in the background sowing the crops, working in factories, or laboring in whatever jobs they could find. The thought of political participation and the ideas of democracy were as remote as distant America. When the peasants heard news of democratic rule in the West, they neither understood its meaning nor comprehended its significance to their traditional ways of living. As the age of democracy grew in other parts of the globe, the masses of Second World countries remained largely isolated and, for the time being, unaffected by the winds of change.

When the Yugoslav Communist Party seized power in 1945, for example, the existing political culture was based on authoritarian, elitist, and nonparticipant norms. Centuries of foreign domination by the Ottoman and Austro-Hungarian empires as well as the more recent periods of nineteenth- and twentieth-century rule under indigenous authoritarian regimes served to mold a resigned, apathetic, and conformist society. The authoritarian Stalinist approach to political life, initially followed by Tito and the Yugoslav communists at the end of World War II, corresponded with the nonparticipant political culture of the past. The masses had never been widely consulted and involved in the affairs of politics before the war and did not really expect to be included afterward.

In Confucian China, the traditional political culture was steeped in the ideal of harmony with nature and a strict, hierarchical set of social and political relations. Power was entrusted to the emperor or empress, his or her supporting officials, and those who had worked their way up the hierarchy through intellectual attainment. To the masses, political power was the right of the emperor; the hierarchy was viewed as natural and the government tended to be remote. On those few occasions when the common peasant or laborer had contact with the government, the authorities appeared unjust and harsh. Because of this experience, the large bulk of the society was resigned to a life of political passivity and acquiescence. In a large peasant society, the common man and woman had little interest in, and few orientations about, politics. An early Chinese communist leader commented on this fact in 1922:

> The peasants take no interest in politics. This is common throughout the whole world, but is particularly true in China. . . . All they care about is having a true Son of Heaven [emperor] to rule them, and a peaceful bumper year.[3]

Mass values about democracy and power in China, Russia, and much of the Second World were shaped by centuries of authoritarian rule. Although the leaders of these countries—the rulers, ministers, counselors, representatives, magistrates, and others who served the empires—possessed a set of political orientations that represented an authoritarian political culture, the masses were characterized by a general absence of political sentiment.[4] They held few political feelings and were uninvolved in politics because of their traditional isolation from political affairs. To transform this massive parochial, nonparticipant sector of society into one that would support and advance the ideas of communist rule was a major task facing the new leaders in the postrevolutionary periods.

Because the leaders of the communist political systems recognized that the building of communism would be difficult, if not impossible, with the political culture (and subcultures) inherited from the presocialist states, they adopted heavy-handed strategies of political socialization to mold the orientations required for their new societies.

Perhaps it should be pointed out that all countries, including the United States, attempt to foster attitudes and beliefs in their people that are supportive of their systems of government. For example, in the United States, children at an early age are taught the Pledge of Allegiance, "The Star Spangled Banner," and the stories of our founding fathers. We may call it civics or citizenship training, but it is political socialization aimed at instructing the newest generation about the values of our political system. The key question in regard to this topic is not whether political socialization exists, for it exists in all societies; we must instead examine who determines what ought to be taught, how it is accomplished, and how far governments go in attempting to change the belief structures of their people.

A variety of different tactics were used over the decades in the Second World countries to reform the minds of the citizenry. After the revolution in China, emphasis was placed on thought reform, self-criticism, and rectification programs; those with "bourgeois mentalities" were given the opportunity to reform themselves and become productive members of Chinese society.[5] In some countries, more coercive methods, such as deportation, imprisonment,

terror, and even death and genocide, were used to mold political cultures. Stalin was notorious for brutal tactics as he ruthlessly sought to transform Soviet society to suit his purposes. Still others used less violent and sometimes more subtle methods. One of Castro's strategies in dealing with Cubans of hostile or nonconforming political orientations was to deport them or simply let them leave. Thousands of Cubans came to the United States during the 1960s and again in 1980 because, among other reasons, they were unable or unwilling to change their beliefs and opinions concerning socialism in Cuba.[6]

There are numerous agents of political socialization (i.e., institutions or instruments by which political values and orientations are transformed) that were at work during the Marxist-Leninist experiments. Among the most important was the family. Although there were some families that were committed to the building of communism in Second World states through the years, there were as many, and perhaps more, who were not. Most families in Second World states historically did more to promote the preservation of traditional (e.g., religious) or familial values than the official, communist values.

One agent of socialization that plagued the socialization intentions of communist leaders was the church. Particularly in the East European states where the Catholic and Orthodox religions are deeply embedded in the cultures of the people, the church proved to be a troublesome institution with which communists had to contend. At some points in communist history, officials undertook aggressive and oppressive campaigns to eradicate religion from their countries. At other points, when they needed to mobilize support for the government and promote unity within the country, they eased their politics of persecution.[7]

After many years of rejecting religion, recent leaders in Second World states have come to accommodate the church. Mikhail Gorbachev was the first Soviet communist leader to meet a Roman Catholic pontiff.

The agent of political socialization that traditional communists took the most interest in and (unlike family life and religion) over which they found it easiest to exert considerable influence was the school. The educational systems in Second World states historically were controlled by the Communist Party. Through the coordinating arm of a central ministry for education, the Communist Parties had great influence in designing curricula, selecting texts, and setting instructional policies within the schools. Although the Party leaders did not typically become directly involved in these activities, they did recommend certain policies, which were implemented through the ministries and by the local organs. The content of courses, textbooks, and the general educational philosophy, however, varied markedly among the different Second World states.

Perhaps the most politicized and ideologically infused education system in communist history was that of the Chinese during the Maoist period (1949–76). During the Great Proletarian Cultural Revolution (GPCR) (1966–69), Maoist doctrine accompanied almost every lesson. In elementary school mathematics, for example, the exploiting capitalist and the downtrodden peasants were typically found in the daily exercises:

PROBLEM: If a peasant works 4 plots of land and the capitalist takes the products of 3, what does that leave the peasant?

The writings of Chairman Mao played a major role in the educational process during the Cultural Revolution. Pictures from China showed the ever-present *Little Red Book* held proudly by the Chinese grade-schooler. Bulletin boards and texts were adorned with pictures of the communist leaders and the slogans they extolled to mobilize the masses. Even at the more advanced levels of Chinese education, including the universities, ideology represented a significant element in the curriculum and course content. One did not even approach the topics of

In Chinese classrooms during the Maoist period, revolutionary posters and slogans accompanied daily lessons. Although the post Mao leaders decreased the emphasis on ideological education, it remains a part of the socialization system.

medicine or physics without recognizing the relevance of Maoist ideology. Western observers witnessed college seminars dedicated solely to the reading of Chairman Mao's revolutionary thought.

Another influential agent of socialization carried out in the past through the schools involved youth organizations. These youth groups ranged from the elementary-grade Young Pioneers to the high-school and college-age youth leagues. Although all Second World states had similar groups, they varied widely in functions and behavior. The Chinese Communist Youth League in the 1970s, for example, constituted the primary training ground for what the leaders called revolutionary successors. It had a militant philosophy and was infused with the Chinese revolutionary spirit. During this period, Young Pioneers in China were even instructed in the arts of making revolution. Whether marching in parades, chanting Maoist slogans, or operating rifles with live ammunition on the firing range, these elementary schoolers were taught the finer points of Maoist strategy for revolutionary warfare.

Social service and political education were, historically speaking, important functions of the organization for teenage youth in the Soviet Union, the Communist Youth League (Komsomol).[8] Former Soviet leader Leonid I. Brezhnev referred to their mission as that of "bringing up youth in the spirit of communist commitment" and of carrying on the "cause of their fathers, the cause of the great Lenin." However, many teenagers in the Soviet Union today seem bored by the group activities; they often complain that they are ineffective organizations for social work and that the activities do not interest them.

The mass media—television, radio, newspapers, books, and the like—historically were also controlled by the Communist Parties and represented important agents of political socialization. In the past, television networks scheduled heavy doses of ideological and political programming. These propaganda programs assumed a variety of formats but always presented the Communist Party, government, and the country's leaders in a complimentary light. Propaganda, historically, has not had the pejorative meaning in Second World states that it typically had held in the West. Lenin felt that all Party members should act as theoreticians, propagandists, agitators, and organizers. Propaganda meant advertising the Communist Party's work in an attempt to win new adherents to the cause. In the past, even those television programs that were expressly intended for entertainment would typically have a political message; the vast majority of novels, short stories, and magazine articles included the same. This concern with ideology had a sobering effect on the written word in all socialist countries. The loading of ideology into almost everything, from newspaper reports to romance novels, severely reduced the quality of writing. Writers unwilling to yield to ideological themes—often some of the very best writers such as Vaclav Havel in Czechoslovakia—were forced to pick other professions to survive.

Although the emphasis was definitely on youth in the socialization process, adults were certainly not ignored. The Communist Parties and trade unions had vast networks concerned with ideological training and propaganda. Often the training was tied to one's job; classes and programs were offered to heighten workers' political consciousness and to call attention to the continuing class struggle. Although many adults ignored such activities, the social pressures were great enough to generate a significant level of participation.

Historically, the primary agent of political socialization in Second World states was the Communist Party itself. As will be noted in more detail in Chapter 4, the Communist Party traditionally controlled public information in the Second World states and, in so doing, played a powerful role in determining what people saw, heard, and learned. Because of their organization and socializing strategy, the Communist Parties attempted to oppose the agents of socialization that ran counter to the desired political culture (e.g., the church, the family) and used those agents that were under their direction (mass media, schools, youth organizations). For example, Communist Party organizations were present in factories, collective farms, and other places of work. Members of these organizations were expected to be exemplary citizens and to set good examples for their peers. In addition, the mere presence of Party members and Party organizations in the work place and throughout the society had a powerful socializing impact of its own. Party propaganda was the responsibility of special departments of the Central Committee in most Communist Parties. "Agitprop" activities (a shortened version of agitation plus propaganda) were controlled by the Communist Parties and furthered by such organizational vehicles as the ZNANIYA (Society for the Dissemination of Political and Scientific Knowledge) Society in the Soviet Union and equivalent organizations in other states.

Finally, in the past when these less coercive agents of socialization failed, the Communist Parties were quite willing to utilize a number of more coercive agencies to deal with citizens who threatened regime goals and political culture. Included in these agencies were local militias, intelligence agencies, and the armed forces. In the Soviet Union, for example, the KGB (Committee for State Security) has been charged with guaranteeing the security of the Soviet state. In exercising this responsibility, the KGB

Science and ideology have coexisted in Soviet education, as shown by the artifacts in this classroom in Moscow. Soviet advances in science attest to the success of its educational system. Success in the area of ideological indoctrination has been far less clear.

(and its counterparts in other Second World states) in the past had wide-ranging authority to combat "counter-revolutionary activities" and "crimes against the state." The frequent presence of unidentified KGB operatives in Communist Party, governmental, military, and other organizations has had a powerful impact on attitudes and behavior in Second World societies.

Now that we have reviewed the traditional political cultures and the historical agents used

to change them, we will look at the type of political cultures the communist leaders have desired.

Desired Political Cultures

Although the question of desired political cultures today is in a state of considerable uncertainty and flux, we can examine the type of political cultures those responsible for the building of communism desired in the past. We can get some idea of what the Soviet leaders wanted by reviewing what they have traditionally referred to as the "Moral Code of the Builder of Communism":

Devotion to the pursuit of Communism; love for the socialist homeland and for the countries of socialism;
Conscientious labor for the good of society; whoever does not work does not eat;
The concern of everyone for the conservation and increase of social property;
A high consciousness of social obligation and intolerance toward infringements of social interests;
Collectivism and comradely mutual aid; one for all and all for one;
A humane relationship and mutual respect among people; one person to another person—friend, comrade, and brother;
Integrity and truthfulness, moral purity, simplicity, and humility in social and personal life;
Mutual respect in family life; concern for the upbringing of children;
Implacable opposition to injustice, parasitism, dishonesty, careerism, greed;
The friendship and brotherhood of all the peoples of the USSR; intolerance toward nationalist and racist hostility;

Implacable opposition toward the enemies of communism; the pursuit of peace and the freedom of nations.

Mao also recognized the importance of political socialization and the desirability of a new political culture. More than forty years ago, he noted:

It is necessary to train a great many people as vanguards of the revolution. People who are politically far-sighted. People imbued with the spirit of struggle and self-sacrifice. People with largeness of mind who are loyal, active, and upright. People who never pursue selfish interests, but are whole-heartedly for liberation of the nation and society. People who fear no difficulties, but remain steadfast and advance courageously in the face of difficulties. People who are neither high or mighty nor seekers after the limelight, but are conscientious and full of practical sense. If China has a host of such vanguard elements, the tasks of the Chinese revolution will be successfully fulfilled.[9]

Like the Soviet leaders, Mao also wanted an ideologically committed and politically active society. Mao placed great emphasis on political participation and, during certain periods of his rule, mobilized what might have been the highest level of mass political activity in modern history. Yet Mao and the Chinese leaders also placed severe limits on the nature of participation. The people were expected to work within the system, and this meant parroting Maoist slogans and supporting the official Party doctrine. There was to be no dissent but rather a united, mobilized populace led by the so-called Great Helmsman, Mao Zedong.

Mao's successors also recognized the importance of political culture to Chinese development and attempted to outline its ideal features. A 1980 statement emphasized the following points:

1. loving the socialist motherland;
2. utilizing Western things useful to the four modernizations and rejecting things unhealthy and against the national spirit;
3. making the ideal of communism a guide to action; and
4. cultivating and strengthening communist ethics.[10]

The political culture desired by the post-Mao leaders has been what we might call both "Red" and "expert." Red means that the culture is to be communist; it should recognize the importance and validity of communism and abide by a code of communist morality. Expert means that the culture also should be based on knowledge, skills, and scientific know-how. The political culture desired in contemporary China is based on many of the ideological principles of the Maoist period but it adds a new dimension—knowledge—which is required by an emphasis on modernization. Although the post-Mao leaders have experimented with the development of a more modern political culture (i.e., less ideology, more skills and knowledge), they have been explicit in setting certain boundaries and reminding the people that the Chinese Communist Party (CCP) is still in charge.

Although the revolutionary changes that came to Eastern Europe at the end of the 1980s have put the issues of political socialization and culture in a state of uncertainty and flux, the desired political cultures of the past show considerable similarity to what was desired in the Soviet Union. Like their Soviet counterparts, through the first few decades of communist rule the East European leaders were intent on molding the dedicated and loyal citizens needed for the building of communism. This would require a "new communist person," one who would support socialism and the Communist Party leadership and contribute unselfishly to the common good.

In the early 1970s Ivan Volgyes conducted a study of these East European socialization efforts.[11] Volgyes' content analysis of East European newspapers identified eight themes that captured what was desired by the Communist Party leaders. Rank-ordered for their importance, from the most frequently found to least found, the themes were:

1. the building of socialism
2. anti-imperialism
3. socialist morality
4. patriotism
5. anti-individualism
6. socialist commonwealth
7. antinationalism
8. anti-Stalinism

This ranking indicates that the leaders' socialization efforts as reflected in East European newspapers in the early 1970s were most concerned with the people's commitment to the building of socialism (or communism). They also desired a commitment to anti-imperialism, socialist morality, patriotism, and other important themes. As we will note later, their efforts did not succeed.

Political Cultures Today

Political cultures in Second World states today are extremely complex and in a state of considerable flux. They are complex because they are a consequence of the traditional and diverse political cultures that preceded the establishment of communism; the revolutionary cultures that Lenin, Mao, and other communist leaders attempted to establish after the advent of communism; and the dramatically changing environments in which individuals and groups find themselves in these states today. Contemporary political cultures are not homogeneous in the sense that everyone holds the values and orientations that were once desired by the ruling elites. Rather, the diverse and heterogeneous political cultures today show all of the complexities, paradoxes, and uncertainties of societies undergoing rapid social, political, and economic change.

Because we want to examine those orientations that most significantly affect politics, we will address those related to the four values outlined in the introduction of this book: power, respect, well-being, and enlightenment. For a political system to allocate these values in an authoritative and peaceful manner, the citizens of a particular state ideally should have reasonably uniform expectations concerning their proper distribution. If 50 percent of the population feels that political power ought to be totally confined to a small number of leaders within the Communist Party, and the other 50 percent strongly feel it should be broadly shared among the entire society or by various opposition groups, it will be difficult for policy makers to satisfy all the people with their decisions. On the other hand, if the society widely shares one distribution or the other, or if its members are largely apathetic, the policy makers will have an easier time governing the society. A useful way of viewing the political cultures, then, will be to examine mass orientations and behavior relating to the four values defined earlier.

Power

The first value and dimension of political culture involves the role of the individual citizen in the political system. Should Soviet, Chinese, or East European citizens be involved, or should they leave political affairs in the hands of a small number of political elites? Should their society be a multiparty system where various individuals and groups can compete democratically for political power? Based on the Marxist goal of worker control and mass participation, traditional communist leaders purportedly wanted to destroy what they perceived to be dictatorial precommunist power relations that prohibited mass involvement in political affairs. These elitist power relations were to be replaced with what they argued would become a more democratic set of social and political relationships. Accordingly, such institutions as legislatures, public courts, and mass organizations were established in all Second World states to facilitate, according to the communists, the goals of worker and mass participation. Although some involved in the early communist experiments may have been committed to developing democratic political cultures and political systems, the totalitarianism brought about by Stalinist rule quashed most hopes surrounding these idealistic goals. What developed were authoritarian political cultures where Party leaders ruled and the rest of society was expected to follow.

Two leading scholars of Soviet political culture used the term *subject-participatory* to describe this aspect of the political culture of the 1960s and 1970s in the USSR.[12] Barghoorn noted "subject participatory denotes the relationship among Soviet citizens of subordination to superiors in one or more bureaucratic chains of command and the obligation of all citizens to do their best to assure the performance of the collective."[13] Barghoorn contended that although some political participation occurred in the Soviet communist past, it did so "within a framework of values, directives, and controls emanating from a ramified national bureaucracy subject to the commands of the Moscow Politburo."[14] Some observers of the Soviet Union feel that participation today is much less controlled than Barghoorn described it in the 1960s and 1970s.

However, it is clear that over the many years of pre- and postcommunist Soviet development, political orientations reflecting the subject-participatory culture have been deeply ingrained in the society. The typical Soviet citizen, whether inhabiting the far eastern reaches of the Russian Republic or the political center in Moscow, possesses a set of beliefs and attitudes defining his or her subject role in the political system.

Gorbachev attempted to change some of this and supported more democratic power relations after coming to power in March 1985. Speaking directly to the question of democratization and perestroika, Gorbachev argued that the Soviet Union could not succeed in restructuring and reforming Soviet society unless the people became more directly involved in political life.

And although Gorbachev and the Communist Party leaders still held the preponderance of power in the late 1980s, important changes were taking place in their and in most other Second World states. Although the Communist Parties wanted to remain the central source of power in the political systems, the leaders recognized the importance of expanding more meaningful mass participation in the affairs of state. This meant giving lower-level socioeconomic and political organizations—and the people themselves—greater opportunities to become involved. It meant making meaningful participation a reality. In this regard, one of Gorbachev's goals was to make the people feel that they had a stake in saving and rebuilding socialism.

What had developed over the years in the Soviet Union and most other Second World societies were feelings of helplessness, passivity, and cynicism among the people. Because the authorities were in charge and the risks of trying to influence policy and bring about change were considerable, most people became politically passive and alienated. Being rational human beings, they concluded that the high costs of trying to participate outweighed any benefits. They blamed, at least privately, their societies' ills on the leaders and were cynical about the leaders' promises and exhortations. This was one of the major obstacles that Gorbachev and reformers like him had to overcome. To build a healthier political culture conducive to Soviet development, they had to convince the people that they were serious about and valued their participation in political life. They had to instill a new sense of pride, involvement, and commitment among the people, and the people had to come to feel that they could contribute to and benefit from the reform process. Some of this began to happen with the reform movement of the late 1980s, but such changes will not come easily or be cost free to the Soviet Union. Political scientists have established that political cultures are slow to change. Yet, although much remains uncertain about how the Soviet people will view participation and power relations in their future, it is clear that change is possible.

Gorbachev's reform program of the late 1980s reminds us that it may be easier to change a leader's ideas about politics than the people's ideas. No one could deny the new ideas coming out of the Soviet Party hierarchy in the late 1980s, but much of the populace remained highly conservative and cautious abut change. Many were afraid of glasnost and democracy. Al-though the Party wanted people to get involved, to do so meant they had to make choices, to take a position, to "stick their neck out." Given past experiences in the Soviet Union, many people were reluctant to do this. However, Gorbachev and the other leaders tried to convince the people that they were serious about democratization and that the people would benefit by becoming more involved in the political process.

Even more significant developments took place in Eastern Europe during the late 1980s. The leaders and the people were viewing Gorbachev's reform efforts and wondering about their relevance in and implications for their societies. Throughout most of the decade, the Polish communist authorities fought to deny the independent labor movement Solidarity an official role in the political process. In the early 1980s, they temporarily imprisoned Solidarity's leader, Lech Walesa, declared martial law, and stood firmly opposed to most efforts to democratize the political process. In this repressive context, Polish political culture grew more and more cynical. The people lost faith in their leaders and political system. They identified more with Solidarity, the Catholic church, and various opposition movements than with the communist leaders. There was an extraordinarily high level of negativism and cynicism throughout the society, and the country was in a crisis and headed in a destructive direction during most of the 1980s. However, toward the end of the decade, the leaders showed greater flexibility toward the possibility of political reform, the role of Solidarity, and the opening of the political system. To bring about progress in Poland, the leaders began to appreciate the need to democratize the political process and convince the people that it was in their interest to participate, and by the late 1980s, the Polish political system was undergoing significant reform.

Soviet May Day parades in the era of glasnost are not the carefully staged displays of Marxist-Leninist and patriotic fervor they once were. At the 1990 parade, an environmentally conscious demonstrator holds a placard that reads "other countries do not know where man breathes so freely," while wearing a gas mask. After years of promoting the Soviet environment as being cleaner than those found in the capitalist West, Soviet officials have more recently admitted that environmental conditions in their country are deplorable and will take years to remedy.

Discussions among the communists, Solidarity, the Catholic church, and others—the so-called roundtable talks of 1989—resulted in democratic reforms, including free elections. These elections brought about a democratic expression of the will of the Polish people and resulted in the rejection of the communist slate of candidates and the first noncommunist government in contemporary Eastern Europe. These and other developments suggest important changes in the values surrounding political power in contemporary Poland.

The people's values about power were changing elsewhere in Eastern Europe in the late 1980s. Gorbachev's glasnost, perestroika, and democratization programs were spreading across the borders into all of the states of the region. The Soviets encouraged East European reform and said that they would not intervene and scuttle the democratization movements as they had been prone to do in the past. These and other factors encouraged a major democratization movement that swept across Eastern Europe and resulted in the dramatic decline of communist rule in 1989. Communist leaders were forced to step down. Citizens took to the streets chanting, "We are the people." Groups of citizens organized opposition parties. Legislatures became meaningful institutions of democratic discussion and policy making. Political cultures were being transformed. The people had become a powerful force in East European politics.

Unlike Lenin and Stalin, who had a deep-seated distrust of the untutored and politically unsophisticated rank-and-file people, Mao was convinced of the need for mass involvement. The adventurous Great Leap Forward and the turbulent Cultural Revolution exemplified the Maoist concept of mass participation. At the height of the Cultural Revolution, Mao orchestrated the induction of a large number of mass elements into the Communist Party hierarchy and gave them positions of Party and government responsibility at all levels. For a time, even the Central Committee of the Communist Party included representatives drawn from model workers among the Chinese masses.

It is, however, inappropriate to equate Mao's emphasis on mass participation with pluralist, participatory democracy. In the final analysis, Maoist participation primarily served as an instrument of legitimation and mobilization. The populace had little or no influence over the decision-making process and had to operate within the parameters of political behavior as defined by the Maoist leaders. Cooperation or recruitment of mass elements was totally at the leaders' discretion. The people's representatives were only a cog in the Maoist political machine and wielded little real power. They were not even allowed to work in the interest of their constituents. They generally occupied a supernumerary position, and when they had outlived their usefulness or when there was a major political reversal, they would be quickly dismissed.

Although it is still difficult to accurately judge to what extent the traditional elitist culture was replaced by the Maoist brand of populism in the 1950s and 1960s, there is reason to believe that some of the young people came to assume somewhat more participatory values and a more active, yet constrained, political role. There was always an undercurrent of opposition in China, but political dissidents were seldom in the national spotlight until the 1980s when they, too, emerged from anonymity and obscurity to be a formidable force. Astrophysicist Fang Lizhi, outspokenly critical of the communist system and ardently supportive of the democratic movement, has been viewed by some as the nation's conscience. Maverick writers like Liu Binyan, Wang Ruowang, and Wu Zhuguang have castigated the radical excesses and perversities of the past and openly deplored the Chinese leadership's procrastination in implementing political reforms. Even prominent Marxist theoreticians, such as Wang Luoshui and Su Shaozhi, challenged some fundamental premises of the official ideology and advocated profound reform of the obsolescent Marxist and Maoist orthodoxy that had put a constraint on Chinese modernization and democratization.

The 1980s were a period of growing openness in China (i.e., until the fateful crackdown that became know as the Tiananmen Square massacre of 1989). During this period, intellectuals and students were demanding more power for the people and a less dictatorial role for the Chinese Communist Party. They wanted to see the value of power more democratically shared, rather than monopolized by the communist elites. Although it was difficult to discern the aspirations of the rank-and-file Chinese, most observers foresaw a trend toward more democratic values in the 1980s, something akin to what seemed to be taking place in the Soviet Union and Eastern Europe.

These hopes and aspirations were brutally crushed in June 1989 when the student occupation of Tiananmen Square in the capital of Beijing was violently put down by the Chinese Army. The students had been demonstrating for democratic reforms and challenged the leadership to make the kinds of changes that were being made in the Soviet Union and Eastern Europe. Although it is too early to assess the full consequences of the Chinese crackdown, it is apparent that the democratic aspirations in Chinese political culture suffered a major setback.

Some have argued that there have always been participatory values in the Chinese communist experience that related to political culture and the political process. Some observers saw Mao's China (1949–76) as a system of mass involvement and referred to it as a mobilization system in which all individuals—leaders and peasants alike—were expected to become actively involved in the struggle for socialist construction.[15] From the early years of Chinese communism until Chairman Mao's death in 1976, Mao was the primary mobilizer and undertook a variety of campaigns and programs to encourage political participation. Following the ideal of populism, the leaders expected all citizens to participate in communal affairs and to serve the people.

Although communist leaders and middle-level political, social, and economic officials tend to support the principles of self-managing socialism, they are still uncertain about sharing policy-making power with the people and relinquishing

their positions of control. They may theoretically share and support the ideals of a more democratic society, but they remain skeptical of the efficiency, effectiveness, and overall feasibility of industrial or multiparty democracy. And although the mass populace tends to distrust the sincerity of its leaders, it also has certain doubts about the desirability of mass democracy. Is it the most efficient and productive system? Do the masses have the knowledge and training to assume such integral responsibilities in political and economic life?

Despite the exceptions in China just discussed, values surrounding power in many of the Second World countries today have an opportunity to change. With the democratic developments in Eastern Europe, for example, people are finding new opportunities to speak out, to become involved in political campaigns, and to vote. These developments are all very new and we are not certain how all of the people will react. We do know, however, that the traditional norms about power relations are changing in these societies and that important elements of the traditional political cultures are undergoing change.

Respect

In his opening remarks at the 24th Congress of the Communist Party of the Soviet Union in 1971, General Secretary Brezhnev spoke of the need for action, "whereby trust in and respect for people is combined with principled exactingness toward them" to create a "businesslike comradely atmosphere." What have trust and respect meant in the Soviet context and why are they important in the building of communism? The qualities of which Brezhnev spoke are a vital element in the political process because they pertain to the subjective feelings governing interpersonal and intergroup relations. Traditionally, citizens in Communist Party states were told to be comrades, which meant that they were to have a common outlook and common interests. To promote comradeliness meant to encourage a common class perspective. Communist citizens were expected to possess similar attitudes and to relate to one another in a respectful, trusting way.

As we observed the ethnic strife that pervaded certain Second World states at the beginning of this decade, we can appreciate the importance of a cohesive community of people who can work together and relate to one another on the basis of trust and respect. Clearly, the diverse peoples of the Soviet Union are still unable to do this. Until Gorbachev came to power, Soviet authorities did everything possible to convince the rest of the world that they had solved their nationality problem. Before the coming of glasnost, Soviet authorities were able to suppress and cover up many of the national cleavages and animosities that existed in Soviet society. However, as Soviet society opened up in the 1980s, it became increasingly apparent that an ideal political culture based on values of comradeliness and goodwill had not been established. Violent displays of ethnonationalism—for example, between the Armenians and Azerbaijanis in the late 1980s—showed that these historical animosities continued to boil. The Estonian, Latvian, and Lithuanian distrust and, in some cases, hatred toward the Russians showed that ethnicity and nationalism still divided people in what is supposed to be a Soviet *union*.

Gorbachev spoke frequently at the turn of the decade about the need of the diverse Soviet people to respect one another. We are one family, he said, and in order for families to survive and flourish, individuals must tolerate and support one another. Given the historical an-

imosities and cleavages in Soviet society, this is no easy undertaking.

Are the Chinese doing any better in developing respectful and comradely relations among their people? In this regard, years ago, Ezra F. Vogel outlined the original Maoist objectives as well as the important changes he thought were taking place during the early period of Chinese communist rule.[16] Vogel described a movement away from what we know as friendship (a personal, private relationship among close companions) to the concept of comradeship. Comradeship in the Maoist context was to be based on a universal ethic in which individuals were to treat all other individuals as equal members of a political community. With the emphasis on collective rather than private relationships, comrades were obligated to mutually reinforcing roles within their society. The emphasis on the collective and helping was reflected in the Maoist slogan and required reading, "Serve the People."[17] In attempting to establish comradely relations of this sort in China, the Western concept of private trust was suppressed. Under the system of comradeship, one would not tell a comrade a secret, something one wanted withheld from others. If a comrade knew, for instance, that you cheated on your income tax or that you took more than your allotment of rice from the storehouse, he or she would be expected to report you to the people's court. If you were found guilty of these transgressions, you would engage in self-criticism and admit to your crime against the people. In attempting to establish a public surveillance system where no indiscretions avoided the public eye, Maoist China tried to build a society free of corruption, crime, and graft. The personal costs reminded some of the coldhearted efficiency of Orwell's "Big Brother," and the long-term benefits were of questionable significance.

Most observers agree that the intensive Maoist political indoctrination failed to dethrone the Chinese traditional culture. Ultimately, it was unable to expunge the faith in interpersonal relationships from the minds of the leaders, not to mention the common people. In the twilight of the Mao era, patronage networks played a pivotal role in political elite recruitment and circulations. After Mao's demise, nepotism and favoritism again gained ascendancy. In many cases, Communist Party leaders seemed to accept ascriptive attributes such as family background and blood lineage in lieu of achievements and meritocratic standards as criteria for political promotion.

In the post-Mao era, the emphasis on comradeship and other more ideological themes decreased. Groupism, altruism, and other desired Maoist values were deemphasized, and materialism and consumerism set in. The post-Mao leadership lifted the taboo against material incentives and encouraged private enterprise, at least on a small scale. "To get rich is glorious" became a leading slogan of the 1980s. The post-Mao ideology posited a stereotype of an exemplary citizen who could reconcile political rectitude with business acumen. In this context, the nation approached a money-making frenzy. The principle of service to the people went into abeyance, and the life of most people, be they student, teacher, worker, or soldier, revolved around his or her performance with respect to finances. At various times, some leaders, obviously overwhelmed by twinges of nostalgia, tried to revive the cult of Lei Feng and Wang Jie, the puritanical heroes whom Mao put forward as paragons of virtue, but these leaders generally ended up as objects of ridicule. Their plan went awry because people dismissed the Maoist values as anachronisms. Some suggest that the Chinese Communist Party's Tiananmen Square massacre of June 1989 proves that the Party's austere socialist values can be imposed only by force.

In Eastern Europe, respect among people, and between the people and communist authorities, declined precipitously in the postwar period. Much of this resulted from the Soviet Union's imposition of a Stalinist model of government on societies that were largely opposed to communist rule. Because the people were forced to accept political and economic systems they despised, they engaged in fraudulence and subterfuge to get around the system. This involved blackmarket financial affairs, bribes, political and economic favoritism, corruption, and the like.

Another feature of the Stalinist model involved the coercive elements of the secret police and political informants. Because many members of the society were on the payrolls of the Communist Parties to keep an eye on everyone from acknowledged dissidents to rank-and-file citizens, there was a continual element of suspicion in many of the interpersonal relationships within the society. Although the official ideology preached comradely relations among the people, this suspicion and other consequences of the Stalinist system did much to impede those relations. There tended to be more fear, distrust, and suspicion than trust, respect, and comradeship in the East European states under communist rule.

There was also little respect between the people and their communist rulers. The people did not respect the communists because they considered them, for the most part, corrupt instruments of Soviet imperialism. As time passed and the communist authorities were unable to provide the socialist paradise they had promised, the people's respect for the leaders declined further. The leaders, in turn, showed little respect for the people. The communist authorities considered themselves the "vanguard of the people" and showed little sensitivity to the needs and concerns of the common people. They became isolated, often living in opulent and privileged settings, and showed little respect for the rank-and-file worker.

Well-Being

What are Second World attitudes and aspirations concerning the value of well-being? What do the people expect in the way of health care, social services, and consumer goods? What are their attitudes concerning a fair and proper distribution of these values? At the 24th Soviet Communist Party Congress in 1971, General Secretary Brezhnev announced, "The growth of the people's well-being is the supreme goal of the Party's economic policy." At the 25th Party Congress five years later, he noted that the most important goal remained "a further increase in the people's well-being." That was to involve improvements in working and living conditions; progress in public health, culture, and education; and everything that facilitates "improvement of the socialist way of life." Similar pledges were given by Gorbachev at more recent Party Congresses. But what do the people think of these pledges and the state of well-being in their society?

First, we should note that the Soviet Union is a welfare state that was founded upon a commitment to meet the needs of its people. It spends the equivalent of billions of dollars on education, health care, social security, and, at tremendous cost, on the massive bureaucracy that coordinates these programs. However, in contrast to the leaders' promises of upgrading the material and social well-being of the Soviet populace, the contemporary scene shows considerable shortcomings. There are critical shortages in housing and basic foodstuffs as

well as poor service in many of those programs (e.g., medical and dental care) the regime has prided itself on the most.

The dominant orientations of the Soviet populace reflect the contradiction between the communist ideal, where goods and services are to be in abundance and allocated on the basis of need, and the Soviet reality of reward on the basis of work. For the most part, the more poorly paid seem reconciled to their less privileged position in the income hierarchy, whereas the better paid tend to believe that a differential system of rewards is the only fair and reasonable way to handle income.

The American visitor views the Soviet living standard as one of general deprivation. To us, the most striking feature of this aspect of Soviet political culture is the general passivity of the population in accepting the status quo. Although there were some strikes and signs of discontent in the late 1980s, most people accepted their circumstances with little hope for change. Most Soviets neither work very hard nor expect very much. A commonly heard saying in the USSR captures the average citizen's values: "We pretend to work and they pretend to pay us." Soviet values are not conducive to fulfilling the productive potential of a country with considerable human and natural resources. These are the values that have contributed to the stagnation of Soviet development.

But how do Soviet citizens view their living standards and their personal well-being? One effort to find out in the 1980s was the Soviet Interview Project (SIP), a major study by Western social scientists to discover from Soviet emigrants how they saw their lives and the Soviet system. The data were gathered from interviews with 2,793 Soviet emigrants who arrived in the United States between 1979 and 1983. There are, of course, biases in a survey of this sort; the respondents were emigrants, which might suggest that they would have attitudes more critical of the Soviet system and quality of life than those of Soviet citizens who did not emigrate. Although these and other possible sources of bias no doubt affected the interview project results, the data do reveal some interesting and useful insights about Soviet political culture.

The Soviet interviewees were positive toward some aspects of their systems and negative about others. For example, the interviewees were asked for evaluations of their standard of living, housing, and other aspects related to the quality of their physical well-being. Although these people had chosen to leave the Soviet Union, they were surprisingly satisfied with their former standard of living, housing, jobs, and health care systems (see Table 3.1). When combining the "very satisfied" and "somewhat satisfied" responses, we see that about 60 percent were satisfied with their standard of living and health care, 70 percent with their housing, and 80 percent with their jobs.

If these Soviet citizens were reasonably satisfied with their physical quality of life, why did they choose to leave the Soviet Union? The interviewers asked this question and found that whereas only 27 percent considered an economic motive as an important reason, more than 40 percent cited ethnic, religious, and political reasons. Interestingly, the Soviet interviewees did not show as much dissatisfaction as we might expect with what we in the West see as an inferior quality of life. There were, however, aspects of the Soviet system that they would have liked to change. When responding to the question posed in Table 3.2, the political system was clearly the leading candidate for change. The other aspects of the Soviet system they would have liked to alter represented a variety of political and economic issues that Gorbachev and the other Soviet leaders are now addressing.

Table 3.1   Self-Assessed Satisfaction SIP General Survey

		How satisfied were you with:				
		Standard of Living	*Housing*	*Goods*	*Job*	*Health Care*
Very satisfied	% =	11.3	23.3	5.1	31.8	19.3
Somewhat satisfied	% =	48.8	43.8	17.8	47.1	42.6
Somewhat dissatisfied	% =	25.2	13.7	23.2	13.5	21.3
Very dissatisfied	% =	14.7	19.2	53.9	7.6	16.8
TOTAL	N =	2,750	2,770	2,738	2,238	2,680
Missing values	N =	43	23	55	555	113

(*Source*) SIP General Survey Codebook. Adapted from Daniel N. Nelson and Roger B. Anderson, eds., *Soviet-American Relations* (Wilmington, Del.: Scholarly Resources Inc., 1988), p. 4.

Table 3.2   What Things in the Soviet System Would You Be Sure to Change?

	1st Answer (%)	2nd Answer (%)	3rd Answer (%)	Total (%)
Political system	27.0	6.6	6.5	40.1
Allow private enterprise	9.3	10.5	9.8	29.6
Control of speech	3.5	8.8	13.6	25.9
Collective-farm system	9.4	9.3	7.1	25.8
Enforce rights	3.5	11.1	10.2	24.8
One-party system	6.3	6.0	4.4	16.7
Economic planning	2.4	3.3	3.8	9.5
Internal passports	1.3	3.6	3.1	8.0
Everything	6.5	0.5	—	7.0

(*Source*) SIP General Survey Codebook. Adapted from Daniel N. Nelson and Roger B. Anderson, eds., *Soviet-American Relations* (Wilmington, Del.: Scholarly Resources Inc., 1988), p. 19.

An important component of this dimension of political culture concerns a society's expectations for the future. Past Soviet policy regarding material well-being has been very sensitive, almost paranoid, on the question of rising expectations. One of the reasons for the Communist Party leadership's traditional reluctance to loosen foreign travel has no doubt been tied to their fear of increased mass expectations, which the government would be unable to meet. Rising and unmet expectations have been more prevalent and, as a result, more of a problem among East European populations, where contact with the West has been greater. In addition, the populations of these countries have been less passive than the Soviet populace and frequently have made their feelings known.

The Polish people have vented their frustrations on numerous occasions. Just before Christmas in 1970, for example, the Polish leaders instituted a major price increase in a variety of foodstuffs. Perceiving a substantial reduction in their level of material well-being, the Polish populace protested the government's policy, rioted in some coastal cities, stopped working, and burned down the Communist Party headquarters in one major city. This action led to the removal of the Party leader, Wladyslaw Gomulka, and abolition of the price increases. The next Party leader, Edward Gierek, attempted a new set of price increases in 1976 and also encountered mass dissatisfaction. The government was forced once again to rescind the increases. Gierek was ousted in 1980 during the workers' strikes, when he, too, proved incapable of meeting the aspirations and demands of the Polish people. The explosions of mass discontent throughout Eastern Europe in 1989 had a distinct economic base and represented the people's rising expectations. The resulting political changes in Eastern Europe call attention to the power of a society's expectations and the impact that orientations concerning the fair and proper allocation of well-being can have on political life.

These developments also have implications for the Soviet Union. As the awareness and sophistication of the Soviet populace have increased with the policy of glasnost, we have seen them develop more critical attitudes and become more involved in important questions of social and political affairs. By 1990, many Soviet officials believed that they were running short on time; if significant improvements were not made in the standard of living, mass unrest would develop in Soviet society.

With the Maoist emphasis on equality and the collectivity, the Chinese people were to deemphasize private material interests and to work for the interests of society as a whole. To solve the problems of mass starvation and the general deprivation that characterized much of Chinese society at the time of the communist assumption of power in 1949, a massive program of economic redistribution was adopted. Because egalitarianism was not previously a dominant part of Chinese political culture, redistribution emphasizing material equality did not meet with universal approval. This became a focal point of Chinese socialization efforts, and during the radical 1966–76 period, the Chinese moved decisively to promote equality of well-being. Subsequently, these values were revised as the leaders moved to establish a link between individual effort and individual reward.

For example, in the 1980s, "from each according to his abilities, to each according to his contribution" was construed as an endorsement and justification of inequality in distribution. People were exhorted to improve their standards of living through hard work and private initiative. They were dissuaded from envying others' affluent lives and told that wealthy people and societies worked hard to earn what they enjoyed. As a result, a new generation of wealthy people began to emerge in China. Although some economic effects of the policy trickled down to the broader population and the regime legislated for some safeguards against the income and social polarization that began to result, relative

deprivation had become a major social problem and irritant in China by the end of the 1980s. A large segment of the population who considered themselves to be the losers in the post-Mao era resented their failure and the beneficiaries of the economic reforms. It was hard for those who became accustomed to more equal distribution in China to acquiesce to the widening gap between themselves and others. In the late 1980s, there were numerous reports of sporadic strikes and demonstrations in protest against the new economic policy.

In Eastern Europe during this same period, societal values concerning well-being were marked by anger, frustration, and hostility toward the communist governments. With stagnant economies and spiraling inflation, standards of living were dropping precipitously. The people were angry and outspokenly critical of their leaders. When East Europeans remembered the better times of the past and looked across their borders at the relative affluence in West European countries, they felt a deep sense of deprivation. The presence of relative deprivation reached revolutionary levels in the late 1980s and contributed to the changes in political leadership and orientation that are described elsewhere in this book.

Today the East European systems appear to be moving in a direction that will take them further away from social equality in well-being. This move in the direction of privatization and away from state socialism inevitably will result in the state having even less control over the growing economic inequalities that are likely to develop. It will be interesting to see how the East European people react to these new developments.

Overall, one gets the impression that self-interest is the dominant value defining well-being in most societies, including the Second World societies. Although there are differences among people and countries, most individuals tend to place their personal interests before those of the collectivity. If the leaders of these states were suddenly to adopt the principle, "from each according to his abilities, *to each according to his needs*," people would probably react according to how this new policy would affect them. If they expected to raise their level of well-being, they would tend to support the new policy. If they were engineers, successful writers, or athletes and already making and enjoying more than they really needed, they would be likely to oppose it. In other words, attitudes and values concerning well-being in most Second World societies may not be all that different from those in the West.

Enlightenment

The final dimension of political culture to be examined concerns the value of enlightenment. After seizing power, communist leaders set out to develop a new set of values, ideas, skills, and behaviors—in other words, a new socialist being—to begin the building of communism. Thus, one way of examining the enlightenment dimension of political culture is to examine the people in terms of a set of standards outlined by T.H. Chen to describe this new being.[18]

1. *Absolute selflessness*. The model Maoist citizen, according to Chen, was to hold no ambitions beyond serving the cause of the revolution and China. In traditional communist ideological parlance, selflessness was an expansive and comprehensive concept signifying unreserved and steadfast commitment to communism, patriotism, and collectivism and unconditional subordination of personal interests to those of the revolution, motherland, and one's peers. Paul Kochakin, a legendary hero in Nikolai Ostrovsky's autobiographical novel

The Making of Steel, became a household name during the Stalinist era in the USSR. The Soviet propagandists conferred an aura of sainthood on him because he personified selfless and wholehearted dedication to the Bolshevik Revolution, for which he sacrificed his youth, his love, his family, and his health.

The Maoist conception of selflessness was capsulized and embodied in Mao's "Three Much Read Articles," which moralized about the desirability of selflessness as a revolutionary virtue. The trio idolized and idealized by Mao—a contemporary soldier, a foreign volunteer doctor, and a fictitious ancient character—were designated as role models for the whole population.

Although the Chinese and other communist leaders sought to instill the quality of selflessness among their citizens, they were largely unsuccessful. Most people living in Second World states are patriotic and may at times be willing to sacrifice their individual interests for what they perceive to be in the best interests of their country. But in everyday life, one gets the impression that they think first of themselves, then of their families and friends, and then perhaps remotely of their fellow citizens and country.

The grandiose Great Leap Forward movement in China, premised on mass spontaneity, voluntarism, and selflessness, ended up a fiasco largely because people placed personal concerns above those of the collective. Major components of the movement, such as communalization, egalitarianism, and abolition of material incentives, did not correspond with people's personal value preferences. No matter how inspiring and uplifting the Maoist exhortations were, the populace was soon disenchanted and demoralized, and the Maoist attempt to ignore technological and physical constraints and build progress on human willpower collapsed.

89

The call for selfless devotion in China rose to a crescendo during the Cultural Revolution. Because the Maoists drew an analogy between self-centeredness and villainy, there was a stigma about showing any concern for oneself. Posters bearing Mao's dictum, "Serve the people," were ubiquitous and people vied with one another in reproaching themselves for their alleged failures to comply with Mao's instruction in a daily liturgy of pledging allegiance to the principle of "combating selfishness." Anyone who had the audacity to openly work in his own self-interests would incur severe criticism and become an object of ridicule. However, this does not mean that Maoist China became a virtuocracy and every citizen a paragon of selflessness. The irony was that as the Maoist moralizing reached its greatest height, the social moral code disintegrated.

During the post-Mao era, the Chinese leadership downplayed the significance of selflessness. Generally speaking, four factors contributed to its decline. First, the value seems to be in conflict with human nature in China. On the one hand, Chinese take pride in helping others. On the other hand, when it comes to a question between personal and public interests, they generally feel that the former should prevail over the latter. Second, a disproportionately large segment of the population lived through the ordeal of persecution and other trials and tribulations during the Cultural Revolution. When their positions were precarious, human instinct for survival would override other considerations, and altruism was considered a luxury they could not afford. Third, the Maoist leaders themselves did not always set a good example. Their addiction to power belied their hypocrisy and selfishness in the eyes of many Chinese citizens. Fourth, continuous emphasis on selflessness would be in conflict with the resurrection of material incentives and private

initiative and stifle efforts to rehabilitate and revitalize the economy.

The political cultures characterizing Soviet and East European societies also fail to show the selflessness desired under communism. In environments of economic hardship and shortage, people have a tendency to put their personal interests before those of others. Self-interests appear to transcend selflessness in most Second World societies today.

2. *Obedience to the Communist Party.* Like selflessness, commitment to the leaders and to the Party was once intended to be a dominant feature of communist political culture. Chen quotes the words of the song "East is Red," which the Chinese children were taught to express their worship of Chairman Mao:

The East is Red,
The sun rises.
China has brought forth a Mao Zedong.
He works for the People's happiness.
He is the people's great savior.

Chairman Mao loves the people,
He is our guide.
He leads us onward
To build the new China.

The Communist Party is like the sun,
Whenever it shines, there is light.
Where there's the Communist Party,
There the people will win liberation.

To instill in the citizenry a deep sense of reverence for and submission to the Communist Party and its leadership, the Maoists portrayed a pantheon of communist heroes. The most prominent among them was Lei Feng, an army squad leader posthumously lionized for his martyrdom, heroism, and selflessness.

Although support and respect for the Communist Parties and leadership have been desired features of all Second World political cultures, they clearly have been absent in most. In many of these countries, the Communist Parties have been totally discredited in the eyes of the people. Why should the people obey a Party that today is generally viewed as having ruined the country? The recent rejection of Communist Party candidates in East European elections has displayed the peoples' values on this issue.

In China, the Maoist regime's political excesses and poor performance over the years, especially during the Cultural Revolution, alienated much of the populace and compromised the Party's reputation. By the eve of Mao's death, both his and the Party's prestige plummeted to a nadir. Popular resentment of endless power struggles and economic shortcomings translated into a skepticism of the political system and its guiding principles of Marxism and Maoism. This was evident from the pervasiveness of what was referred to as the three crises in China—the crises in trust, confidence, and credibility—that jeopardized the legitimacy of the regime.

After Mao's death, the pragmatic and reform-minded leadership mounted strenuous efforts to redeem the Communist Party's damaged reputation. It repealed many unpopular Maoist policies as an antidote to political radicalism. The new regime's initial success in economic reconstruction, development, and depoliticization at first won support. However, as the economic reform ran into difficulty and caused dislocation and inflation, more and more people began to voice their grievances against the post-Mao regime as well. The Chinese Communist Party's image was further damaged as a result of its brutal suppression of the democratization movement in 1989. Although it is too early to determine the full implications of the Party's crackdown on Chinese political culture, most analysts feel it has turned more of the Chinese people against the Party.

3. *Class consciousness*. The model communist citizen was also to be on guard against remnants of the class struggle, such as bourgeois ideas at home and abroad, and the global threat of capitalist imperialism. Because of intense indoctrination by the schools, the arts, and the media during the Maoist period, the Chinese were immersed in class-struggle thinking and were expected to assume a political consciousness as part of their belief systems.[19]

There is little evidence to suggest that class consciousness is of any real significance in the belief system of the majority of people living today in Second World societies. Although most Soviet students have been taught to explain in class terms the Great Patriotic War or race relations in Africa, it is not something they think of frequently or feel strongly about; the same holds true for the Chinese. In contrast to Mao's China, where the people were continually warned of class enemies and where class warfare was said to rage endlessly, there is today a much more relaxed atmosphere surrounding the idea of class struggle in the Second World states.

4. *Ideological study*. Ideological study in Mao's China meant the study of Mao Zedong's political writings; the works of Karl Marx, Friedrich Engels, and Joseph Stalin; and contributions by certain other Chinese Party officials. At the height of the Cultural Revolution (1966–69), the Maoist cult surrounding ideological study achieved unprecedented heights; there was saturation of Maoist ideology in every aspect of an individual's life. Mao's teachings became the ultimate ethical code for the whole nation. Everybody had to make a daily ritual of reading his *Little Red Book*, a collection of revolutionary aphorisms and moral precepts. Academic work in all fields became an exegesis of the Maoist scriptures, and the quality of scholarship was evaluated

During Mao's reign, art and culture in China were expected to communicate the goals and values of the revolution. "The Red Detachment of Women," a folktale made into a revolutionary ballet, exemplifies the adoration of Mao and his *Little Red Book*.

on the basis of the ability to recite Maoist tenets. Whereas almost all books were labeled as remnants of feudalism, capitalism, and revisionism and withheld from publication and circulation, Mao's works came out in stunning profusion and inundated the nation.

After the post-Maoist leadership embarked on the reform and modernization policies, ideology no longer dominated the national agenda. Although the Chinese communist leaders claimed to have inherited Mao's ideological mantle and paid lip service to it, they renounced the primacy of the Maoist dogma. Few Chinese people bothered any longer with

ideological study and redirected their efforts at staying clear of the political authorities and making money. Mao's books were largely ignored and could no longer be found in the average Chinese household.

After the mass demonstrations and political protests of spring 1989 had been brutally suppressed by the Chinese army, the Chinese Party leadership turned back to ideological training and indoctrination in an effort to prevent future dissent and unrest among Chinese students and workers. The old ideological works that had largely been in storage throughout most of the post-Mao period reemerged in classrooms and factories across China. Courses in communist ideology once again became a required part of university curricula; workers once again had to partake in ideological sessions at their place of employ. While commitment to ideological training on the part of the Party may not have been as strong or as fervent in the post-Tiananmen period as it was in Mao's heyday, ideology had once again become an integral part of the Party's plan for political control and socialization of the Chinese people.

Ideological study today has become passé in the Soviet Union and is rejected in Eastern Europe. Although the Soviet school curricula contain Marxist-Leninist requirements, students and teachers generally oppose it and want to see ideological study reduced. Ideological study has been more strenuously opposed in Eastern Europe. Noting that about one-fifth of their college classroom hours were devoted to the study of Marxism and that most other classes were taught from a Marxist perspective, Hungarian students demonstrated in 1988, resisting this form of governmental control of their curriculum. Likewise, during the height of the Solidarity movement in the 1980s, the independent union of Polish university students pressured the government into removing classes on dialectical materialism from the required curriculum. As a result of the revolutionary changes that swept across Eastern Europe in 1989, there is now very little communist ideological study in any of these Second World systems.

5. *Labor and production.* The new communist citizen in Mao's China was expected to thrive on, and enjoy, manual labor. During the Maoist period, for example, all students were required to engage in productive labor for the state in addition to their normal academic study. Schools and universities were to become centers of production as well as centers for learning. Mao's China was a picture of men and women at

work: peasants marching in the fields, students and laborers working side by side in farms and factories.

The drive to indoctrinate the higher-educated stratum of society in the importance of manual labor culminated in the massive "sending-down" campaigns before and during the Cultural Revolution. Compulsory participation in productive labor was consonant with the advocacy of Maoist anti-intellectualism and populism. It was designed to humiliate the presumably arrogant intellectuals, eliminate a divorce of theory from reality, and bridge the gap between the urban and rural areas. Mao's insistence on political reeducation through productive labor demoralized and antagonized those in the scientific and technological professions whose contributions were subsequently solicited for the modernization efforts. The Maoist strategy interfered with routine scientific and technical work. Later, the post-Mao leadership revoked the Maoist prescriptions and exempted students and professionals from the bulk of their duties involving manual work. Recently, however, Communist Party officials have raised alarm about a new tendency among young students to despise manual labor. To remedy the situation, in the late 1980s, some educational systems began to alternate classroom instruction with field experiences on farms and in factories. This trend gained added support in the repressive environment following the Tiananmen Square crackdown.

6. *The Red/expert blend.* The enlightened socialist citizen was also to be both committed to communist ideology (i.e., Red) and an expert, with specific skills and talents that would contribute to the construction of communism. The different blends of Redness and expertness seen throughout communist history, however, have illustrated some significant contrasts among the various Second World states. Mao's China in-

variably placed greater emphasis on the ideological side (Red) and less on the technical, scientific aspects (expert) of socialist construction. During this period in China, the "Red and expert" formula served as a theoretical justification for the denigration of technocrats and intellectuals and the domination of workers over professionals. In practice, political virtuocracy invariably took precedence over meritocracy. Lack of professional competence seldom disqualified a politically reliable candidate from recruitment or promotion.

For most of its history, the Soviet Union took a more middle-of-the-road position. Although the Soviet leadership did not emphasize the value of extreme Redness, neither did it allow the more unfettered development of the technocratic experts; what it did was emphasize both. The enlightened citizen was to be not only ideologically committed but also trained and educated to bring the most advanced skills and training available to his or her work setting. The new emphasis on glasnost in the Soviet Union suggests that this and other dimensions of Soviet political culture are changing. The East European states began making decisions in the 1980s that placed greater emphasis in their political cultures on technical merit and productivity and less emphasis on ideological considerations. This trend was given a big boost with the political revolutions of 1989. Red was out, and professional merit was in. Most of the East European leaders and people came to the conclusion that the heavy emphasis on Redness in their postwar societies was one of the significant factors that led to economic stagnation and social malaise. If you do not have well-trained and competent people involved in development programs, they concluded, it is difficult to compete in the increasingly competitive global economy.

In concluding our discussion of enlightenment, we should call attention to the recent developments in Eastern Europe that are likely to have significant implications for the enlightenment element of political cultures in that part of the Second World. As this book was being written, the Berlin Wall was coming down and formerly repressive states like Romania were opening their borders to allow free passage of their citizens in and out of the country. Although it is difficult to predict where these and related changes will lead East European countries, and what impact this will have on the political cultures of their societies, we can be assured that in the 1990s the attitudes and values surrounding enlightenment likely will be changing. The heavy emphasis on communist ideology appears to be a thing of the past, as these societies are beginning to experiment with elements of pluralist democracy including multiple parties, free elections, and noncommunist governments. Although difficult challenges face these societies as they attempt to rebuild their political cultures and systems, exciting opportunities clearly exist.

Subcultures, Countercultures, and Dissidence

Although the postwar Second World leaders were dedicated to building unified, communist political cultures in their societies, they came to realize that it was an impossible task. Most of these societies are complex and heterogeneous and contain a variety of subcultures, countercultures, and dissidents within their broader populations. Although these individuals and groups may share certain values with the dominant political culture, they also hold many distinct values of their own.

Subcultures can be based on a diverse set of characteristics. We can divide populations geographically and find distinct subcultures; we can also divide societies by age, social or occupational attributes, ethnic differences, and so forth. Another meaningful and useful way to explore subcultures is by dividing societies into political elites and masses. The masses, for example, hold values that are often quite different from those held by the political elites. The presence of subcultures, countercultures, and dissidence in China is particularly interesting in view of Maoist efforts to wipe out the old and create a new communist political culture. Even during the most repressive days of the Maoist period, individuals and groups challenged the ideology and values that the regime tried to impose. In 1955, Hu Feng, a celebrated literary figure who had won recognition as the Chinese Communist Party's poet laureate, dissented from the Maoist policy on literature and art issues, articulated the embittered literary workers' resentment of the authoritarian Communist Party controls, and stated their demands for the stoppage of unwarranted Party surveillance. The fact that the Communist Party had to respond not only by putting Hu behind bars but also by launching a nationwide political campaign to round up his followers was clear proof of the existence of an anti-Party subculture within cultural and educational circles during the Maoist period.

Then, during the liberalization drive in 1957 (generally referred to as the Hundred Flowers Movement) many Chinese began to speak out during this fleeting Maoist period of glasnost. Inspired and emboldened by the Maoist leaders' conciliatory gestures approving of a new openness, a significant number of China's political, economic, cultural, educational and scientific elites came out to voice their disillusionment with the communist regime's shortcomings and their skepticism about the feasibility of communism. The vehemence and scale of criticism provided considerable evidence of the intensity and significance of the anticommunist subcultures. In panic and with great exasperation, the Maoist leaders decided to strike back. As a result, the so-called Anti-Rightist crackdown ended the short-lived Hundred Flowers Movement and was used as an instrument for retribution for political dissent and heresy. Mao found the dissidents guilty of maligning socialism, opposing the Communist Party's development strategy, and advocating anticommunist ideology. In the face of repression in subsequent years, the Chinese counterculture replaced their frontal attack with subtle, circuitous criticism in articulating their political and ideological preferences.

In the post-Mao period, the criticism became more open. Some writers and scientists, like Liu Binyan, Wu Zhuguang, Wang Ruowang, and Fang Lizhi, delved into the Chinese communist experience to identify and expose the problems inherent in the Chinese communist system. Their views and opinions were echoed by thousands of young students and intellectuals. They won considerable support for their courage and became national celebrities among their subcultural supporters. The conservatives among the communist elites resented their "pernicious" influence and had many of them purged in early 1987 on a charge of agitating for student demonstrations in support of liberalization and democratization. Student demands for democracy and reform grew, however, resulting in the violent confrontation between students and communist authorities in June 1989 in Tiananmen Square. The authorities used military force—the Peoples' Liberation Army (PLA)—to quash the democracy movement, pushing it underground and to foreign lands. Some of the students came to the United States, where they set about organizing change for China from abroad.

In the late 1980s, other subcultures, some of which were diametrically opposed to communist values, gained ascendancy in China. Some were motivated by materialistic and consumer concerns. Materialism seemed to be triumphing over revolutionary asceticism. Many of the younger generation, who did not live through the ordeal of precommunist chaos and famine, were no longer inspired by revolutionary ideals; rather, they were obsessed by desires for modern comforts and consumer goods such as color TVs, refrigerators, stereos, and bigger apartments. Patriotism and ethnocentrism seemed to give way to worship of the West. Many Chinese young people had a fixation with Western culture and art and made a fetish of imported goods. Dazzled and mesmerized by the affluence of the West, many young Chinese were ready to desert their motherland mired in poverty and backwardness in search of their fortunes in foreign lands.

The late 1980s saw a mass exodus of Chinese students and people from all walks of life to the United States, Japan, and Europe. Still more were biding their time, anxiously awaiting their exit visas. Many government-sponsored students chose to be expatriates after completion of their studies abroad. The number of international marriages skyrocketed because they were an avenue for emigration to and resettlement in the West.

Other Chinese were motivated out of concerns for democracy and human rights. Many thoughtful young men and women were exposed to Western ideology and dismissed Marxism and Maoism as irrelevant anachronisms. Adoption of Western philosophy and democratic concepts was very much in vogue in China in the late 1980s. It would not be an overstatement to say that the existentialist Paul Sartre, psychoanalyst Sigmund Freud, and the Soviet leader Mikhail Gorbachev had a far larger following than did any Chinese among the educated young people of China.

Finally, in China, many of the ethnic minorities have remained tied to their subculture value systems. During the first few years of communist rule, the regime gave preferential treatment to the minority nationalities and showed remarkable tolerance for their indigenous values, habits, and customs. Later, however, as minority leaders demanded more administrative autonomy and cultural tolerance, the Communist Party rescinded its original conciliatory and concessionary policy and decided to clamp down on ethnic opposition. It orchestrated a crusade against local nationalism and purged many officials who were of ethnic extraction. Ethnic insurgency erupted in many areas during the period of economic depression in the late 1950s and early 1960s, in protest against communist interference in religious, social, and cultural life and the majority Han's colonization of their homelands. The government resorted to brutal force in suppressing a variety of rebellions—for example, in the theocracy Tibet.

In the Soviet context, political subcultures, countercultures, and dissidence also can be viewed in a variety of different ways. There are differences based on age (e.g., youth culture), religion (e.g., Jews, Moslems, Christians), and political persuasion (e.g., democratic pluralists versus totalitarian communists). Frederick C. Barghoorn has distinguished different political subcultures on the basis of social structure.[20] Classifying Soviet society in terms of intelligentsia, workers, and collective farmers, Barghoorn identified attitudes and behaviors that distinguish each group from one another and from the dominant political culture. According to this approach, different orientations toward politics are largely defined by one's position in the social structure. Because the intelligentsia are a somewhat privileged stratum in Soviet society, they have higher levels of education and sometimes expect higher levels of power, respect, and well-being than do the less privileged and less educated sectors.

Subcultures can also be distinguished in different age groups in the Soviet Union. Interviews conducted in 1988 by the Soviet Institute of Sociological Research revealed that different age groups held rather different values about important aspects of the Soviet system (see Table 3.3). Younger people were far more skeptical than the older generations about the ability of the one-party system to promote democracy. The younger were more supportive of multicandidate elections and more tolerant of street demonstrations to air grievances. Surprisingly, perhaps, the old were more supportive of Gorbachev and his policy of perestroika. As the

Table 3.3   Voices from Moscow: What They Say about Their System

	Age				
	18–29	*30–44*	*45–64*	*65+*	*Total*
One-party system in U.S.S.R. promotes development of democracy					
Agree	46%	50%	53%	60%	51%
Disagree	34	32	25	13	28
Elections to regional Soviet should be conducted under a multicandidate system					
Yes	80	83	76	65	77
No	2	3	5	4	4
Interests of minority groups in U.S.S.R. are infringed on					
Not at all	61	65	65	84	66
Partially	27	22	20	6	20
Severely	4	2	1	1	2
It is acceptable for people with grievances to hold street demonstrations					
Yes	44	40	34	13	35
No	49	48	56	75	54
Support Gorbachev's domestic policies					
Completely	65	74	85	94	78
Less than completely	32	23	14	4	19
Support perestroika					
Strongly	65	66	83	83	73
With reservations	31	33	13	11	23

Based on a poll of Moscow residents conducted by The Institute of Sociological Research of the Soviet Academy of Sciences for The New York Times and CBS News. A total of 939 Moscow residents were interviewed by telephone on May 7, 8, 14, and 15, 1988.
(*Source*) The *New York Times*, May 27, 1988.

data in Table 3.3 indicate, different generations can hold rather different attitudes about politics in Second World states.

Subcultures can also be distinguished on the basis of nationality. Because there are so many nationalities and ethnic minorities in the Soviet Union, there are many national subcultures. These nationalities produce beliefs, values, and opinions that can have a powerful impact on politics. The Baltic nationalities had such an impact in the late 1980s. Representing formerly independent states, nationalities like the Estonians, Latvians, and Lithuanians hold values that place great emphasis on national autonomy. They want the Soviet state to provide them with more political, economic, and cultural freedom to promote their national interests. Such values have motivated the Baltic nationalities to make a number of demands on Moscow, including requests for independence.

National subcultures, then, can hold rather different preferences about the allocation of such values as power, respect, well-being, and enlightenment. On the issue of power, for example, many national groups—such as the Baltic nationalities, the Georgians, the Armenians, and others—feel that their power ought to be expanded. They feel that the Soviet state has concentrated far too much power in the central government in Moscow. They also feel that they have not received the respect that is due them. In their opinion, the central authorities have suppressed their national cultures and contributed to the Russification of their territories. They also believe that their well-being has been stunted through the economic system imposed on them by Moscow. And, finally, through the communist controlled information and socialization policies of Moscow, they have not been allowed to mold the enlightened citizenry that will serve their national interests and cultural development. As a result of such values, a number of Soviet nationalities

are making demands of great significance to the political process and to the future of the Soviet state. In fact, such values are of an intensity and character to threaten the very existence of the Soviet Union.

Similar national subcultures exist in other Second World states. Yugoslavia, for example, has a number of nationalities that are finding it very difficult to coexist and cooperate in the Yugoslav federation. Because of cultural, religious, and economic differences, these groups hold political orientations that contrast, and often conflict, with one another. Some of the groups (e.g., the Albanians) who inhabit less developed areas of Yugoslavia feel that the government should do more to equalize the level of well-being among different national regions.[21] Because their levels of well-being are considerably below those in the more developed regions, they feel funds should be taken from the developed regions and invested in their areas to aid social and economic development.

These and other differences of opinion associated with nationality in Yugoslavia are reflected in both elite and mass political cultures, and on many occasions they have resulted in political conflict pitting one republic or group of republics against another. Many Albanians in the province of Kosovo demonstrated and rebelled on numerous occasions in the 1980s to indicate Albanian dissatisfaction with their situation in the Yugoslav union. Other festering inter-national disputes and animosities were rekindled. By the end of the decade, the historical Croatian-Serbian feud was boiling. Croatians were increasingly outspoken about their fears of Serbian dominance in the Yugoslav union. With the country on the verge of economic collapse, ethnonationalism was ripping the delicate fabric of the Yugoslav state.

There were many other cleavages expressed in East European political cultures in the 1980s. Most of them were repressed and kept out of the press and public eye by the communist authorities. However, with the opening of these societies in the late 1980s, the full meaning and significance of the cultural differences came into public view. There were differences between generations, national and religious groups, and social classes. Perhaps the most significant differences had to do with the precise political values that were to guide East Europe's experiments with political democracy and economic reform in the 1990s. Although there was considerable sentiment to move in the direction of multiparty democracy and market-oriented economies, there were significant differences when it came to specifics. Many of these societies were rejecting communism but had much to do to create new democratic political cultures.

We thus can conclude this chapter by noting that the communists did not succeed in creating a new communist person and new political cultures. Although one could observe a certain level of conformity and even some level of acceptance and support of the ideals and values of the regime among the people throughout most of the Second World states in the past, there was little real progress in the development of unified and genuine communist political cultures.

In their book written more than ten years ago on political culture and political change in Communist Party states, Archie Brown, Jack Gray, and others summarized the results of considerable research on this question.[22] In all of the countries examined, there was little evidence to suggest that communism had been able to change human nature and political culture in a fundamental way. We should acknowledge that the amount of time devoted to communist change has been relatively brief when viewed in the course of human history and that more fundamental changes may still come about in the countries that remain communist; however, their and our conclusions still raise some important questions about the creation of communist political cultures. Because Second World leaders have been unsuccessful in creating their desired political cultures, they must make decisions in environments marked by considerable differences of opinion on the proper distribution of such values as power, respect, well-being, and enlightenment. This means that policies will be made in a politicized environment where different groups and individuals will prefer different decision and policy outcomes. Like the historical and socioeconomic forces reviewed in Chapters 1 and 2, the attitudinal and behavioral forces reviewed here are contextual determinants of considerable importance to politics and policy making in Second World states.

Suggestions for Further Reading

Avis, George, ed., *The Making of the Soviet Citizen: Character Formation and Civic Training of Soviet Education* (London: Croon Helm, 1987).

Black, Cyril E. and **Thomas P. Thornton,** *Communism and Revolution: The Strategic Uses of Political Violence* (Princeton, N.J.: Princeton University Press, 1964).

Brown, Archie, *Political Culture and Communist Studies* (London: Macmillan, 1984).

Brown, Archie, and **Jack Gray,** eds., *Political Culture and Political Change in Communist States,* 2nd rev. ed. (New York: Holmes & Meier, 1979).

Chen, Theodore Hsi-en, *The Maoist Educational*

Revolution (New York: Praeger, 1974).

Curry, Jane Leftwick, *Dissent in Eastern Europe* (New York: Praeger Publishers, 1983).

Dallin, Alexander and **George W. Breslauer,** *Political Terror in Communist Systems* (Stanford, Calif.: Stanford University Press, 1970).

Gorbachev, Mikhail, *Perestroika: New Thinking for Our Country and the World* (New York: Harper & Row, 1987).

Lenin, Vladimir I., *Imperialism: The Highest Stage of Capitalism* (New York: International Publishers, 1939).

Matthews, Mervyn, *Education in the Soviet Union: Policies and Institutions since Stalin* (London: Allen & Unwin, 1982).

Metzger, Thomas A., *Escape from Predicament: Neo-Confucianism and China's Evolving Political Culture* (New York: Columbia University Press, 1977).

Mickiewicz, Ellen P., *Split Signals: Television and Politics in the Soviet Union* (New York: Oxford University Press, 1988).

Millar, James R., ed., *Politics, Work, and Daily Life in the USSR: A Survey of Former Soviet Citizens* (Cambridge, Mass.: Cambridge University Press, 1987).

Nelson, Daniel N., *Elite-Mass Relations in Communist Societies* (London: Macmillan Press, 1988).

Nove, Alec, *Glasnost in Action* (Winchester, Mass.: Unwin Hyman, 1989).

Ramet, Pedro, *Religion and Nationalism in East European Politics* (Durham, N.C.: Duke University Press, 1985).

Remington, Thomas F., *The Truth of Authority: Ideology and Communication in the Soviet Union* (Pittsburgh: University of Pittsburgh Press, 1989).

Solomon, Richard H., *Mao's Revolution and the Chinese Political Culture* (Berkeley: University of California Press, 1971).

Tucker, Robert C., *Political Culture and Leadership in Soviet Russia: From Lenin to Gorbachev* (New York: Norton, 1987).

Volgyes, Ivan, ed., *Political Socialization in Eastern Europe* (New York: Praeger, 1975).

Welsh, William A., ed., *Survey Research and Public Attitudes in Eastern Europe and the Soviet Union* (Elmsford, N.Y.: Pergamon, 1980).

White, Stephen, *Political Culture and Soviet Politics* (New York: St. Martin's Press, 1979).

Notes

1. Gabriel A. Almond, "Comparative Political Systems," *The Journal of Politics,* 19(3)(1956): 395.

2. Gabriel A. Almond and Sidney Verba, *The Civic Culture: Political Attitudes and Democracy in Five Nations* (Princeton, N.J.: Princeton University Press, 1963).

3. Chang Kuo-tao, cited in Jerome Chen, *Mao and the Chinese Revolution* (London: Oxford University Press, 1965), p. 193.

4. An authoritarian political culture represents a set of beliefs and attitudes supporting or at least tolerating nondemocratic political rule.

5. Robert J. Lifton, *Thought Reform and the Psychology of Totalism: A Study of "Brainwashing" in China* (New York: Norton, 1961).

6. See Richard R. Fagen, *The Transformation of Po-*

litical Culture in Cuba (Stanford, Calif.: Stanford University Press, 1969).

7. Stalin's persecution of religion was abandoned in 1941 in an effort to foster greater support and national unity to address the Nazi threat. Nikita S. Khrushchev resumed the more oppressive policies and initiated a campaign (1960–64) to eliminate religious life completely from the Soviet Union. Gorbachev relaxed the oppressive policies again in the late 1980s.

8. In the Soviet Union, the Komsomol accepts people of ages fourteen to twenty-eight; the Pioneers, nine to fourteen; and the Octobrists, seven to nine.

9. Cited in "Transform Schools in to Instruments of Proletarian Dictatorship." *Peking Review* 19(11)(1976): 7.

10. Wang Renzhong, "Striving for the Future of Socialist China," *Beijing Review* 23(24)(1980): 16–19.

11. Ivan Volgyes, "Political Socialization in Eastern Europe," *Problems of Communism*, 23(1): 51.

12. The term *subject-participatory* comes from Almond and Powell's three basic varieties of political culture: a "parochial" political culture where individuals manifest little or no awareness of the national political system; a "subject" culture where individuals are oriented to the political system and the impact it has on their lives but are not oriented to participation; and a "participant" political culture of individuals oriented to engage actively in the political process. (Gabriel A. Almond and G. Bingham Powell, Jr., *Comparative Politics: A Developmental Approach* [Boston: Little, Brown, 1966].)

13. Frederick C. Barghoorn, *Politics in the USSR*, 2nd ed. (Boston: Little, Brown, 1972), p. 23.

14. Ibid., p. 25; the Politburo is the highest decision-making authority within the Communist Party.

15. Mobilization systems utilize government control to activate the people in the quest for high-priority goals. See Franz Schurmann, *Ideology and Organization in Communist China* (Berkeley: University of California Press, 1966).

16. Ezra F. Vogel, "From Friendship to Comradeship: The Change in Personal Relations in Communist China," *The China Quarterly* 21 (1965): 46–60.

17. "Serve the People" was one of the three political writings that was required by the Chinese government for all citizens.

18. These six standards are drawn from Theodore Hsi-en Chen, "The New Socialist Man," in C. T. Hu, ed., *Aspects of Chinese Education* (New York: Columbia University Press, 1969), pp. 88–95.

19. The arts in China were viewed as a forum for heightening the class consciousness of the masses during Mao's time. Revolutionary operas and ballets were written to convey the themes of class struggle and consciousness.

20. Barghoorn, op. cit., pp. 48–86.

21. The autonomous province of Kosovo, inhabited primarily by Albanians, was rocked by rioting and demonstrations in the 1980s as Albanians sought a greater share of resources in the Yugoslav federation.

22. Archie Brown and Jack Gray, eds., *Political Culture and Political Change in Communist States*, 2nd rev. ed. (New York: Holmes & Meier, 1979).

C H A P T E R 4

COMMUNIST PARTIES AND THEIR POWER: PAST AND PRESENT

The late 1980s were a period of incredible change for the Communist Parties of the Second World. Most of the Second World societies in Eastern Europe, for example, saw their top Party leaders overthrown. Thousands of Party officials in Eastern Europe were voted out of office in competitive elections. All of the East European Communist Parties were either seriously weakened or destroyed, and a proliferation of noncommunist parties emerged in the region. By 1990 in most Second World states, Communist Parties were no longer the sole and uncontested holders of power they had been throughout the postwar era.

Because it is difficult to anticipate what will happen in the 1990s, much of this chapter will be devoted to the past. We need to examine the characteristics of one-party rule and why it has recently failed in so many Second World states. We will also look at membership in the Communist Parties and other issues such as organizational structure, personnel, and past Party rules and practices. Then we will examine the revolutionary changes of the late 1980s and what they have meant to Communist Party rule

in the Soviet Union, China, and the countries of Eastern Europe.

Historical Setting

Karl Marx and Friedrich Engels provided the practioners of communism precious little guidance concerning the proper organization of the postrevolutionary Marxist state. "Now that we've won, what do we do?," Vladimir Ilyich Lenin and Leon Trotsky asked themselves after the Bolshevik victory in 1917. How should they organize political power and activity to solve the pressing social and economic problems facing the Russian state?

Lenin understood the importance of political organization. As one leading scholar put it:

One trait that made [Lenin] a pioneer of twentieth-century politics was his insight into the crucial role of organization. Lenin realized that . . . all human activities . . . are carried out in and through organizations and associations.[1]

In what is perhaps his most important work, *What Is to Be Done?*, Lenin recognized the need for a particular type of organization that could be used to facilitate the revolutionary goal of socialist construction. Years before the Russian Revolution, Lenin's political organization, the Communist Party, was created and molded into a highly centralized, authoritarian, and militant "party of a new type"[2] and one that became the sole guardian of communist political rule.

Under Lenin's leadership, the Communist Party represented the key institution for consolidating power and forging the messianic construction of communism. Using great organizational and leadership skills and adhering to the ruthless principle that the ends justify the means, Lenin concentrated political power within the organizational structure of the Party. What was initially viewed by the Bolsheviks as the dictatorship of the proletariat became, for all intents, a dictatorship of the Communist Party. During the Leninist and Stalinist stages of development, the Party grew into a dictatorial, bureaucratic organization that controlled the goals, actions, and policy outcomes of the Soviet political process.

Lenin attempted, however, to include some semblance of democratic values within the Party dictatorship by adopting the principle of democratic centralism. This formula represented an intended merging of both democratic and centralistic (or dictatorial) powers, in which members of the Party were encouraged to debate policy matters freely until the point of decision. Once a vote had been taken and a decision was made, however, centralism was required and further discussion and debate, outside normal Party channels, was forbidden. Although this principle did allow some level of democratic debate within the Party, it did not alter the underlying primacy of dictatorial Communist Party rule, in which a small minority of the state's population monopolizes the primary institution of political power. One-party rule administered according to the principle of democratic centralism was the single most distinguishing characteristic of traditional Second World communist political systems.

The traditional supremacy of the Communist Party as an omnipresent and omnipotent decision-making body manifested itself in several important ways. First, the Party ensured its domination and control over the political system through a fusion of the Party and government. Second, the Party controlled the national economy through state ownership and central planning. Third, the Party had the nation's armed forces at its disposal; and fourth, the Party imposed its official ideology on the population through political indoctrination and enforcement of stringent rules outlawing ideological heresy.

Communist Party Membership in the 1980s

Who belonged to Communist Parties before the major changes of the late 1980s? As Table 4.1 indicates, only a small minority of Second World societies were members of ruling Communist Parties. In the mid 1980s, membership ranged from a high of about 16 percent in Romania to a low of 0.1 percent in Cambodia. Why did so few people belong to the Parties? There were a variety of reasons for the minority status of the traditional Communist Parties. First, the leaders wanted it that way. They preferred minority Parties that supposedly included only the most dedicated, ideologically committed citizens. This made it easier to maintain Party discipline and purity and to ensure the Party's role as the so-called revolutionary vanguard of the society. Second, Party membership was often

Table 4.1   Communist Party Membership in the 1980s

Country	Communist Party Name	Party Membership	Communist Party Membership as Total Percent of Population
China	Chinese Communist Party	46,001,951	4.3
USSR	Communist Party of the Soviet Union	19,037,946	6.7
Romania	Communist Party of Romania	3,640,000	15.9
North Korea	Korean Workers' Party	2,500,000	11.7
East Germany	Socialist Unity Party	2,324,386	14.0
Yugoslavia	League of Communists of Yugoslavia	2,168,000	9.3
Poland	Polish United Workers' Party	2,130,000	5.6
Vietnam	Vietnamese Communist Party	1,900,000	3.0
Czechoslovakia	Communist Party of Czechoslovakia	1,705,490	10.9
Bulgaria	Bulgarian Communist Party	932,055	10.4
Hungary	Hungarian Socialist Workers' Party	870,992	8.2
Cuba	Communist Party of Cuba	523,639	5.1
Albania	Albanian Party of Labor	147,000	4.8
Mongolia	Mongolian People's Revolutionary Party	88,150	4.4
Laos	Lao People's Revolutionary Party	40,000	1.1
Cambodia	Khmer Communist Party	7,500	0.1

(*Source*) Richard F. Staar, ed., *Yearbook on International Communist Affairs* (Stanford, Calif.: Hoover Institution Press, 1988).

demanding and not many people wanted to do it. Members were expected to serve as model citizens and often found their lives scrutinized by other Party members. Finally, many people were reluctant to join Parties that were viewed as bankrupt or discredited political organizations by large sectors of society.

There were a number of factors, however, that still led some people to join the Party, and at least three should be mentioned. First, some individuals were achievement oriented and had high aspirations for success. Joining the Party could open doors that might otherwise be closed. Second, some joined the Party because of the political influence it provided them. If in the past one wanted to pursue a career in politics or in some line of government service, membership in the Party was practically mandatory. In many cases, it gave a person leverage in competing for positions in traditionally nongovernmental sectors. Finally, there were always some who joined because of a spirit of communist conviction. Committed to the Marxist-Leninist doctrine, they felt that the best way to promote communism and the betterment of society was within the organizational structure of the Party.

The Communist Parties attempted to attract members from all sectors of their societies, although most had difficulties keeping the peasant and workers' ranks sufficiently high to justify their proletarian basis and heritage. At one time or another, most of the Parties had to undertake campaigns to increase the number of peasants, workers, and minority nationalities among their memberships. The substantial increase (over 8 percent) in worker representation in the Community Party of the Soviet Union (CPSU) between 1957 and 1980 was the result of a recruitment campaign begun by Party leaders Nikita Khrushchev and Leonid Brezhnev to increase working class involvement.

Procedures governing entrance into the Parties varied somewhat from country to country and over time. The procedures followed in the Soviet Union in the 1960s and 1970s, however, are fairly representative and illustrate the general standards that were maintained. When an individual wanted to join the CPSU, he or she had to be recommended by three persons, each of whom must have been a Party member for five years and known the candidate for at least one year. Once the application was prepared and brought before the local primary Party organization, a two-thirds majority vote was required for admission as a candidate member. After serving for one year in this provisional status—a period when the candidate's work was closely monitored by superiors—the application was again voted on by members of the local primary organization. If the individual received a two-thirds vote, his or her file was sent to the next Party level (usually city or district), where it was normally approved.

It was not always easy to join a Communist Party. In Maoist China only a small fraction of candidates whose applications were forwarded with grassroot endorsements were considered and accepted for membership. An exhaustive, thorough scrutiny of background and commitment preceded a final decision on the candidate's fate. Many aspirants and hopefuls were screened out for trivial defects in character. In the 1980s, the eroding prestige of the Chinese Communist Party (CCP) greatly dampened the popular enthusiasm for Party membership. Although the post-Mao leadership lifted many restrictions on induction and actively solicited applications from intellectuals, the number of newly filed applications steadily declined. Most people balked at the prospect of joining the Party because they felt that only those who wanted to ingratiate themselves into the Party's favor and advance their careers at their friends' and co-workers' expense would still be interested in Party membership. By the end of the 1980s, the question of Party membership generated increasing cynicism and skepticism throughout the Second World. What was once hailed to be an honorable and responsible act of service to one's country had, in the eyes of most, become an act of self-aggrandizement and delusion. As we will see, there are several reasons for this and most of them represent a serious indictment of the quality of Communist Party rule.

Organizational Structure

Primary Organizations

Figure 4.1 illustrates the typical organization of the traditional Communist Party, from the lowest-level primary organization (what formerly were called the local Party cells) to the highest-level Party leader. The organizational structure of the Party approximated a pyramid, at the bottom of which were thousands of primary organizations based in factories, schools, collective farms, and the like. When an individual joined the Party, it was this local organization that received and processed the application. Recruitment of new members and ideological work (spreading official propaganda, political education, and so on) were major responsibilities of the primary organizations. These organizations also served as ideological caretakers within factories, schools, and other institutions as they tried to propagate attitudes and behavior corresponding to the Party's expectations. By linking every social, economic, and territorial unit within the state, the primary organizations were intended to provide the central Communist Party with a communication network that reached to the grassroots of their society. There

were over 400,000 primary organizations in the Soviet Union in the late 1980s.

One distinctive feature of the Chinese Communist Party (CCP) organizational policy during the Maoist era was the fusion of the Party, local government, and economic management at grassroot levels. For a long time, local Party leaders (called Party secretaries) served in important supervisory and management capacities in addition to concurrently acting as ideological watchdogs for their superiors. There was a positional overlap and the Party leadership always exercised authority in local administration and management. Non-Party managers, directors and superintendents were generally figureheads and performed largely ceremonial duties. The rationale for totally integrating the Party organization into government and administration was the perceived need for unified leadership under the control of the Communist Party.

The usurpation of administrative powers by Communist Party leaders and committees represented costly and unwarranted intervention into purely technical and professional affairs. These Party officials ended up making decisions in areas that were often beyond their true responsibilities and capabilities. Significantly, the reform movements of the 1980s in China, Eastern Europe, and the Soviet Union featured a bifurcation of Party and government administration. Deng Xiaoping and Mikhail Gorbachev both were ardent proponents of the separation of Party and government. Deng was explicit about his endorsement of reduced Party control over economic enterprises in comments he made in 1986:

The substance of reform should primarily be separating the Party from government administration, finding a solution to how the Party should exercise leadership, and how to improve leadership.[3]

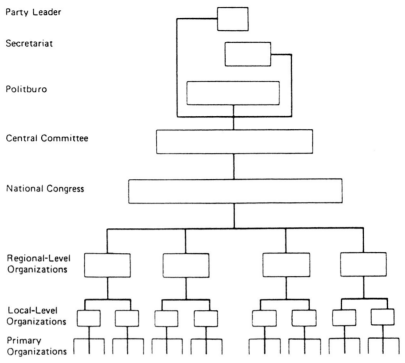

Figure 4.1 Communist Party organizational structure.

Although the 1989 crackdown and reversal of the reform programs in China raised certain questions about the Chinese communist commitment to this principle, most observers expect the trend to continue. Of course, more than a few former Party functionaries appeared unreconciled to the erosion of their powers, and there has been evidence suggesting that the policy favoring a separation has been opposed, circumvented, and boycotted in China.

Regional- and Local-Level Organizations

Traditionally, the vast majority of Party members worked in part- and full-time capacities within the regional- and local-level networks. The central Communist Party organization provided the regions—the republics and provinces—with a certain degree of autonomy in the administration of Party affairs. These regional organizations typically coordinated their own Party conferences and had organizational structures that closely corresponded with those of the national Party organizations.

The regional-level Party organizations in the Soviet Union had always been based on a federal structure. At the regional level, the Parties of the fifteen Soviet republics—for example, Russia, Armenia, Estonia, and so forth—had the highest status. A major issue for the Soviet Union as it entered the 1990s was the relationship between the central and republic Party organizations. Some regional Communist Party organizations, such as that of the Lithuanians, declared their independence from the Communist Party of the Soviet Union (CPSU).

Next in order of importance were the regions and areas within the Soviet republics, followed by the towns, rural and urban districts, and so on down the list. Each of these units had its own Party organizations and networks, including full-time committees, officials, and elected delegates to represent the unit at the next highest level.

The Communist Party in China (CCP) was also divided into regional and local Party networks. The degree of regional Party autonomy had been hotly debated in China and had been subject to the shifting desires of the central Party leaders. During the initial stage of the Great Proletarian Cultural Revolution (1966–69), for example, the provincial Party structures were assaulted and dominated by both the national leaders and such grassroots groups as the Red Guards. In the 1980s, the provinces regained some semblance of regional autonomy and became a stronger force in making policy within their respective regions. Many of the leaders who emerged in the post-Mao era gained their experience in the regional organizations.

The Yugoslavs traditionally had the most formalized and autonomous regional Party organizations. Each of the six republics (Bosnia-Hercegovina, Croatia, Macedonia, Montenegro, Serbia, and Slovenia) and two autonomous provinces (Kosovo and Voyvodina) had regional congresses, central committees, and the usual executive Party organs. Meeting regularly, these organs and their members had considerable power in determining regional Party policy. In fact, the central Party organization lost power in the political arena over the last few decades and that of the regional Party organizations

grew. The republics' vigorous pursuit of regional interests resulted in a high level of interregional conflict, leading many to remark that Yugoslavia long had, in reality, a de facto multiparty system—that is, the Croatian Communist Party, the Serbian Party, and so forth.

National Party Congress

In all traditional Communist Party states, delegates from the regions and lower-level organizations gathered every four or five years to attend the national Party congresses. Called the All-Union Party Congress in the USSR and the National Party Congress in China, these large and highly ceremonial meetings were filled with considerable Party fanfare.

In theory, the delegates came to the national congresses to elect the new Central Committee that would serve until the next congress. In fact, however, the slate of candidates was typically prepared in advance by the leaders themselves, which resulted in the unanimous election of the official slate. Traditionally, rank-and-file delegates had little, if any, effect on the selection of their highest leaders. The content of the speeches, the selection of the Central Committee, and the congress in general was carefully orchestrated by the top Party leadership.

Some of this began to change in the 1980s. By the end of the decade, Party congresses in the Soviet Union and China were meetings of considerable importance and called attention to the dramatic changes taking place in the politics and policies of communist states. The 1986 27th Party Congress of the CPSU in Moscow marked the end of the Brezhnev and the beginning of the Gorbachev era. In power as Party leader for about one year, Gorbachev used the 27th Congress as an opportunity to outline his vision for Soviet reform. To do so took considerable time. Gorbachev's opening speech ran five and one half hours and addressed all major aspects of Soviet foreign and domestic policy.

The 27th Congress also approved a new set of Party rules outlining the rights and duties of the Party member and adopted a Party program that outlined the need for perestroika and radical reform of the economy. The 27th Congress endorsed the 12th Five Year Plan for the 1986–90 period and a document charting Soviet social and economic plans to the year 2000.

Gorbachev and the Party leaders convened another important meeting called a Party con-

ference (rather than congress) in June 1988. By convening the 19th Party Conference, the first such meeting in forty-seven years, they reintroduced the convention of holding Party conferences at intervals between the Party congresses. Among other important developments, the 1988 Conference offered valuable insights into the politics surrounding Gorbachev's reform program. For example, whereas most of the Party leadership seemed to support perestroika and economic reform, some Party conservatives, such as Yegor Ligachev, were highly skeptical

Gorbachev confers with Yakovlev and Ligachev at the historic Communist Party Conference in June 1988.

about Gorbachev's goals surrounding glasnost and democratization. The debates were critical, spontaneous, and often electrifying. For the first time in history, Communist Party policies were being debated in more open and democratic ways, in full view of the world and an astonished Soviet television audience.

By the time the 28th Party Congress convened in Moscow during July 1990, the divisions apparent within the CPSU at the 19th Party Conference had grown deeper and become more clearly defined. Again before the people of the Soviet Union and the world, Party leaders argued vehemently with one another over the future course and pace of reform the Party should undertake. Conservative delegates castigated Gorbachev and his reform program for abandoning Marxism-Leninism. Radical delegates demanded that the Party embrace social democracy and relinquish its control over state resources. Near the end of the Congress, Boris Yeltsin, an outspoken member of the radical faction of the Party, announced his decision to quit the Party from the rostrum of the Congress. Following his announcement, instead of returning to his seat, Yeltsin dramatically walked out of the hall where the delegates had convened. Several other members of the radical reform faction of the Party later joined Yeltsin in renouncing their Party membership. The 1990 Soviet Party Congress demonstrated the extent to which the traditional communist principles of democratic centralism and Party solidarity before the public had been abandoned by members of the CPSU in the Gorbachev era.

An important Party congress was held in China in the late 1980s. Meeting in Beijing from October 25 to November 1, 1987, the 13th Party Congress of the CCP addressed the major question of Chinese reform. To open the congress, then General Secretary Zhao Ziyang presented a report to the approximately 2,000 as-

sembled delegates entitled "Advance Along the Road of Socialism with Chinese Characteristics." Zhao emphasized that China was in the primary stage of socialism and would continue to be so for at least another 100 years. He noted that the primary stage of socialism was a long-term and necessary transitional stage, which China had to go through to build communism from a backward, underdeveloped economic base. Zhao outlined the Party's goal to turn China "into a prosperous, strong, democratic, culturally advanced, and modern socialist country" of the future. Zhao was ousted in the aftermath of the Tiananmen Square massacre in 1989 and had little time to see his vision realized.

Central Committee

Because of their large size, the infrequency of their meetings, and the fact that the highest-level leaders were making the decisions, the national Party congresses traditionally had little meaningful power as policy-making bodies. Although affected by some of the same factors, the Central Committees were far more influential bodies. The Central Committees were large, generally ranging from 100 to 300 members within the different states, but not nearly so enormous as the Party congresses that supposedly elected them. Meeting periodically, usually every few months or so, the Central Committees theoretically were considered the most important Party organization within their states. The traditional Central Committee of the CPSU historically had been the organ that directed the considerable activities of the Party and of the local organs. This involved selection and appointment of leading personnel; direction of the work of central governmental and public organizations; creation and direction of various Party organs, agencies, and enterprises of the Party; appointment of the editors of the central newspapers and magazines operating under Party control; and allocation of funds from the Party budget.

Historically, the Central Committees in all Second World countries were vested with a number of important functions. First, the Central Committees were required to ratify Politburo decisions to give them legitimacy. Second, with their memberships recruited from all parts of the country, the Central Committees served as an effective and important link between the apex of the political pyramid and its base. Third, Central Committee membership was one of the highest accolades for Party veterans. The Party honored its outstanding members with Central Committee membership in recognition of their meritorious service. Fourth, tenures as Central Committee members were also part of the apprenticeship to top Party and governmental positions.

The Central Committees historically were the conclave of the country's most influential and powerful people. Among its members were the leading personnel of the central and regional Party apparatuses and government agencies. The Committees also embraced national dignitaries and prominent figures from the military, industrial, and intellectual sectors; in short, they assembled in their midst the highest bureaucrats and functional elites who ran the country.

The memberships and meetings of the Central Committees in the 1980s reflected the important changes taking place within Second World systems. In April 1989, Mikhail Gorbachev and his associates engineered a sweeping purge of 110 of the 301 members of the CPSU Central Committee. The removal of the Brezhnevites, or what were called the dead souls—from the title of the novel by Nikolai Gogol—included such Party stalwarts as Andrei Gromyko, long-time Foreign Minister of the Soviet Union, and Nikolai Tikhonov, former Prime Minister of the Soviet

state. This 1989 meeting was also noteworthy for the startling outpouring of opinion, which was published in great detail in the Communist Party newspaper *Pravda*. Although many of the speeches and discussions were in support of the Gorbachev reform policies, many regional Party officials used the occasion to criticize the central Party organization—and implicitly Mr. Gorbachev himself—for mismanaging the economy, undermining the authority of the Party and the military, and allowing for a dangerous rise in nationalist sentiments. Like other aspects of Soviet politics, Central Committee meetings became more open and democratic.

At the 28th Soviet Party Congress in July 1990, delegates to the Congress directly elected the Party leader and the Politburo for the first time. Previously the delegates to the Congress had elected the Central Committee which in turn chose the Party leader and members of the politburo. The change in voting procedures made it increasingly unlikely that the Central Committee could again oust a Party leader, as it had done Nikita Khrushchev in 1964, in the future. By mid 1990, the Soviet Central Committee had lost many of its traditional powers.

Politburo, Secretariat, and Party Leader

Although in theory the Central Committees held considerable power throughout communist history, they did delegate the bulk of it to the bodies and individuals they elected—the Politburos, the Secretariats, and the Party leaders (see Figure 4.1). The Politburo was an exceedingly important decision-making institution with a great deal to say concerning who got what in Second World states. Generally meeting at least weekly, this group of Party members traditionally was responsible for transacting the highest level and most important business on the nation's agenda. The Politburos were considered the most significant and powerful policy-making bodies in Second World states.

Formal power to make policy was given to the Politburo, but the Secretariats had considerable power and important responsibilities of their own. The Soviet Party statutes in the 1980s noted that the CPSU Secretariat was to direct the Party's work and organize the fulfillment of Party decisions. As the organizational arm of the Politburo, the Secretariats supervised the implementation and execution of Party policies. Meeting almost daily, these bodies occasionally overshadowed the Politburos, particularly in times of crisis, by making policy proposals, issuing decrees, and ensuring administrative execution.

These high-level Party bodies were subject to considerable change in the past and are likely to be subject to even more in the future. The Chinese Communist Party (CCP) Central Committee Secretariat was abolished in 1967 and reestablished in February 1980. During that period, the Politburo Standing Committee, often thought of as the Secretariat but, in fact, a different body and more powerful than the CCP Politburo, indeed was the most important decision-making body in China. During the unstable period following Mao's death in 1976, for example, the Politburo Standing Committee convened an enlarged Politburo session and undertook a number of important actions of great consequence to the future course of Chinese politics. Perhaps the most important was the purging of Mao's wife, Jiang Qing, and three additional members of the CCP Politburo, the so-called Gang of Four. In the 1980s the CCP Central Committee Secretariat once again became a major locus of power. Because of the absence of formal rules outlining the sharing and use of power in the upper Party echelons as well as a general disregard for statutes and

rules during times of crisis, the power relationships between these highest organs were always rather fluid.

As a result of their heavy supervisory, implementation, and execution functions, the Party Secretariats controlled and relied on large bureaucracies to assist them in these tasks. The bureaucracies were divided into departments organized according to broad policy areas. In the CPSU Secretariat in 1989, for example, Viktor Chebrikov was in charge of legal policy; Yegor Ligachev, agricultural policy; Vadim Medvedev, ideology; and Aleksander Yakolev, international policy. Generally, each member of the Secretariat was in charge of a certain department and specialized in that department's designated policy areas. In overseeing policy implementation and execution in these different departments, the secretaries had a major impact on the policy process.

Also elected by the Central Committees, the Party leaders—at the beginning of 1990, Mikhail Gorbachev in the Soviet Union and Jiang Zemin in China—traditionally have been the highest ranking officials in their states, outranking the top government officers, such as the President or the Premier. The first among equals in their states and in their Parties, the Party leaders presided over the work of the Politburos, controlled the central Party apparatus, and acted as the primary spokespersons for the Party and for the state.

Because political power was heavily concentrated in the hands of the top Party leaders during the decades of traditional Communist Party rule, these leaders had a deep impact on the governing of Second World systems. Lenin was the supreme leader of Russia from 1917 to 1924.[4] After Joseph Stalin's assumption of power (he became General Secretary of the Party in 1922), the position of Party General Secretary soon overpowered all other political offices, including the leading government positions. In his so-called last testament, Lenin warned his associates against the appointment of Stalin as General Secretary, noting that Stalin already had become too powerful and did not use his power with sufficient caution. Shortly before his death, Lenin added a postscript to his testament, suggesting that Stalin be removed from his post. As history shows, Stalin was not dislodged; rather, he decisively moved to increase his power within his role as General Secretary of the CPSU.[5] Under his administration, the role of Party leader became the dominant position in Soviet politics, a pattern that held until 1990, when the Soviet Union continued to consider political reforms that would lead to a different constellation of power.

After Stalin's death in the spring of 1953, a power struggle between Nikita S. Khrushchev and a number of high CPSU officials ensued. Having a solid political base by virtue of being a member of both the Secretariat and the Politburo, Khrushchev soon became the dominant figure and had his title upgraded to First Secretary.[6] Unlike Stalin's leadership as General Secretary, however, Khrushchev's was never as totalitarian and autocratic. Not only was he less powerful, but his reign of power was shorter. In the fall of 1964, while on vacation in the Crimea, Khrushchev was summoned back to Party headquarters in the Kremlin and ousted from his job. Because of shortcomings in his agricultural policy, the embarrassment and failure of the Cuban missile episode, the bifurcation of the Party, and other alleged shortcomings, the career of the impulsive Khrushchev was abruptly brought to an end.[7] Replacing Khrushchev as head of the CPSU was Leonid I. Brezhnev, who headed the Party for two decades, longer than both Lenin and Khrushchev. Beginning his leadership of the CPSU under Khrushchev's former title of First Secretary,

Brezhnev assumed Stalin's upgraded title of General Secretary in 1966 and the state presidency in 1977.[8]

In November 1982, General Secretary Brezhnev died at the age of 75. Considerable attention focused on the Kremlin as the Soviet leaders prepared to choose a successor. American Kremlinologist Myron Rush noted that the most striking feature of the Brezhnev succession was the absence of clearly qualified candidates who possessed not only good health but also broad political experience.[9] Many of the candidates were older than Brezhnev; others had careers that were highly specialized. Brezhnev's apparent choice for a successor was Konstantin Chernenko, who had the unfortunate image of being Brezhnev's aide and an undistinguished staff man who had never been the responsible head of a high-level Party or government organization. Despite Brezhnev's apparent desire to make Chernenko his heir, Yuri Andropov, former head of the Soviet Committee for State Security (the KGB), decisively moved to assume the top Party spot. Having capitalized on Brezhnev's physical frailties and political vulnerabilities during the final years of the former Party leader's life, Andropov brought some strong qualifications to the job. Described by Kremlinologist Rush as highly intelligent, dispassionate, and cool under fire, the 68-year-old Andropov quickly took over the top Party and government positions, something that had taken Brezhnev thirteen years to accomplish. Once in office, Andropov sought to wipe out corruption and turn around the Soviet Union's decline.

However, Andropov's reign was short-lived. By August 1983, nine months after assuming Brezhnev's mantle, Andropov had disappeared from public view. According to official medical reports, Andropov had developed serious kidney problems; his condition sharply deteriorated in January 1984, and he died the next month.

Many predicted that the Soviet Union would then turn to a younger successor, perhaps the 53-year-old Mikhail Gorbachev or the 61-year-old Grigori Romanov. However, the CPSU Politburo stuck with the most experienced generation and chose Brezhnev's original heir, 73-year-old Konstantin Chernenko. However, Chernenko also proved to be a short-term leader and thirteen months later succumbed to ill health. Having long suffered from emphysema, Chernenko died in March 1985.

Soviet leadership then underwent a swift, and what proved to be a far-reaching, transformation in the course of a single day. Chernenko's death was announced in the afternoon of March 11, 1985, and by evening, Mikhail Gorbachev was installed as the new CPSU General Secretary. A native Russian, Gorbachev was born in 1931 in the Stavropol region, an agrarian area in the Russian heartland. According to his official biography, his parents were peasants and he worked on local collective farms as a youth. Bright, talented, and ambitious, Gorbachev went to study law at Moscow University in 1955. Unlike previous high CPSU officials, most of whom had little advanced education, Gorbachev earned a degree from Moscow University and another degree, in agricultural economics, from a correspondence school. Representing a new kind of Soviet leader, Gorbachev was the first leader to come from a generation that did not take part in World War II and the first who had received a full education in the postwar era.

After graduating from Moscow University, Gorbachev went back to Stavropol and began his rapid climb up the political ladder. He first became head of the Komsomol, later took charge of the collective farms in the region, and then, in 1970, became First Secretary of the Communist Party in Stavropol. In 1978, he was brought to Moscow to fill the vacant post of the CPSU Central Committee Secretary for Agriculture. The next year, in a remarkable and meteoric rise, Gorbachev was catapulted into the CPSU Politburo, first as a candidate member and, in 1980, as a full member. Although passed over for the top job when Brezhnev died in 1982 and again in 1984 when Andropov died, he used the time to acquire more experience and to expand his power base. During this period, Gorbachev acquired considerable responsibility for matters concerning the economy, culture, ideology, personnel, and various aspects of international affairs.

When Chernenko's health began to fail in 1984 and 1985, forcing him to drop more and more of his official activities, Gorbachev assumed a leading role in the work of the CPSU Secretariat and Politburo. Although a power struggle was being waged behind the scenes at the highest levels of Soviet politics, the political momentum was very much on Gorbachev's side. Working to his advantage were personnel changes made during Andropov's brief tenure. Andropov brought a number of younger people into the top Party leadership who were natural allies to Gorbachev. By the time Chernenko's health failed, and with KGB support and the acquiescence of the Soviet army, Gorbachev had assumed an almost unassailable position.

Although the Politburo vote making Gorbachev the Party leader was not unanimous, Gorbachev quickly became a powerful leader. Two weeks after taking power, he began a campaign to sweep out incompetent, corrupt, and aging Party officials and replace them with younger, better educated, and more technocratic-minded successors. Gorbachev was now in charge, and Soviet communism was in for a period of substantial change.

Along with Gorbachev came new ideas and thinking. The new thinking involved *glasnost*, increased information and honesty in public life, *perestroika*, a restructuring of the economy, and *demokratizatsia*, a democratization of political life. Gorbachev proved to be a remarkable tactician in furthering these revolutionary objectives in the early days of his rule. He demoted or ousted his opposition and in rapid succession introduced a panoply of new reforms. By the end of the 1980s, he had set off a chain of events that would transform the Second World and the nature of Communist Party rule.

In a deft play of power in 1988, Gorbachev took over the governmental position of President with the forced retirement of 79-year-old President and Politburo member Andrei Gromyko. (This will be discussed in more detail in the next chapter.) Gorbachev also engineered other changes in the Politburo, including the retirement of the 74-year-old Mikhail Solomenstev and 68-year-old Anatoly Dobrynin, foreign policy specialist and former ambassador to the United States who apparently lost his position due to the rapid rise of a close Gorbachev associate, 64-year-old Aleksandr Yakovlev. A strong ally of Gorbachev's, Yakovlev took over the top foreign policy job in the Secretariat and assumed the powerful number-two position behind Gorbachev in the Politburo. To bring additional new blood and support for his reform program into the Politburo, Gorbachev elevated the 59-year-old Vadim Medvedev to full Politburo membership, allowing him to bypass his normally expected service as a nonvoting candidate member. Promoted to candidate membership was the 59-year-old Aleksandra Biryukova, who became the first woman to serve on the CPSU Politburo in twenty-seven years.

Until September 1976, the People's Republic of China had known only a single leader of the Chinese Communist Party (CCP). As one of the founders of the CCP in 1921, this leader, Mao Zedong, held a variety of positions in the Party before becoming its head during the period of the Long March (1934–35). When the People's Republic was proclaimed in October 1949, Mao concurrently became Chairman of the Republic and Chairman of the CCP. The Chairman of the People's Republic was considered the head of state in China, putting Mao in charge of a number of executive and ceremonial responsibilities. Giving up the head-of-state role in 1959, Mao remained the reigning head of the CCP until his death in 1976.

Although choosing Mao's successor was a favorite pastime of many Sinologists, most were surprised when Hua Guofeng, a relatively unknown Party official from the province of Hunan, assumed the dual roles of Chairman of the CCP and Premier of the State Council in 1976. Hua's meteoric rise was generally believed to be the result of an effort to break a stalemate in an intra-Party factional fight over succession. From the outset, both Hua's heir apparency and the authenticity of what was purported to be Mao's message, "With you [Hua] in charge, I am at ease," which Hua used to legitimize his leadership, were challenged. Lacking a power base of his own and experience at the helm, Hua was predestined to be a transitional leader. Deng Xiaoping, the resilient and pragmatic leader, and the so-called moderates in the CCP—those who opposed the ideological excesses of Maoism and favored more pragmatic reforms to modernize China—skillfully challenged and successfully dislodged Hua from his leadership posts.

In September 1980, Hua resigned as Premier in favor of Zhao Ziyang, then a member of Deng's moderate coalition. Although Hua cited the Party principle of collective leadership (to be discussed later in this chapter) as the reason for his resignation, it was apparent that he was

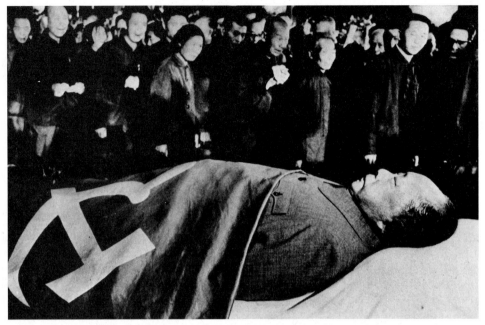

Chinese mourners file by Mao's body at his funeral in September 1976. At that very moment, an intense struggle for succession was underway. It resulted in the elevation of Hua Guofeng to take on Mao's mantle and the purging of the "Gang of Four," which included Mao's wife, Jiang Qing.

losing a struggle for power with the moderates. Two months later, Hua also resigned the Chairmanship of the CCP's Military Commission and, most importantly, the overall Chairmanship of the Party, which went to another member of the moderate coalition, Hu Yaobang. These demotions were officially announced in June 1981, when a lengthy Party resolution critically assessed both Mao and Hua. Hua was charged with fostering a cult of personality, propagating erroneous policies and opposing correct ones, and committing other transgressions.[10] The changes in the CCP leadership put the moderates Deng, Zhao, and Hu in a position of dominance in the Chinese political structure.

After Hua was deposed, the moderate coalition split into two factions, the reformists and the conservatives, with the top leader, Deng Xiaoping, as the ultimate arbiter. The reform-oriented Party leader, Hu Yaobang, was soon on a collision course with the more conservative senior leaders. Hu favored a quickened tempo of reform and rejuvenation of China's political system; the conservatives wanted to go slow. In late 1986 and early 1987, student demonstrations provided ammunition for the conservatives opposing Hu's political and economic reforms. They capitalized on Hu's reluctance to crack down on the dissident students and accused him of favoring "bourgeois liberalization." In a cacophony of malicious attacks, the Politburo stripped Hu of his Party leadership and designated Zhao Ziyang as his successor at the Party's 13th Congress in 1987.

Zhao was also a reformer, and his Party leadership was also short-lived. Once again, student demonstrations brought down the CCP's Party leader. What started out as student demonstrations praising Hu Yaobang, who had died on April 15, 1989, became a major democratization movement involving millions of Chinese, primarily students, in the hearts of major Chinese cities most notably in Tiananmen Square in the center of Beijing. Party leader Zhao Ziyang was tolerant of the demonstrations and wanted to avoid the use of force in bringing them to an end. Others, including longtime leader Deng Xiaoping and the conservative Premier Li Peng, were more concerned with stability and called in troops to quash the student demonstrations. Behind the bloody violence in Tiananmen Square was an intense power struggle, which led to the ouster of Party leader Zhao Ziyang and the appointment of his successor, the 62-year-old Jiang Zemin, the Party leader from Shanghai.

Deng Xiaoping, Zhao Ziyang, and Li Xiannian stand side by side at an anniversary celebration of the Chinese Revolution. As a consequence of the political protests and conservative backlash of spring 1989, Zhao was removed from his position as General Secretary of the Chinese Communist Party.

The power struggles and leadership changes taking place in the Soviet Union and China in the 1980s provided an important lesson about Communist Party rule in Second World states. We sometimes had the impression that communist leaders, once in power, were firmly in command. Although they did have considerable power at one time, once Second World states began to reform, that power became increasingly fragile.

Past Party Rules and Practices

Unlike Western political parties, the traditional Communist Parties required more from their members than occasional financial contributions, verbal support, and turnout at key elections. What was expected of Soviet Party members in the 1980s was outlined in the CPSU Party Rules. Parts I and II of the rules set down the rights and responsibilities of members and described the procedures for admission and expulsion. Parts III to VI of the rules described the structure and powers of Party organs and the principles guiding Party elections, leadership, and decision making. Parts VII to IX explained the CPSU's relationship to government, to the Komsomol, and to the military.

Party members in China were also guided by certain rules and obligations in the 1980s. These included:

1. To adhere to the Party's political and ideological line of Marxism-Leninism–Mao Zedong thought.
2. To uphold collective leadership and oppose the making of arbitrary decisions by individuals.
3. To safeguard the Party's centralized leadership and strictly observe Party discipline.
4. To uphold Party spirit and eradicate factionalism that undermines the Party's unity.
5. To speak the truth, match words with deeds, and show loyalty to the cause of the Party and to the people.
6. To promote inner-Party democracy and to take a correct attitude toward dissenting views.
7. To guarantee that the Party members' rights of criticism, policy formulation, and implementation are not encroached upon.
8. To provide genuine democratic elections within the Party and give full expression to the voters' wishes.
9. To criticize and fight against such erroneous tendencies as factionalism, anarchism, and extreme individualism and evildoers such as counterrevolutionaries, grafters, embezzlers, and criminals.
10. To adopt a correct and positive attitude toward comrades who have made mistakes.
11. To accept supervision from the Party and the masses and to see that privilege seeking is not allowed.
12. To study hard and become both Red and expert in order to contribute to the four modernizations.[11]

A variety of procedures and practices also were important to traditional Communist Party life and politics. Collective leadership was one practice and was intended to avoid a return to the highly dictatorial, "one-man" rule of Joseph Stalin. Therefore, decision making in Party organs at all organizational levels was to be a collective exercise. Although Party leaders and secretaries were the first among equals, they still had to gain the support of their peers. Although the so-called one-man rule under Stalin truly never was a reality, it led all states, in the post-Stalin era, to more fully embrace the principle of collective rule.

Democratic centralism was supposed to be another important practice at work in the Communist Parties of Second World states. Developed by Lenin to reconcile both freedom and discipline, democratic centralism was based on the following principles: (1) election of all Party bodies, (2) accountability of Party bodies to their organizations and higher bodies, (3) strict discipline of the minority to the majority on all decisions, and (4) the binding of decisions of higher bodies on lower bodies. Theoretically, there were to be both democratic and centralistic elements in these principles. In actuality, centralism and control usually prevailed.

Another past practice or set of practices is noteworthy, partly because of the general absence of Party rules and partly because of the changes taking place today in Communist Parties. This concerns the problems of circulation and rotation of Party leaders and the issue of succession once leaders die or are removed. The Yugoslavs did the most in the past to formalize both rotation and succession of Party leaders.[12] Until the changes of the late 1980s, efforts in most of the other states to formalize turnover within Party organs were largely ineffective. For example, at the 23rd Congress of the CPSU in 1966, Brezhnev and his colleagues abolished the requirement (adopted at the previous Congress in 1961) that there would be a regular, specified turnover in Party leadership bodies. The requirement was intended to avoid the election of the same leaders time after time and to bring some new blood into decision-making circles. Little came of the 1961 proposal, but in the late 1980s Gorbachev proposed secret balloting and a choice of candidates in Party elections within the context of his democratization and political reform program. Gorbachev's belief that the average citizen and Party member must be given a greater sense of participation began to affect the traditional principles regarding the selection of Party leadership. In this regard, Gorbachev is quoted as saying, "A house can be put in order only by a person who feels he is the owner."

In May 1988, the CPSU Central Committee approved proposals that limited service of all Party officials to two consecutive five-year terms. Election for a third consecutive term required approval by no less than 75 percent of the membership of the relevant Party organization. The proposed limitation covered membership in the CPSU Secretariat, the Politburo, and even the office of General Secretary, the post occupied by Mikhail Gorbachev. Much remains to be done to make genuine elections and term-of-office limitations a reality, but in the late 1980s there was evidence that the Soviet Party leaders were serious about these proposals.

Another traditional Party practice was called nomenklatura. Nomenklatura referred to a list of positions, both in the Party and in society at large, that the Party maintained and for which Party approval was necessary before personnel changes, removals, or replacements could be made. The nomenklatura list in the USSR included an extensive list of high positions in the military, scientific organizations, the mass media, and other important sectors of Soviet life. This practice allowed traditional Communist Parties to control appointments to key positions throughout their societies. Party officials actively used the nomenklatura practice in the past to remove undesirables, select officials who met Party standards, and control appointments to the most important positions in society.

The importance of the nomenklatura practice, and certainly the number of positions on the list, began to decline in the 1980s throughout most of the Second World states. At the 13th Party Congress in 1987, China endorsed plans to reduce the number of jobs whose hiring was controlled by the CCP.[13] As the East European

Communist Parties began to crumble in the late 1980s, one of the first practices to be discarded was the nomenklatura system. Changes also are being contemplated in the Second World states where Communist Parties remain in control.

Recent Developments

Soviet Union

Mikhail Gorbachev has faced opposition from within the Communist Party of the Soviet Union since he was chosen as the Party General Secretary in March 1985. Originally, Gorbachev's opposition within the Party consisted of holdovers from the Brezhnev era: Party careerists who profited from the corruption allowed under Brezhnev and refused to acknowledge the need to reform once Brezhnev left the political scene.

By the time the 27th Party Congress of the CPSU concluded in February 1986, Gorbachev and his Party supporters had been able to remove most of the old Brezhnev guard from power and put in their place younger officials who recognized that if the Soviet Union was to maintain its stature as a superpower into the twenty-first century, both the Soviet state and the Soviet Communist Party would have to undergo a lengthy period of reform and renewal.

The replacement of the Brezhnevites by Gorbachev did not signal an end to opposition to his reform policies within the Party, however. Where reformers had been united in their common pursuit of removing the old Brezhnev guard from power, once that goal had largely been accomplished, the unity of the reform movement collapsed within the Party. Some Party officials began to assert that Gorbachev was proceeding too quickly and too broadly with his perestroika and glasnost reforms. Party leaders like Yegor Ligachev, a reformer himself in comparison with

many of the ousted Brezhnevites, began to criticize Gorbachev for trampling upon the memory of those who had worked so hard to achieve the ideal state of communism in the Soviet Union before he came to power.

Gorbachev faced opposition from Party conservatives who resisted reform, but he also came under attack from other factions within the Communist Party, who believed that his reforms were not radical enough to solve the pressing problems that the Soviet Union was facing in the late 1980s and continues to face in the 1990s. Party leaders like Boris Yeltsin and economists and academicians like Abel Aganbegyan and Oleg Bogomolov grew increasingly frustrated with the slow pace of the reform process under Gorbachev.

Since the ouster of most of the old-guard Brezhnevites from the CPSU in the first year and a half of his rule, Gorbachev has strived to keep himself in a moderate, middle-of-the-road position relative to his critics from both the radical and conservative reformist factions within the Party. He has become a master at playing one faction off the other, always reserving for himself and his supporters the role of final arbiter between competing factions.

Gorbachev has made sure that he has kept the middle ground for himself by lashing out against conservatives and radicals alike when he has felt his role as Party leader being challenged. For example, in 1987, Boris Yeltsin, a radical reform member of the ruling Politburo and Party leader in the city of Moscow, was removed from his positions of authority by a temporary coalition formed between conservative reformers and Gorbachev and his supporters. In this instance, Gorbachev saw Yeltsin as too radical a proponent of change and aligned himself with conservatives like Ligachev to remove Yeltsin from power. By so doing, Gorbachev appeared as a moderate relative to Yeltsin and could not be targeted by conservatives as being too far out on a limb in pursuing his visions of glasnost and perestroika.

Unfortunately for Gorbachev, Boris Yeltsin did not fade into anonymity after he was stripped of his power base within the Party in 1987. In subsequent years, Yeltsin ironically became a primary benefactor of Gorbachev's efforts to transfer the locus of Soviet power from the Party to revamped and more powerful governmental institutions. In 1989, Yeltsin was elected to the Congress of People's Deputies and became a leader of a radical bloc of deputies within the new legislature. His political comeback and outspoken criticism of both the Party and Gorbachev's reform program proved immensely popular with the Soviet people. In 1990, he was elected as the new President of the Russian Republic and renounced his Party membership, proclaiming that he no longer intended to serve the interests of the Party, but rather the people. While Gorbachev had effectively removed Yeltsin as a threat to his role as leader of the Party, via his reforms he had created a new power base, the Soviet government, from which Yeltsin could once again challenge his role as supreme leader of the Soviet Union.

In 1988, following a series of attacks by conservatives on his policies of perestroika and glasnost in newspapers around the Soviet Union, particularly in Leningrad, Gorbachev, in coalition with radical reformers, took action against the recognized head of the conservative opposition within the Party, Yegor Ligachev. Ligachev had been serving as head of the ideology department within the Secretariat of the CPSU. The head of the ideology department had long been recognized by Western Kremlinologists and Sovietologists as the second most powerful position within the Soviet Communist Party, behind only the position of General Secretary. The powerful and respected Mikhail

Suslov served as ideology chief under Brezhnev for many years, and Gorbachev himself served in this coveted position under Chernenko.

From his position as the number-two Party man, Ligachev could wield considerable power to subvert and even challenge Gorbachev's reform policies. During a Central Committee plenum in 1988, Ligachev was demoted from his position as ideology chief to that of agricultural secretary, the same position Gorbachev had held when he first arrived on the national political scene in 1980.

At the 28th Party Congress, Ligachev with the support of his conservative allies set out to recapture his number two position within the Party. The title and nature of the number two Party position had changed since Ligachev lost it in 1988. Since Gorbachev had assumed the new, more powerful presidency of the Soviet Union, he had found it increasingly difficult to manage the day-to-day affairs of both the Soviet state and Party. He decided to concentrate his time and energy in his role as head of state and turn day-to-day management of the Party over to a deputy Party leader. This new deputy Party leader position became the second most important in the Party, replacing that of ideology chief. At the 28th Party Congress, unable to unseat Gorbachev as Party leader, Ligachev sought election as deputy Party chief in the hopes that he could control day-to-day management of the Party and move the Party in a more conservative direction. Gorbachev opposed Ligachev's candidacy and supported Vladimir Ivashko, an ally and fellow reformer from the Ukraine. Ivashko defeated Ligachev by a vote of 3,109 to 776. Following his defeat and exclusion from the Politburo by the 28th Congress, Ligachev returned to his home in Siberia to pen a book.

The actions taken by Gorbachev against Yeltsin and Ligachev can be seen as two very bold and shrewd political moves. By playing the radical and conservative factions of the Party against each other, Gorbachev was able to secure his position as Party leader by holding onto the political middle ground. Gorbachev's strategy was very similar to that employed by Stalin in his battles against both Trotsky and Bukharin following Lenin's death in the mid-1920s.

Until February 1990, Gorbachev's political balancing act between radical and conservative critics had worked marvelously. By that time, however, the middle ground in which Gorbachev had anchored his policies had eroded. The Soviet Communist Party had become polarized. The radical reformers increasingly had become more radical in their policies, whereas the conservatives had become more and more conservative. One group of reformers had gone so far as to organize their own caucus, the Democratic Platform, within the Party, which called for "radical reform of the Soviet Communist Party in the direction of a completely democratic parliamentary party, acting in a multiparty system."[14] In such conditions, it becomes almost impossible for a middle-of-the-road, moderate position to win the day because the constituencies to which the moderate leader must make his case hold too-extreme views. In the words of the British Sovietologist Peter Frank, "The center ground became depopulated, leaving Gorbachev satisfying neither the reformist radicals nor the traditional conservatives."[15]

Therefore, by February 1990, Gorbachev had to make a choice as to which camp he wanted to join, the radical reformers or the conservatives. At the Central Committee plenum held from February 5 to 7, Gorbachev did so; he chose to count himself as a radical reformer. He primarily did this by endorsing and seeking the removal of Article 6 from the Soviet Constitution. Article 6 of the Soviet Constitution read:

The leading and guiding force of Soviet society and the nucleus of its political system, of all state organizations and public organizations, is the Communist Party of the Soviet Union. The CPSU exists for the people and serves the people.

The Communist Party, armed with Marxism-Leninism, determines the general perspectives of the development of society and the course of the domestic and foreign policy of the USSR, directs the great constructive work of the Soviet people, and imparts a planned, systematic and theoretically substantiated character to their struggle for the victory of communism.

All party organizations shall function within the framework of the Constitution of the USSR.

Article 6 of the Soviet Constitution guaranteed the Communist Party of the Soviet Union a monopoly of political power within the country. Opposition parties were not allowed, and only the Communist Party could control the government. The willingness of Gorbachev and the CPSU to have Article 6 withdrawn from the Soviet Constitution had tremendous significance. It meant that after more than seventy years of one-party dictatorship, political pluralism and a multiparty state in the Soviet Union now were possible. Suddenly, the Soviet people had a number of political parties from which to choose. This led Aleksandr Yakovlev, a key supporter of Gorbachev, to note that Soviet society itself "will now decide whether it wishes to adopt our [the CPSU] policies."[16]

In addition to advocating the removal of Article 6 from the Soviet Constitution, Gorbachev also took radical measures related to the powers of the CPSU Politburo, the traditional base of Soviet communist power. Following Gorbachev's lead, the delegates to the 28th Party Congress elected a new 24-member Politburo in July 1990, which by design included him as the national Party leader and the Party leaders of the fifteen Soviet republics. The new Politburo was quite different from a traditional Soviet Politburo in that it had twice as many members; was elected by delegates to the Party congress, rather than the Central Committee; was not dominated by Great Russians; did not include many Party leaders who held high positions in the Soviet government; and met monthly instead of weekly. Before and during the Congress, Gorbachev argued that the Soviet government, and not the Party's Politburo, should decide state policy. He insisted that the Politburo be relegated to a role of setting long-term goals for the Party and for the state. By electing more disparate, and less influential individuals to the Politburo, delegates to the 28th Party Congress apparently obliged their Party leader.

In the late 1980s, another challenge to Gorbachev's role as Communist Party leader and to the integrity of the Party itself emerged in the Soviet Union. Rather than being concerned with the pace and comprehensiveness of perestroika and glasnost, reforms largely targeted at Soviet society and the Soviet state, as the radical and conservative reformist factions within the Party had been, this new challenge was directed more toward internal Party policy, came from nationalist forces at the regional Party level, and pitted the local Communist Parties in the Soviet republics against the Russian-dominated central Party hierarchy in Moscow.

In late 1989 and early 1990, the Soviet Republic of Lithuania in a series of startling moves abolished the local Communist Party's monopoly of power; created a multiparty system with a legislature composed of freely elected representatives; held the first freely contested, multiparty elections in Soviet history; and, on March

11, 1990, declared itself independent from the Soviet Union.

To be competitive in the February 1990 elections for the newly created Lithuanian legislature, the Lithuanian Communist Party on December 20, 1989, declared itself independent from the Communist Party of the Soviet Union. Agirdas Brazauskas, the leader of the Lithuanian Communist Party, justified his Party's move by underscoring the power of Lithuanian nationalism and the belief that any political party viewed by Lithuanians as being under the control of Moscow and Great Russians stood little chance of ever hoping to accumulate power within an independent, pluralist Lithuania. Lithuanians despised Great Russian control over their land. They believed that they had been an occupied country since Stalin forcefully annexed the independent Republic of Lithuania into the Soviet Union in 1940.

In respect to the violent turmoil that engulfed the Soviet Republics of Armenia and Azerbaijan in the late 1980s, the local Communist Parties in those two republics largely lost their ability to rule autonomously. Regional Party leaders frequently were caught between taking orders from Moscow and appealing to popular pressure to fan the fire of ethnic unrest throughout the Caucasus. In most cases, they chose the latter course and even instigated some of the ethnic violence in the region. Although the CPSU claimed to retain dejure rule over Armenia and Azerbaijan, defacto local rule was in the hands of the Armenian National Movement and the Azerbaijani People's Front, aggressive popular-front organizations that had more than a few local Communist Party members included in their membership.

Gorbachev's response to the challenge posed by rebellious regional Communist Parties was, not surprisingly, one of moderation. He neither approved of regional fragmentation of the CPSU, as local leaders like Brazauskas and the Estonian Communist Party leader Vaino Valjas would have liked him to, nor forced submission of the regional Parties to Moscow's control, as many CPSU leaders in Moscow, particularly of Great Russian heritage, wanted. He adopted a wait-and-see, middle-of-the-road position.

As with his position concerning the pace of his economic and political reforms at the state and societal level, however, it is most probable that in the future Gorbachev will have to make a choice between two polarized alternatives to reconcile national differences in the CPSU. He will have to either allow regional Communist Parties to go their separate ways from CPSU control in Moscow altogether or crack down on the regional Parties, purge the nationalist leaders of those Parties, and impose Party discipline through leaders imposed by Moscow.

Eastern Europe

As the year of 1989 commenced, it was fair to say that the Soviet Union led all of the Second World states of Eastern Europe in terms of its commitment to democratic reform, openness, and economic restructuring. By the end of March 1990, however, Hungary, Poland, Czechoslovakia, and East Germany had passed the Soviet Union on the road to political pluralism and a market-oriented economy; Bulgaria, Yugoslavia, and Romania had at least caught up to the USSR, and only Albania remained lagging behind, a position to which the small Balkan country had by now grown quite accustomed.

In discussing the impact of recent developments in Eastern Europe on the Communist Parties in the region, perhaps the best way to proceed is chronologically, touching upon key events affecting the Parties in the various countries as they happened in time. Before beginning the discussion, however, one should keep in mind that as this book goes to press, the different states and Communist Parties in these societies are at different points along the road to institutionalized political pluralism and market economies. To date, most of the paths that Eastern European countries have been taking to reach their destination have been similar in nature. None, however, has yet reached the end of the road, and pitfalls and curves may befall these countries before they finally do reach their sought-after destination of a democratic, market-centered political and economic system.

As mentioned earlier, as 1989 opened, all of the Eastern European states were more or less ruled by traditional Communist Party regimes. Conditions of a one-party dictatorship and of a centrally planned economy predominated; opposition parties to communist rule were banned, and the government and legislatures of these countries were under the control of the Communist Party.

Hungary's Communist Party took the initial bold step in 1989 by agreeing in February to allow the creation of independent, opposition political parties within the country. The Polish Communists followed the Hungarian lead in April by signing an agreement with Solidarity, the historically persecuted Polish opposition trade union movement. The Polish government legalized Solidarity and called for the holding of elections in which Solidarity could run for 35 percent of the seats in the lower house (the Sejm) and all 100 seats in a newly created upper house (the Senate) of the Polish legislature. In May, the Hungarians dismantled the barbed wire fence along their border with Austria, becoming the first Soviet Bloc country to open its border with Western Europe.

At this point in the discussion, perhaps an important question needs to be raised. Why would a traditional Communist Party willingly agree to legalize opposition parties that might pose a challenge to their rule? This question is not an easy one to answer. In Poland, Hungary, and the other states of the Warsaw Pact, communist rule was never legitimate in the eyes of the majority of the population. Communist rule was a product of Soviet aggression following World War II. Most people did not believe in the communist ideology, and whenever the opportunity to revolt presented itself, as in 1956 in Hungary and 1980 in Poland, some brave souls did so. With the rise of Gorbachev in the Soviet Union and his advocation of perestroika, glasnost, and democratization, it became increasingly difficult for the East European Communist Party leaders to toe the old line of the Brezhnev era in their respective countries. The people became more and more frustrated with communist rule as it became increasingly incapable of meeting their needs—economic, spiritual, or otherwise. Before 1989, all of the Eastern European countries were in a state of stagnation relative to their Western European counterparts. Factions within the East European Communist Parties began to develop that advocated adoption of policies similar to those being advocated in the Soviet Union. By early 1989, the reform factions within several of the Eastern European Communist Party states were assuming the mantle of Party control. The first tangible expressions of the ascendency of the reformers to power in Poland and Hungary were the Parties' allowance for the formation of a legal opposition.

After the legalization of Solidarity in Poland, the call for semifree elections by the Polish Communist Party, and the Hungarians dismantling of their barbed wire border with Austria, all of Eastern Europe—Party leaders and citizens—as well as the industrialized advanced world, turned toward Moscow to see if these liberalizing measures would be tolerated. In all previous instances in the postwar era when

states of Eastern Europe attempted to do away with the one-party dictatorship of the Communist Party, Moscow had intervened to militarily quash the liberalization movements. The impact of Gorbachev's decision not to intervene to stop the initial liberalization measures of the Hungarians and Poles in the first few months of 1989 on reformist communist officials in other Parties around Eastern Europe, and the subsequent popular revolutions that were to take place later in the year, cannot be underestimated. To put it simply, if Moscow had desired to keep traditional communist regimes in place in Eastern Europe, they would probably still be there today. Fortunately for the people of Eastern Europe, Moscow made the decision to forego its European empire.

As 1989 moved into the summer season in Eastern Europe, more and more events took place that indicated that fundamental and substantial change would be taking place in these societies in the months ahead. In the Polish elections in June, the Polish Communist Party suffered a humiliating defeat when candidates endorsed by Solidarity won 260 of the 261 seats they were allowed to contest. In July, the Polish parliament elected the Polish Communist leader, General Wojciech Jaruzelski, as President of Poland, but in August, Solidarity refused to enter a coalition government with the Communist Party, formed a coalition with two smaller parties, and formed the first noncommunist government in Eastern Europe in postwar history under the leadership of Prime Minister Tadeusz Mazowiecki. In September, the Polish Parliament confirmed a twenty-three member coalition cabinet put forth by Mazowiecki. Only four of the cabinet posts in the Mazowiecki government went to members of the Polish Communist Party.

In October, the Hungarian Communist Party, officially the Hungarian Socialist Workers' Party, renounced Marxism and renamed itself the Hungarian Socialist Party. The Hungarian communists' renouncement marked the first time a ruling Communist Party had turned away from its fundamental ideology. Later in October, Hungary proclaimed itself a free republic. In late March 1990, freely contested elections for the national Hungarian parliament took place, with a number of new parties and the former Communist Party, under its new name, sponsoring candidates. The Hungarian Socialist Party won less than 11 percent of the total vote, trailing far behind two center-right parties, the Hungarian Democratic Forum and the Alliance of Free Democrats.

During September and October 1989, thousands of East Germans fled their country to West Germany via the new opening in the Iron Curtain along the Austro-Hungarian border. Later in October, about 100,000 people joined a prodemocracy protest in Leipzig that resulted in the removal of longtime Communist Party leader Erich Honecker. In November, the country's borders and the Berlin Wall were opened. In early December, the East German parliament voted to change the constitution and eliminated the Party's guaranteed monopoly of power. In March 1990, free, multiparty elections to the Volkshammer, or parliament, were held in East Germany for the first time. Fully 93 percent of the electorate turned out to vote. The Communist Party of East Germany, after changing its official name from the Socialist Unity Party to the Party of Democratic Socialism, earned just 16 percent of the vote in the March elections, coming in third behind the Christian Democratic Union led by Lothar de Maiziere and the Social Democratic Party led by Ibrahim Bohme. The Party of Democratic Socialism garnered only sixty-five out of 400 seats in the new parliament, a far cry from the dictatorial control it had held over the East German parliament for more than

forty years. The new Communist Party leader, Gregor Gysi, aimed to position the Party as the primary opposition force in the future.

In just six months, members of the East German Communist Party went from total control over their state, to a role of minor opposition in a new pluralist government, to wondering, toward the end of March 1990, if there even would be an East German state in coming years, as German reunification and Chancellor Kohl loomed ever closer on the horizon.

On November 17, 1989, hundreds of demonstrators in a huge crowd gathered at an officially approved student rally in Prague, Czechoslovakia, were clubbed and teargassed when riot police crushed the peaceful demonstration. Two days later, more than 10,000 people held a prodemocracy rally in Prague, at which the reform movement Civic Forum was founded. On November 20, more than 200,000 people demonstrated in Prague, demanding free elections and the resignations of hard-line communist leaders. On November 24, the masses were granted their wish, as Communist Party General Secretary Milos Jakes and other hard-line leaders resigned. By the end of November, the government of Czechoslovakia had scrapped a provision in its constitution ensuring a leading role for the Communist Party. By the turn of the new year, Alexander Dubcek, the father of the Prague Spring in 1968, was serving as Prime Minister of a provisional government that included both communists and members of Civic Forum. Vaclav Havel, the playwright dissident who had been imprisoned on numerous occasions over the previous two decades by the traditional Communist Party leadership, was serving as President of Czechoslovakia.

In early November 1989, the head of the Communist Party of Bulgaria for more than thirty-five years, Todor Zhivkov, was ousted and replaced by the moderate Petar Mladenov.

Thousands of demonstrators pack Wenceslas Square in Prague resulting in the resignations of Czechoslovak Communist Party leaders in November 1989.

On December 11, Mladenov proposed that Bulgaria hold free elections and remove the Party's monopoly on power from the constitution as soon as possible. Mladenov later became the President of Bulgaria. He had to resign his position, however, after the political opposition in Bulgaria obtained a videotape of Mladenov asking his Party colleagues the question "Shouldn't we bring the tanks in?" during a 1989 antigovernment demonstration. The exposition of scandal for political gain and public accountability, two characteristics of Western politics, had come to Bulgaria.

In late November 1989, Nicolae Ceausescu, by this time the last Communist Party dictator remaining in the Warsaw Pact states, categorically rejected the democratic reforms being adopted elsewhere in Eastern Europe. By Christmas night, Ceausescu along with his wife Elena had been convicted of treason by a revolutionary tribunal and been shot to death. The fall of Ceausescu, unlike the fall of every other traditional Communist Party regime in Eastern Europe during 1989, was not peaceful. Scores were killed as Ceausescu's dreaded Securitate, the secret police, tried to halt their dictator's demise by shooting down protestors in Bucharest and Timisoara and later waging open warfare with the Romanian Army as it heroically abandoned Ceausescu in favor of the Romanian people.

Following Ceausescu's demise, state power in Romania fell into the hands of the eleven-member executive board of the Ruling Council of National Salvation. The National Salvation Front outlawed the Romanian Communist Party in January 1990 and promised to hold free elections in Romania. The primary leaders of the Front, including its President Ion Iliescu, its Prime Minister Petre Roman, Silviu Brucan, and Cazimir Ionescu, all were former communists who worked for Ceausescu at one point but were discredited and removed from office before his fall.

There was some question as this book went to press as to whether the Council of National Salvation in Romania was truly representative of the democratic interests of the Romanian people or whether it was just a new group of communists attempting to seize power and reestablish a one-party dictatorship in Romania. The Front's decision to hold a monopoly of state power until elections could be held and its harassment and intimidation of fledgling or reborn opposition parties like the Peasants'

Party, Liberal Party, and Social Democratic Party raised doubt as to whether the revolutionary violence in Romania was yet over and whether a few more steps had to be taken by the people of Romania before they could achieve their goal of a pluralist democracy.

On January 22, 1990, the Yugoslav Communist Party voted to give up its forty-five-year monopoly on power and to permit a new political system in which other parties could compete. The League of Communists of Yugoslavia, the official name of the Yugoslav Communist Party, was, like most other Communist Parties in Eastern Europe, in a state of crisis. The Yugoslav Party crisis, like the crisis within the Communist Party of the Soviet Union, was a product of many factors, including strong nationalist divisions within Yugoslavia and the desire of regional Communist Parties representing different national groups to separate themselves from the national Party. The Slovenian Communist Party declared itself independent from the League of Communists of Yugoslavia as the 1990s opened, and other regional Parties are likely to do so in the future, further amplifying the disintegration of the Yugoslav Communist Party into independent factions divided along both Communist/Social Democratic lines as well as ethnic/national lines.

Finally, as this book goes to press, the small Balkan country of Albania remains the odd man out in Eastern Europe. Albania is unique in the Second World in that after Stalin's death no moderation of the repressive Stalinist communist model took place as it did in all other Second World states around the world. Albania chastised its communist brethren for their heresy and withdrew from the international communist community to pursue an austere isolationist course. That course remained remarkably steady for over forty years, although under Party leader, Ramiz Alia, some moderation took place in the late 1980s and early 1990.

Under Alia, who in 1985 replaced Enver Hoxha, the longtime Albanian Communist Party leader, Albania abandoned its strict isolationism and opened diplomatic relations with some countries, most notably the Federal Republic of Germany; relaxed travel and emigration restrictions for its people; and increased Albanian society's access to Western consumer goods, including televisions. The Albanian people, largely by watching Italian, Greek, and Yugoslav television, became aware of their relative backwardness compared to the rest of Europe. Viewing Alia's moderation of orthodox Stalinism as an opportunity to pursue their freedom, the Albanian people by the start of the 1990s were seeking to bring political change to their country. Mass protests and strikes erupted throughout the country in 1990 and many Albanians sought refuge in Western embassies, hoping to gain safe passage out of their country. With the world watching, a reluctant Albanian leadership allowed many of its citizens to emigrate.

China and Other Second World States

Following the June 1989 crackdown by the People's Liberation Army on the massive student demonstrations in Tiananmen Square in Beijing and in other major cities around China, the Chinese Communist Party entered a period of retrenchment, relative to the reforms made in political and economic policies in the country throughout most of the 1980s. With Deng Xiaoping ailing from both the frailties of his advanced age and the loss of his role of final arbiter between radicals and conservatives in the Party, with the purging of Zhao Ziyang and most of his supporters from the upper echelons of power following the Tiananmen massacre, the conservative Premier Li Peng has ascended to new heights of power since June 1989.

Under the direction of Li Peng, the Chinese state and the Chinese Communist Party have implemented policies to rejuvenate ideological steadfastness of cadres in the face of perceived threats from "bourgeois liberalism" both at home and abroad. Ideological training has been stepped up at universities throughout China in an attempt to subdue the source of pressure for democratic change that erupted in the spring and summer of 1989. Student leaders of the democracy movements have fled China; gone into hiding in China; or been arrested, sentenced, and, in some cases, put to death for their revolutionary fervor. Similar to these leaders of the democracy movement, the spirit among the Chinese people for change once again has become latent and gone underground. It would be a mistake to conclude that it has disappeared, however. When the time is right, perhaps at the time of Deng's passing or during the next power struggle behind the doors of the Great Hall of the People, the democracy movement in China will once again come into the open and press even harder for change. Until such a time for opportunity presents itself, Tiananmen Square likely will remain quiet.

Traditional Party leaders at the helm of Communist China, North Korea, and Vietnam currently are keeping a watchful eye on the events transpiring in Outer Mongolia. The Mongolian People's Republic is a relatively obscure Second World state sandwiched between the Soviet Union and China, with a human population of about 2 million and a sheep population of close to 13 million. By the end of March 1990, the Mongolian People's Revolutionary Party (the Communist Party of Mongolia) had brought to East Asia political and economic reform comparable to that taking place in Eastern Europe and the Soviet Union. The ruling Politburo under the direction of Party leader Jambyn Batmonh had agreed to give up its monopoly on power and proposed that Party officials and dissidents work together on a new constitution. This constitution would allow for rival political parties to compete in democratic elections to the Great People's Hural, the national legislature. Batmonh also called for an Extraordinary Party Congress to convene in April 1990 to choose a new Central Committee and agree on a new Party policy, including an official name change of the Party to the Mongolian People's Party. As if Outer Mongolia were an infected neighbor, China looked cautiously on the changes taking place in that country in early 1990. China seemed preoccupied with the possibility that unrest in Mongolia could spill over and cause unrest first among the 3 million ethnic Mongolians living in China and then, more significantly, among the Chinese population at large.

Besides the maintenance to date of traditional Communist Party regimes in China, North Korea, and Vietnam, momentum for reform also has been lacking in Cuba. Fidel Castro remains the communist dictator in Cuba. One would think, however, that Castro's anxiety over a potential coup against him has been increasing, in light of the defeat of Daniel Ortega in the February 1990 elections in Nicaragua, the violent overthrow of fellow dictator Nicolae Ceausescu in Romania, the increased efforts by the United States to broadcast news into Cuba via both Radio and Television Marti, and the reluctance of the Soviet Union to continue their massive funneling of aid to the Caribbean island nation. Castro and his regime have been increasingly dependent on this aid in recent years, as the Cuban economy continues to stagnate and world commodity prices for sugar, Cuba's chief export, continue to flounder.

Conclusion

If Lenin, Trotsky, and other founders of the original Communist Party in Russia were to come back today and see the present condition of the Communist Party of the Soviet Union—not to mention the international communist movement as a whole—they most likely would shake their heads in disbelief and disgust. They would no longer consider the Party they founded and the Parties they directed through the Communist International, or Comintern, as being communist anymore.

The nineteenth-century ideas and philosophies of Marx and Engels always have had and continue to attract their followers. In the late nineteenth and early twentieth centuries, the original proponents of Marxism and their descendents split into different factions. Each faction represented a different interpretation of Marxist philosophy. The two predominant factions both within Russia itself and internationally were the social democratic and communist traditions.

Too often today, people identify Marxism only with communists and Communist Parties. In point of fact, such democratically and pluralist-inclined organizations as the Labour Party in Great Britain and the Social Democratic Party in the Federal Republic of Germany can trace their political roots back to Marx just as easily as can any Communist Party. The split that generated the development of independent, social democratic and communist traditions of Marxist thought occurred both over the speed with which the "dictatorship of the proletariat" was to be established in a country and the degree to which nationalism and national institutions

were to be respected by proponents of Marxist philosophy.

The original position of most Marxists was that Marxist political parties should engage in social democratic practices, that is, come to power legitimately in countries through national electoral processes. They would do so by respecting the existing political institutions of the state and by working with political parties in coalition to create conditions in the society that would eventually lead to the establishment of the "dictatorship of the proletariat" and advancement toward the communist ideal as originally defined by Marx.

The social democratic parties that exist today in Western Europe to an extent have perverted the original Marxist social democratic tradition, in that they do not seek or see in the future the establishment in their respective countries of Marx's dictatorship of the proletariat. Although they in essence have abandoned the Marxist dialectic claiming that history will end with the establishment of communism, they have not abandoned the emphasis that Marx put on the importance of the physical and economic well-being of the society as a whole, and on the welfare of the working class in particular. Social democratic parties in Western Europe have been largely responsible for the creation and protection of the welfare state in their societies in the post–World War II era.

In the early 1900s, a small minority of Marxists became dissatisfied with the social democratic Marxist tradition of their movement and developed an independent effort. This new movement called for the rapid and revolutionary accumulation of state power and the creation of a dictatorship of the proletariat in a country, irrespective of national laws, institutions, and customs. These more radical Marxist followers were led by Lenin and Trotsky. Lenin and Trotsky despised both social democracy and nationalism. Social democracy was too passive and weak for the communists; they believed that Marx's ideal state could be achieved forcefully and quickly in societies if a true dictatorship of the proletariat or "party of a new type" existed.

Lenin and Trotsky did not think of people as being divided into different nations and ethnic groups. They believed that people were primarily divided by different social classes. To them, workers in Germany had more in common with workers in Great Britain than with Germans of the bourgeois class. Lenin and Trotsky believed that the upper classes used patriotism and nationalism to keep workers from identifying with each other on a universal class basis. As a result, they felt that nationalism had to be eradicated so that workers could properly develop their class consciousness and unite in opposition to the bourgeoisie.

As we have seen in this chapter, a number of Communist Parties in Second World societies today have willingly abandoned their position as "dictatorships of the proletariat" in their countries in favor of participating in a multiparty system. Some have abandoned the communist tradition of Marxism and adopted the social democratic tradition. By definition, then, they are no longer Communist Parties as the founders of the communist movement conceived of Communist Parties. In addition to turning toward social democracy, many present-day Communist Parties have embraced nationalism. In societies that blame traditional communism and communists for their sorry standard of living, some of these parties see nationalism as the one potential platform that might help attract voters in future competitive elections. As one can see, Lenin and Trotsky would not be pleased with what happened to their tradition of Marxism in 1989 and with what likely will continue to happen to it throughout the 1990s.

Suggestions for Further Reading

Beck, Carl, et al., *Comparative Communist Political Leadership* (New York: McKay, 1973).

Bialer, Seweryn, *Stalin's Successors: Leadership, Stability, and Change in the Soviet Union* (Cambridge: Cambridge University Press, 1980).

Borkenau, Franz, *European Communism* (London: Faber and Faber, 1953).

Breslauer, George W., *Khrushchev and Brezhnev as Leaders: Building Authority in Soviet Politics* (Winchester, Mass.: Allen & Unwin, 1982).

Brown, Archie, ed., *Political Leadership in the Soviet Union* (Bloomington, In.: Indiana University Press, 1990).

Bunce, Valarie, *Do Leaders Make a Difference? Executive Succession and Public Policy under Capitalism and Socialism* (Princeton, N.J.: Princeton University Press, 1981).

Carter, April, *Democratic Reform in Yugoslavia* (Princeton, N.J.: Princeton University Press, 1982).

Conquest, Robert, *Power and Policy in the USSR: The Struggle for Stalin's Succession, 1945–1960* (New York: Harper & Row, 1967).

Djilas, Milovan, *The New Class* (New York: Praeger, 1957).

Hahn, Werner G., *Democracy in a Communist*

Party: Poland's Experience since 1980 (New York: Columbia University Press, 1987).

Hill, Ronald and **Peter Frank,** *The Soviet Communist Party,* 3rd ed. (Winchester, Mass.: Allen & Unwin, 1986).

McCauley, Martin and **Stephen Carter,** *Leadership and Succession in the Soviet Union, Eastern Europe, and China* (New York, M.E. Sharp, 1986).

Miller, R. F., J. H. Miller, and **T. H. Rigby,** *Gorbachev at the Helm: A New Era in Soviet Politics* (London: Croon Helm, 1987).

Rush, Myron, *How Communist States Change Their Rulers* (Ithaca, N.Y.: Cornell University Press, 1974).

Rusinow, Dennison, *Yugoslavia: A Fractured Federalism* (Washington, D.C.: Wilson Center Press, 1988).

Schapiro, Leonard B., *The Communist Party of the Soviet Union* (New York: Random House, 1970).

Schulz, Donald E., and **Jan S. Adams,** eds., *Political Participation in Communist Systems* (New York: Pergamon, 1981).

Terrill, Ross, *Mao: A Biography* (New York: Harper & Row, 1980).

Voslensky, Michael, *Nomenklatura: The Soviet Ruling Class* (New York: Doubleday, 1984).

Notes

1. Alfred G. Meyer, *Communism,* 4th ed. (New York: Random House, 1984), p. 46.

2. For a discussion of Lenin's "party of a new type," see Bertram D. Wolfe, "Leninism," in Milorad M. Drachkovitch, ed., *Marxism in the Modern World* (Stanford, Calif.: Stanford University Press, 1965), pp. 76–84.

3. *Beijing Review* (20), May 18, 1987: 16.

4. Lenin was referred to as Premier, because he was chairman of the Council of People's Commissars and also a member of the Politburo, which at that time had no formal head.

5. Stalin ruled in the dual position of head of both Party and state. Although the tendency in most Second World states during the post-Stalin era was to divide these posts, General Secretary Leonid I. Brezhnev combined them once again in 1977 by assuming the ousted Nikolai V. Podgorny's role as President. Brezhnev's successors, Yuri Andropov, Konstantin Chernenko, and Mikhail Gorbachev, also assumed both positions.

6. Georgi M. Malenkov initially replaced Stalin as head of both Party and state. His leadership evolved into a triumvirate in which he shared power with Vyacheslav M. Molotov and Lavrenti P. Beria. Beria's arrest and Khrushchev's rapid ascent to increased power in 1953 led to Khrushchev's election as First Secretary in September of that year.

7. Khrushchev lived out the remaining years of his life in retirement on the outskirts of Moscow, in a dacha (country home) supplied by the state.

8. For an excellent review of the Brezhnev era, see Jerry F. Hough, "The Man and the System," *Problems of Communism* 25 (2) (1976): 1–17.

9. Myron Rush, "Succeeding Brezhnev," *Problems of Communism* 32 (1) (1983): 2.

10. See "The Resolution on Certain Questions of Our Party since the Founding of the People's Republic of China," *Beijing Review* 24 (27) (1981): 10–39.

11. "Guiding Principles for Inner-Party Life," *Beijing Review* 23 (14) (1980): 11–20.

12. In 1978, Tito suggested that yearly rotation should be applied to almost all LCY organs, from the commune to the federation. In 1979, the Central Committee endorsed the practice. See Stephen L. Burg, "Decision-Making in Yugoslavia," *Problems of Communism* 29 (2) (1980): 1–20.

13. See John P. Burns, "China's Nomenklatura System," *Problems of Communism* 36 (5) (1987): 36–51.

14. *Time*, February 19, 1990: 35.

15. *The Observer*, January 28, 1990.

16. *The New York Times*, August 2, 1990: 1.

CHAPTER 5

GOVERNMENT IN THE SECOND WORLD: PAST AND PRESENT

If Second World states historically were ruled by Communist Parties, what was the function of their governments? Were the Party and government distinguishable in any important ways? Which was more important in shaping overall state policy and influencing policy outcomes?

In many of the Second World countries we are studying, the revolutions of 1989 and the elections of 1990 brought fundamental changes to the governmental process. What exactly did these changes entail? Have actors and institutions outside the Party become more powerful than they once were in these states? If so, how and why?

We will address the questions posed above in this chapter. We will do so by first examining how institutional and power relationships traditionally were structured in Second World states. We will describe the traditional methods of government that were utilized in the majority of Second World states before the events of the late 1980s and early 1990s. And we will analyze how one particular state, the Peoples Republic of China, still practiced such methods as the 1990s commenced.

Next, we will take an in-depth look at the impact the various reform programs of Mikhail Gorbachev have had on conventional methods of government in the Soviet Union. Finally, we will take a close look at the major changes that in the late 1980s and early 1990s altered the processes of government in the states of Eastern Europe. We will analyze the reforms that have been undertaken and the means by which they have begun to be formalized and institutionalized in states such as Poland, Hungary, and Czechoslovakia.

Traditional Processes of Government in the Second World

The Relationship between the Party and Government

In traditional communist political systems, the Communist Party led and set policy while the government followed and implemented policy. Traditional communist governments were designed to take policy directives of the Party and translate them into the rules and regulations that organized socialist life. Darrell Hammer, an American Sovietologist, once described this relationship by quoting an authoritative Soviet text: "No important decision is ever taken by an organ of government, or by an administrative organ, without corresponding instructions from the Party."[1]

Constitutions in traditional communist political systems outlined a set of government institutions of significance to the policy process. Conventional communist constitutions called for representative assemblies with legislative authority. Many included provisions for a collegial or collective head of state, usually called a presidium, that possessed legislative authority in addition to administrative responsibilities. Most established executive or ministerial bodies, typically called councils of ministers, which were entrusted with the functions of policy implementation and execution.[2]

Because the idea of separation of powers was rejected as a bourgeois theory, the government assemblies, presidiums, and councils set up by the constitutions of traditional communist states were dominated by the Communist Parties. Communist Party centralism and terrorism—not democracy or constitutional liberalism—were the underlying features of the processes of government in the most orthodox Second World states.

Party leaders believed that if they created constitutions and institutions patterned along Western lines, they could disguise the Party dictatorship that really existed in their states. They saw in the promulgation of constitutions and the establishment of parliaments opportunities to insulate the Party from criticism at home and abroad.

The creation of a subservient government gave the Party many advantages. When Party planning or policy resulted in popular discontent at home, the Party could blame the government for poor implementation of Party policy, rather than having to accept the responsibility. If a Party leader did not want to agree to an internationally popular proposal put forth by the West or an international organization, he or she could use the government at his or her disposal to scuttle it, instead of doing so directly.

Conventional Communist Party leaders viewed governmental institutions as necessary administrative tools, but when those institutions obstructed revolutionary politics or became outmoded, they were simply ignored, altered, or dismantled. The reasons are manifold as to how political leaders vested with overarching powers could ignore or restructure the government. In addition to the fact the Communist Party controlled the government, the populace had little if any influence on key political processes. Party leaders could with impunity overstep their authority or arrogate to themselves executive powers that were not constitutionally established.

There largely were no prescriptive rules and norms in traditional communist political systems that specified and defined the scope of the respective functions, powers, and responsibilities of the Party and government organizations. This allowed the Party leaders much latitude in making decisions. The subordination or subservience of the state bureaucracy to the Party also helped to assure the Party a ruling monopoly and hegemony over the policy-making process.

Past observers of traditional communist political systems called attention to the close relationship between the Party and the state bureaucracy and described it as inseparable or as an interlocking directorate: "The central Party organs give guiding instructions to the ministries . . . while not restricting their operational independence."[3] This overlapping and interlocking relationship between Party and bureaucracy in the past applied to all levels of conventional communist government. From the federal level down through the local villages, Communist Party members staffed all the organs of the Party and the state administration.

Traditional Government Structures in the Second World

To develop a better understanding of the setting in which governmental processes took place in traditional (i.e., pre 1990) communist political systems, we need to describe in more detail the government structures and institutional actors that were part of such systems. Therefore, in this section of the chapter, we will take a closer look at such orthodox communist state actors as the legislature, the council of ministers, the state bureaucracy, and the defense council to see the role and function these institutions played in the government of traditional Second World states.

Legislature. The legislative body of the traditional communist government may have been designed to mirror a Western parliament, but unlike a Western parliament, the conventional communist legislature was not a significant policy-making body that could initiate and independently decide on legislation. Rather, the traditional legislature was a ceremonial organ, whose primary functions were to ratify policy proposals of the more powerful Party organizations, such as the Politburo, and to legitimate the actions of the Communist Party.

The political impotence of the legislatures in traditional Second World states was indicated by the unusually short time they were in session; typically, they met once or twice a year, usually for less than a week each time. Representatives in these ceremonial bodies never debated or disagreed on the passage of legislation; all of their votes were unanimous.

Deputies were elected to traditional communist legislatures for a set term, on the basis of universal suffrage and secret printed ballots. Although only one name usually appeared on the ballot for each official position, election returns made public by communist state governments often showed that 99.9 percent of the population consistently voted in national elections. They did so for the simple reason that traditional Communist Party doctrine considered voting an obligation. Communist Party pressures were great, and citizens felt obligated to vote.

A more important stage in selecting deputies to a traditional communist legislature occurred before the election itself. Selection of the official slate appearing on the ballot was very much engineered and controlled by the Communist Party. Names forwarded to electoral commissions to be placed on the ballot were almost always determined from nomenklatura lists maintained by the Party.

More so than the legislature as a whole, the smaller presidium of the traditional communist legislature, which was usually elected by the larger legislature, was a relatively influential body within most conventional communist political systems. Much more professional and less diverse in membership than the legislature, the presidium usually had the right to conduct legislative affairs and make decisions while the legislature itself was not in session. As a result of the short and infrequent meetings of traditional communist legislatures, this provided presidiums with enhanced responsibility and power.

Western observers often gave the title of president to the chairman of the presidium of the national legislature of a communist state,

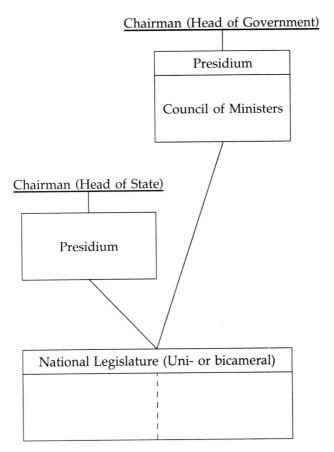

Figure 5.1 The structure of a traditional Second World government.

although the power of the office was nowhere near that of the president of the United States or the president of France. Historically, in most communist states, whoever held the chairmanship of the presidium of the national legislature was considered to be the head of state.

Council of Ministers. The executive arm in traditional communist political systems, the council of ministers, was generally composed of the heads of all ministries, chairpersons of regional councils of ministers, and chairpersons

of important state committees. The chairman of the council of ministers, the prime minister, was legally head of government in most traditional Second World states. Because the traditional council of ministers had a large number of members, a smaller body, the presidium of the council of ministers (not to be confused with the presidium of the national legislature) often acted in the council's name.

The council of ministers and the ministries were important government institutions in conventional communist political systems, both in theory and in reality. Typically, the presidium of the council was constitutionally prescribed the powers and responsibilities for issuing decrees, in a fashion similar to the presidium of the national legislature; it directed and coordinated the work of the national ministries and carried out the plans of the Party.

State Bureaucracy. Conventional communist state bureaucracies were enormous. Adhering to the leading role of the Communist Party in social and economic development, Party leaders established massive bureaucracies to carry out their messianic visions of building communism. For example, there were many commissions, councils, ministries, and committees under the umbrella of the council of ministers. All of these bodies had their own bureaucracies, with hundreds and often thousands of additional offices, committees, and assorted bodies. Many employed hundreds of thousands of civil servants and had administrative structures that stretched throughout the country.

The state bureaucracy included many ministries with their own areas of responsibility and specialization, e.g., Foreign Affairs, Defense, Agriculture, and Health. Each was headed by a minister and thousands of officials. There was little mobility from ministry to ministry within the traditional communist bureaucracy, as there historically has been among departments and agencies of the United States government. Traditional government officials usually were knowledgeable specialists who worked their way up the bureaucratic ladder within a particular ministry. The primary function of these ministries was to implement and coordinate Party policy in their specialized areas and supervise activities at the regional and local levels. The large industrial and agricultural bureaucracies within conventional communist systems often became highly specialized, compartmentalized, and parochial.

A ministry common to all traditional communist states was the ministry of planning. The ministry of planning's responsibilities were much heavier and larger than those of the Office of Management and Budget in the United States. A large ministry with numerous deputy ministers, the ministry of planning primarily was charged with the planning and coordination of the complex and cumbersome centrally controlled economic system common among conventional communist states. Every year, the ministry of planning in each traditional communist state had to set, review, and confirm production and prices for hundreds of thousands of goods.

In addition to ministries, the state bureaucracy in conventional Second World states consisted of a number of important commissions, such as the military-industrial commission. The military-industrial commission usually cut across ministry or departmental lines. This commission was in charge of the defense industry, a very high-priority sector of most traditional communist states. The military-industrial commission worked closely with other state ministries and bodies to ensure preparedness in the defense sector.

Defense Council. One key position of power familiar to Americans that we have not identified yet as existing within conventional communist political systems is that of commander-in-chief. Party leaders in traditional communist states historically did not want outsiders to know either who or what policy-making body would be at the helm of state in times of crises or national emergencies. The office that held the responsibilities of commander-in-chief was never identified in any conventional communist constitution.

138

Through careful analysis of historical communist political behavior, however, Western observers were able to learn of a very secret organ of power within traditional communist political systems: the state defense council. They also discovered that the chairman of this council held the powers historically reserved for a commander-in-chief. The exact composition and functions of the state defense council in traditional Second World governments were never very clear. Most observers believed that the council was chaired by the leader of the Communist Party, the General Secretary, and included such key positions as the minister of defense, the head of the secret police, the foreign minister, and the chief of the military's general staff. It has long been thought that the council primarily was created and designed to assume supreme authority in the event of war, extreme international tension, or national emergency. It was never as clear, however, as to what the role of the state defense council played in peacetime. Some believed it was the key policy-making body in traditional communist states, more powerful than even the Politburo or the Secretariat. Others were equally convinced that the defense council remained dormant in times of peace and was only activated and convened in a crisis situation.[4]

The Party, the Military, and the Secret Police: A Fragile Truce

Owing to communist sensitivity, internal security, and regime stability, the state security apparatus had a special role in traditional communist politics, far greater than that of the Federal Bureau of Investigation or the Central Intelligence Agency in the United States.

Most traditional communist states had two types of secret police forces. One typically was a security organization designed to spy both at home and abroad. The other was more of a national guard, designed to quash dissent and restore order when popular discontent got out of hand. Traditionally, the security organization was an independent state committee within the government, whereas the militia-styled force was part of the interior ministry. The security organization was the more powerful of the two.

Because traditional Second World states had closed societies, Party dictatorships, and lacked institutionalized means for leadership succession, the importance of the security apparatus in the process of government cannot be downplayed. The security apparatus kept tabs on everyone—ordinary citizens, dissidents, military and bureaucratic personnel, and even top Party leaders.

When a power struggle arose within the Party, as it inevitably would, the faction that had the security apparatus on its side had a powerful ally in its bid for power. If it was successful in its struggle, it had clear knowledge that it had better keep the security apparatus happy or it might lose its next bid.

Because of the information it had in its files, the security apparatus had considerable ability to influence Party power struggles. The Party, however, was not so foolish as to open itself up to potential overthrow or dominance by the security apparatus. The security apparatus in traditional Second World states was kept in line by the Party in a number of ways. First, the security forces were controlled by both a department within the Central Committee Secretariat and the council of ministers. In addition, there usually were two other departments within the Central Committee Secretariat whose sole purpose was to keep tabs on the activities of the security apparatus—one department to track domestic agents, the other to track agents abroad. Finally, the Party would try to prevent any potential coup by the security apparatus by placing its leaders into choice Party positions, so they also would have a stake in the future of the Party.

The security apparatus was not the only state actor in pursuit of state power that the Party had to worry about staging a coup against it. The military also was a potential threat. The military was a very significant actor in conventional communist political systems, if for no other reason than it was the only institution that, if not held in check or pacified, had the power to overthrow the Communist Party, government, and secret police.

Because the military had the potential to be such a powerful force on the political stage, the Communist Parties in nearly all conventional communist political systems took calculated steps to insure that the military establishment remained, like the security organization, under its watchful eye. The Party primarily did this in two ways. First, it established watchdog departments within the Central Committee Secretariat to monitor the activities of the military, and second, it played the military off the security apparatus, by allowing the apparatus to infiltrate both the armed services themselves and the military intelligence.

To conclude, there were three institutions capable of exercising state control in traditional communist political systems: the Party, the military, and the security apparatus. The Party maintained control over policy making, the military had the guns, and the security apparatus had knowledge of who had done what when. These three pillars of power constantly vied against each other for power. If one looked like it was accumulating too much power, the other two would gang up against it and restore a balance of power among all three institutions.

Historically, in most Second World states, the Party was first among equals primarily because the military and the security apparatus hated each other more than they hated the Party. The one common interest the three actors had was keeping the population suppressed, for if the population was aroused, it could shift the balance of power among the three state actors in favor of one or in favor of the people or oppositional groups outside the ranks of power. The overthrow of Nicolae Ceausescu by the Romanian army, and the popular revolutions in Poland, Hungary, and Czechoslovakia in late 1989 all are classic examples of what can happen to the fragile balance of power among the Party, the military, and the security apparatus when the people force themselves into the power equation of a traditional communist state.

China 1990: A Case Study of Traditional Communist Government

Despite the fact that the preceding outline of traditional methods of communist rule was placed in the past tense, those methods have not been abandoned by all Second World states and they could make a return appearance in some of the states that in recent years have undertaken reform processes. One case in particular that demonstrates that traditional communist methods of government have not yet departed the Second World is that of China. Let us now look at China to see how the generalized methods of communist rule that were developed in the first part of this chapter apply to her specific story.

Communist Party control over the Chinese government takes two important forms. First, Party officials concurrently serve as government officials. For example, the People's Republic President in 1989, Yang Shangkun, also held Communist Party posts in the Politburo and the Chinese Communist Party Central Military Commission. Occupancy of dual positions in the Central Committee of the Communist Party by vice-premiers, councilors, and ministers of the State Council within the government is taken for granted in China. Second, Party committees and their secretaries supervise and monitor routine government operations and report to the central Party authorities.

Although the post-Mao moderates have made the separation of Party and government functions a top priority in their efforts to reform the Chinese political process, they have brought relatively little change to traditional power relationships. Many Party functionaries have been ambivalent toward the moderates' plans for political reform. Little progress has been made in this direction, especially at the top and medium levels of the Chinese government. If in the future China were to resume a reformist

political strategy that was comparable to the one it had appeared to assume in the late 1980s until the Tiananmen Square massacre, the role and significance of government institutions in the Chinese political process might increase.

In constitutional terms, the National People's Congress is the Chinese legislature. The NPC is a unicameral legislature because Chinese Party leaders want to promote the point that their state operates on the basis of a unitary system. The constitutionally prescribed functions of the NPC are discussing and ratifying Party and government reports, state plans and legislative drafts, and electing and approving government officials.

The 1982 constitution refers to the NPC as the highest organ of state power in China. In reality, however, it is far less significant. Although it is supposed to convene yearly, the constitution provides the nation's leaders with

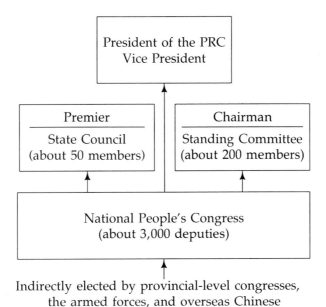

Indirectly elected by provincial-level congresses,
the armed forces, and overseas Chinese

Figure 5.2 The structure of the Chinese government.

considerable flexibility for canceling or postponing meetings of the NPC.

Representatives to the NPC are elected for five-year terms by the provincial-level congresses, the armed forces, and overseas Chinese. The NPC elections are indirect in the sense that rank-and file citizens do not cast ballots for specific candidates. The nomination, selection, and election of delegates in China are handled through organizations in a way that is heavily dominated by the Chinese Communist Party.

The real function of the NPC has been to symbolize the regime's legitimacy and popular base. It is intended to provide the political system with a democratic facade and serve as an instrument for ratifying (some might say rubber-stamping) Party resolutions into law. Virtually all Party and state apparatuses traditionally have been immune to NPC oversight and surveillance.

The presence of a large number of Party and government officials in the NPC detracts from its utility as a mechanism for checks and balances. The typical NPC session shows submissive deputies vying with each other in paying homage to the Party and its leaders. The unanimity with which Party decisions are passed is suggestive of the NPC's unquestioning obedience and subservience to the Party.

However, for a time during the reformist period in the 1980s, NPC deputies no longer were content with this submissive position and tried to seek autonomy and assert their authority. For example, in 1986, the NPC withheld ratification for a controversial bankruptcy law because many deputies had misgivings about its efficacy and social implications. Some proponents of an overhaul of the Chinese political system during this period even envisioned a reincarnation of China's legislature as an effective and independent locus of power, accountable to its constituencies and capable of

effecting substantial results. However, few optimists remained, at least in the short term, after the Tiananmen Square massacre and the 1989 reassertion of traditional Communist Party authority.

The Standing Committee exercises most of the important functions of the NPC. A smaller body of high officials who frequently meet in Beijing, the Standing Committee has a compact, cohesive, and permanent structure with a membership of approximately 200, enabling it to exercise more effectively the NPC's formal powers of legislation and oversight. It also enjoys a certain degree of autonomy because a stipulation in the Chinese Constitution precludes other state officials from becoming eligible for its membership. Because it has potential as a genuine parliamentary body, some reformers in the late 1980s were contemplating amendments to the existing Chinese Constitution to transform the Standing Committee into a regular parliament that would hear and examine government reports and inspect and inquire about the performance of state organs. Once again, however, the bloody crushing of the student demonstrations in Tiananmen Square in June 1989 put an end to such talk of reform.

The head executive body, and the most important one in the Chinese government, is the State Council. From its inception in 1954 until early 1976, the State Council was headed by Premier Zhou Enlai. Upon Premier Zhou's death in 1976, Hua Guofeng became the new premier and leader of the State Council. In 1980, Hua was ousted, and the premiership was passed to Zhao Ziyang, an energetic reformer. After his election as Party Secretary General in early 1988 and in compliance with injunctions in force at that time against simultaneously holding both dominant Party and governmental positions, Zhao resigned his premiership in favor of Li Peng, a Soviet-trained engineer-turned-bureaucrat and the adopted son of the deceased Premier Zhou Enlai. Interestingly, Li Peng, in concert with Deng Xiaoping, was a primary player in bringing about the backlash against Zhao and his reformers in the spring of 1989.

The State Council consists of the premier, four vice premiers, half a dozen state councilors, and numerous heads of ministries and commissions. Many of the high Party leaders simultaneously hold positions on the State Council. Unlike the NPC, the State Council always has been and continues to be an important organ in Chinese politics. Although hardly an independent decision-making body, the State Council plays a significant role in the governing process because the Party cannot dispense with the expertise of its professionalized and specialized staff.

The State Council is particularly important in the implementation of Chinese Communist Party policy. As the highest executive body, the State Council directs and supervises the Chinese administrative structure. Assuming the responsibility for implementing the Party's policy proposals and for coordinating the economy and foreign and domestic affairs, the State Council shares political power with the CCP Politburo and Standing Committee. Under Zhao's stewardship in the late 1980s, the State Council distinguished itself as a bulwark of modernization and reform.

Above the State Council is the president of the Republic (head of state), a post that is different than that of chairman of the Standing Committee of the National People's Congress. In 1988, the president of the Republic post was assumed by Yang Shangkun, a member of the Politburo. Mao held this post from 1954–59 and passed it on to Liu Shaoqi, who held it from 1959–66, when he was purged. The post was abolished but restored in 1982, when Yang's

predecessor, Li Xiannian, assumed the head-of-state role.

In the 1980s, although moderate and reformist Chinese leaders presided over the elimination and merger of many ministries, the Chinese bureaucracy today still remains large and highly entrenched. The State Council directs numerous ministries. For example, one of them, the State Planning Commission, was established in 1952 as the Chinese ministry responsible for the planning of the state-run economy. The Chinese bureaucratic system is characterized by higher levels of provincial power than is seen in most traditional communist systems. Both the national ministries and the provincial organs can serve as powerful actors in the Chinese governmental process.

The Chinese military, the People's Liberation Army (PLA), has historically played a more important role in Chinese politics than militaries in other traditional communist states. During the civil-war years in China, the CCP and the PLA were indistinguishable; during Mao's reign, the PLA clearly was the most powerful bureaucracy in politics. Deng Xiaoping, the supreme leader in China in the 1980s, primarily owed his status and power to the ranks loyal to him within the PLA. Because of its willingness to implement a Deng-ordered crackdown on demonstrations and dissent in 1989, the PLA's power once again appeared to be on the rise.

Because of the closeness between the military and the Party in China, the security apparatus, which includes the People's Armed Police, historically has been weaker than the average security apparatus in a traditional Second World state. The relative weakness of the Chinese security apparatus vis-à-vis the PLA can be seen in the Party's response to both actors failing to promptly carry out orders relative to the crushing of the student demonstrations in Tiananmen Square. Both actors hesitated, and there was insubordination in the ranks of each, yet, only the security apparatus was significantly purged by the Party after order had been restored.

Governmental Reform in the Soviet Union

"The most perilous moment for a bad government is when it seeks to mend its ways. Only consummate statecraft can enable a king to save his throne when, after a long spell of oppressive rule, he sets to improving the lot of his subjects."[5]

—Alexis de Tocqueville

Since Mikhail Gorbachev first came to power in 1985, he has proposed a number of reforms targeted at the traditional method of government dominant in the Soviet Union since Joseph Stalin. Each of the reforms Gorbachev has proposed to date may be placed into one or more of four broad classifications: democratization, economic and political restructuring (perestroika), openness (glasnost), or "new thinking." Gorbachev has referred to the implementation of the four types of reform as being absolutely essential, if the Soviet Union ever is to break the shackles of its traditional methods of government and become a "rule of law state," characterized by the "direct involvement of the Soviet people in politics."

This section of Chapter 5 will be devoted both to outlining the goals of the various reform programs identified and to analyzing how much progress Gorbachev and his reform-minded allies have made in implementing them. What successes and what failures have Soviet reform communists experienced in attempting to implement their reform programs? Have the ac-

tions of Soviet reform communists matched their stated goals? Have they been practicing what they preach? How strong are the challenges to continued reform communist rule in the Soviet Union from both traditional communist and anticommunist forces? Let's take a look.

Outline of Reforms

The stated purpose of Gorbachev's democratization and restructuring reforms has been to break down in an orderly and evolutionary (as opposed to revolutionary) manner the monopoly of power that the Communist Party of the Soviet Union has enjoyed for more than 70 years in all aspects of social, political, and economic life, and to transfer that power to a reformed, restructured, and revitalized Soviet government. This reformed government would be held accountable to the Soviet people at large—and not to the Party—so that the Soviet Union finally might escape the spiritual and economic stagnation that has plagued it and achieve its true potential as a Great Power, not just a superpower, in the twenty-first century.

Policies of openness and toleration toward an independent press, political opposition groups, and free debate over the Soviet Union's past and future have been looked upon by reform communists in the Soviet Union both as a means to win popular support for their programs in the face of traditional communist opposition and as a means of generating new and fresh ideas that may cure the Soviet Union of its spiritual and economic malaise.

In an attempt to create a calm international environment conducive to the long-term growth of their domestic reform programs, as well as from a desire to transfer scarce economic resources to those programs so that they may have a fighting chance for success, Gorbachev and his allies in the Party and government have advocated a conciliatory, benign Soviet approach to international affairs. Disarmament proposals and announcements of Soviet intentions to demobilize forces, cut defense spending, and alter traditional military doctrine have emanated from the Kremlin on a fairly consistent basis since Gorbachev came to power in 1985.

Taken together, all of the offers, proposals and concessions the Soviet Union has made related to defense and foreign policy make up a package of substantial reforms in their own right. These are a different breed of reform than the programs described above, however, for they generally are believed to be sought after by Soviet leaders not for their own sake, but rather as a means to help support other, more domestically focused reforms. The term usually attached to this outwardly focused reform package of defense cuts and benign Soviet behavior around the world is "new thinking."

Not surprisingly, reaction in the West to the "new thinking" line promulgated by the Kremlin has been mixed. Some have viewed Soviet offers and moves such as its withdrawal from Afghanistan, its abandonment of the Brezhnev Doctrine in Eastern Europe, and its signing of the INF Treaty with the United States as proof positive that the Soviet Union is sincere in its attempt to alter its aggressive international tendencies of the past.

Others are not so sure that overall Soviet strategy has changed as much as the tactics used to implement that strategy. They view "new thinking" as a Soviet strategy designed to gain a breathing spell, a *peredyshka*. During this "breather," they will seek a "realignment of the correlation of forces" (i.e., strengthening of Soviet military power) in a manner that will make them even stronger in the future, when they will decide to return to their more traditional foreign and defense policies of expansion and coexistence.

Implementation of Reforms

Culminating, on December 1, 1988, a hotly contested two-year process of discussion and debates, the Supreme Soviet (the name of both the traditional and the reformed legislative body in the Soviet Union) adopted institutional changes which were envisioned by Gorbachev and his fellow reformers as the first phase of a concerted and serious attempt to reform and reorganize the Soviet government and the broader political system. Gorbachev described the changes as a major step leading to the democratization of Soviet society.

Among other things, the political reforms created a new national parliament with broad legislative authority; competitive elections and limited terms of office; a powerful, expanded post of President; and enhanced responsibilities for executive bodies of the central government.

The reforms called for by Gorbachev in 1988 began to be implemented in 1989. First, a new 2,250-member unicameral legislature called the Congress of People's Deputies was created and seated by means of competitive elections. Deputies were selected for membership in the Congress on the basis of secret balloting in multiple candidate elections held throughout the country in the spring of 1989.

By arrangement, 750 deputies were selected from all-union public organizations. One hundred of these seats were reserved by law for candidates from the Communist Party, whereas the other 650 were allotted to organizations such as trade unions, cooperatives, youth leagues, and scientific groups. Another 750 seats were assigned to territorial districts, each with 257,300 voters. The residents in a given territorial district then voted in competitive elections to see who would be their district's representative to the Congress. Finally, the last 750 seats were allotted to regional units of the

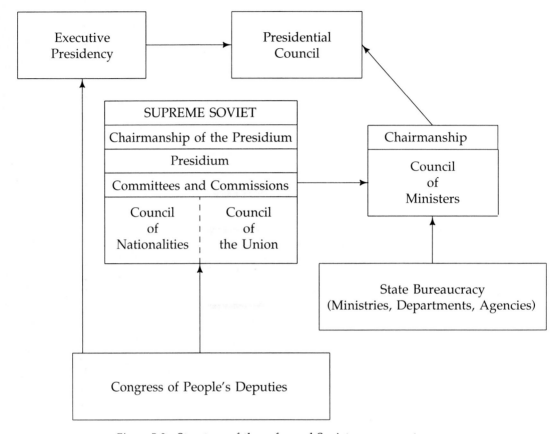

Figure 5.3 Structure of the reformed Soviet government.

Soviet federal structure. For example, each union republic received 32 seats. The union republic then held 32 elections within its borders to determine who its representatives would be.

The first Congress of People's Deputies convened in Moscow on May 25, 1989. The Congress is considered to be the highest state body in the Soviet Union and meets once or twice a year to establish state priorities in economic, social, political, and defense spheres.

In January 1989, the Communist Party selected its deputies to the Congress of People's De-

puties. First, nominees were submitted to the CPSU Politburo by the CPSU Central Committee and the Central Committees in the constituent republics. In a four-hour meeting on January 10, 1989, the Politburo alone chose the deputies who would represent the Party in the Congress, leaving the Central Committees and others with no say in the final selection process. Although all Party members had a chance to be nominated, and 31,500 were purportedly nominated from across the country, Gorbachev and the central Party leaders, particularly those in the Politburo, kept the authority for themselves to decide who the Party's representatives would be.

Some aspects of the 1989 election of the 1,500 deputies from territorial and regional jurisdictions to the Congress of People's Deputies suggested more democratic developments. The late Andrei Sakharov, a nominee for the citywide Moscow seat along with Boris Yeltsin, the former Politburo member, and Vitaly Vorotnikov, a member of the Politburo at the time, drew enthusiastic pre-election support. Sakharov's support motivated Yeltsin and Vorotnikov to take their chances in other electoral districts. Subsequently, however, Sakharov withdrew from the territorial election on the principle that he should have been a nominee of the Soviet Academy of Sciences, which had been assigned a number of seats on the basis of its status as an all-union organization.

Sakharov ultimately was elected by the Academy of Sciences, and Yeltsin won by an overwhelming margin in his electoral district. Many higher Party leaders were soundly rejected by the voters, indicating that new democratic trends had been set in motion in Soviet society.

Once the new Congress of People's Deputies had been seated, it elected a reconstituted, streamlined 542-member Supreme Soviet. Unlike the traditional Supreme Soviet that it replaced, the reconstituted Soviet meets twice a year for two or three months' duration, rather than its typical one- or two-day, twice-a-year sessions of the past. The new Supreme Soviet did keep the bicameral structure of its predecessor. One house of the new Supreme Soviet is called the Council of the Union, and the other is called the Council of Nationalities. Both houses of the new Supreme Soviet have 271 members.

Delegates to the Supreme Soviet come from the ranks of the Congress of People's Deputies. The Congress puts forth its own nominees and then votes. Those chosen move on to become

President Gorbachev presides over a meeting of the Congress of People's Deputies, an institution of increasing importance in the USSR. The late dissident and People's Deputy Andrei Sakharov stands at the podium, addressing the Congress.

members of the Supreme Soviet while simultaneously maintaining their seats in the Congress.

Twenty-three permanent committees and commissions are attached to the Supreme Soviet. Their responsibilities include not only preparation of legislation for consideration by the Supreme Soviet but also oversight of key executive actors who are responsible for implementation of the legislation once it has become law. For example, the Supreme Soviet Committee on Defense and State Security oversees the Soviet armed forces, internal police, and security apparatus.

The Supreme Soviet has a Presidium. The Presidium of the Supreme Soviet is a collegial body whose membership includes the Chairman of the Council of the Union and the Chairman of the Council of Nationalities, the two houses in the Supreme Soviet, the chairmen of the Union-republic supreme soviets, and the chairmen of the permanent commissions and committees of the Supreme Soviet. The Presidium of the Supreme Soviet is headed by a Chairman, who is elected by the Congress of People's Deputies from within its own ranks. The Chairman of the Supreme Soviet acts as the parliamentary speaker for the Supreme Soviet. In spring 1990, the Chairman of the Presidium of the Supreme Soviet was Anatolii Lukyanov.

The initial reforms of the Soviet constitution adopted in 1988 established the Chairman of the Presidium of the Supreme Soviet as President of the Soviet Union. The 1988 amendments to the Soviet constitution conferred important levers of state power on the Presidium of the Supreme Soviet as a whole and its Chairman in particular. For example, the right to declare war or to proclaim a state of emergency was granted to the Presidium. Its Chairman had the right to negotiate and sign international treaties, and from the General Secretary of the Party, he took control over the State Defense Council.

In March 1990, however, the Congress of People's Deputies approved new amendments to the Soviet constitution. These new amendments created a new executive Presidency within the Soviet government. This new Presidency was designed to stand alone, independent of the Presidium of the Supreme Soviet. Shortly after its creation, Mikhail Gorbachev assumed the mantle of the new Presidency, giving him the top leadership positions in both the Communist Party and the government in the Soviet Union.

The executive Presidency of the Soviet Union is an extremely powerful office as designed by the 1990 amendments to the Soviet constitution. The President of the Soviet Union has the power to propose legislation, negotiate treaties, overrule decisions of state bodies if they violate the constitution and endanger people's rights and freedoms, veto laws passed by the Supreme Soviet (the veto may be overridden by a two-thirds vote by each house), declare war, and to declare a state of emergency or martial law (but only after a warning to the republic concerned and the consent of that republic's presidium, or approval by a two-thirds vote in each house of the Supreme Soviet). In addition, the Soviet President is considered to be the Commander-in-Chief of the Soviet armed forces and the head of state.

The President of the Soviet Union can be removed from office by a two-thirds majority vote of the Congress of the People's Deputies, but it must be proved that he has violated the Soviet constitution. There is no provision for removing the President for immoral or irrational behavior. Although Gorbachev was elected President by the Congress of People's Deputies, plans have been drawn for the next election to the post to be held on a direct, popular-vote basis. The anticipated date of that election is late 1994, with the new popularly elected President entering office in early 1995 to serve the first of two possible five-year terms.

Along with the new office of the President, the constitutional amendments of 1990 provided for the creation of a new consultative body, the Presidential Council, to advise the President. This body appeared to be designed to take over the tasks reserved in the past for the Politburo of the Party and the State Defense Council. In other words, it is very powerful. Its membership is at the discretion of the President, except for the Chairman of the Council of Ministers (the prime minister), who must be included by design.

The Supreme Soviet elects the Council of Ministers, a body that does not appear that different from its traditional predecessor. Headed by the Prime Minister (Nikolai Ryzhkov in March 1990), the Council includes about a dozen first deputy prime ministers and deputy prime ministers, as well as various ministers and heads of other government bodies. What is different about this body is the process by which it is appointed. In the past, members of the Council of Ministers were handpicked by the top Party leaders. In 1989, the Supreme Soviet began playing a key role in determining the elections and confirmation of the new Council of Ministers, going so far as to reject 12 nominees from the Communist Party itself.

A final institution important in the new Soviet government is the Council of the Federation. The Council of the Federation includes the President of the Soviet Union and the presidents of the fifteen Soviet republics. Because the reformed and new governments of the individual republics of the Soviet Union were demanding greater autonomy from Moscow and indigenous political and economic control in the late 1980s and 1990, the Council of the Federation is likely to take on increased importance as the 1990s progress. Having the power to formulate treaties between the Soviet national government and the republics, the Council of the Federation will play a major role in any attempt on the part of Soviet leaders to create a loose confederation of sovereign states out of the union of socialist republics that has existed in the country since 1922. In such a confederated political order, the foreign and defense policies of the individual republics would likely be controlled by the national Soviet government, while the individual republics would maintain autonomy in other policy areas.

The inaugural sessions of the new Congress of People's Deputies and the reconstituted Supreme Soviet were televised across the entire USSR, and what the people witnessed was amazing. Heated debates about the most important and sensitive political issues, pointed criticism of higher Party officials, including Mikhail Gorbachev himself, and dramatic statements both for and against further reform. The stark contrast between the former, traditional Supreme Soviet and its vibrant, more democratic successor was apparent to all who witnessed the historic sessions of 1989.

Although significant democratization of the Soviet government has been undertaken, it would be inaccurate to say that the separation of powers and the checks and balances that have been built into the reformed Soviet political system have come anywhere close to approximating the pervasiveness of such principles in the political systems of the United States and other First World countries. The Communist Party of the Soviet Union remains very powerful in the Soviet Union, and the reforms that have been implemented in the Soviet government have had its blessing. What will happen when the government defiantly challenges the will of the Party is yet to be determined.

The will of the government has yet to deviate from the will of the Party largely because there are still so many Party members occupying key positions in the reformed Soviet government. The Party holds a vast majority of the seats in both the Congress of People's Deputies and the Supreme Soviet. The President, Prime Minister, and Chairman of the Presidium of the Supreme Soviet all are leaders of the Communist Party. Many departmental secretaries of the CPSU

Central Committee Secretariat serve as Chairmen of Supreme Soviet committees.

It should be duly noted, however, that the Communist Party that dominates the reformed Soviet government is far different from the Party that controlled the more traditional one. The CPSU is not the monolithic force it once was. The principles of democratic centralism and unity through terror are no longer applicable to the Party. The CPSU is highly factionalized. Party members are divided over the pace of social, economic, and political reform and over the resurgence of nationalism that has occurred throughout the Soviet Union during the reform era. The Party is so factionalized that it is no longer possible to talk, as was done traditionally, about "the will of the Party."

Threats to Reform

The reform communist leaders in the CPSU have had to deal with significant opposition to their programs of democratization, restructuring, openness, and "new thinking" from traditional conservatives, radical liberals, and ardent nationalists, both from within their Party and outside of it.

The reform communists' frustration and anxiety with their more doctrinaire brethren stem from the difficulty they have had in getting their reform proposals implemented through traditional channels and methods of communist rule. In many instances, lower-level Party and traditional state officials have not had the same enthusiasm for change and reform of the traditional Soviet economic, political, and social system that the leaders on high have. Party and state bureaucrats have enjoyed the perks granted to them by the old system. Why would someone want to implement reforms that might cost them their jobs and positions of power?

As Mikhail Gorbachev began in the late 1980s to scale back military spending and the role of the military in Soviet affairs, he encountered a certain amount of resistance within the military. So far, Gorbachev and the Communist Party have been firmly in control. However, the Soviet military remains a powerful actor, and we can expect them to continue to compete for what they consider their fair share of Soviet resources.

Gorbachev has long tried to eliminate the retrenchment and inertia toward his reforms from within the ranks of the Party and traditional state bureaucracies. During the first several years of his regime, he attempted to do so through a purging of personnel from within the traditional political system. When that didn't work, it is argued, he decided to create a new system, which would move the locus of power out of the bureaucracy and into the hands of a reformist government.

In fact, many Western analysts believe that Gorbachev's primary motivations in restructuring the Soviet government have been to eliminate the threat to his reforms posed by traditional conservatives within his Party. By proposing and then occupying the powerful Presidency, Gorbachev, they believe, has created an alternative power base for himself, independent from the Party, that might enable him to maintain his power even if he should be removed from his position as Party General Secretary by a conservative coup within the CPSU Central Committee.

Unfortunately for the reform communists, radical reform factions have developed within the Communist Party and in the new institutions of the reformed Soviet government that want to go much further and much faster than they do in reforming the political and economic system away from traditional methods of communist rule. One example is the Interregional Deputies Group in the Supreme Soviet. The

Group backs a political platform that advocates a free-market system and 100 percent popular-vote elections for the Soviet Union.

Many members of the Interregional Deputies Group were dissatisfied with the powers granted to the executive Presidency by the constitutional amendments of 1990. During debate over the amendments in the Supreme Soviet, they argued that expanded presidential power was not consistent with the reform communists' stated goal of democratization. Some warned that the expanded presidential powers set dangerous precedents for the future.

Another force that has threatened the programs of the reform communists is the intense mass appeal of newly emerging noncommunist national fronts, informal groups, and political parties within Soviet society. Taking advantage of the relaxation of repression in the age of glasnost and the repeal of constitutional provisions prohibiting political parties other than the CPSU, new political movements and organizations sprang up throughout the Soviet Union in the late 1980s and early 1990. Many of these new rivals to Party rule seek not the reform of the traditional communist Soviet political system but its overthrow (see Figure 5.4).

In an era of increasing national consciousness in the Soviet Union, the new political parties and mass movements of the Baltic republics have been particularly critical and outspoken of centralized communist rule. During the reformed Soviet government's consideration of constitutional changes in early 1990, for example, legislators from the new political parties in the Baltic republics made dramatic appeals and proposed reforms that would give their republics greater say. Initially, the non-communist leaders of the Baltic republics just asked the Supreme Soviet to pass reforms that would give the republics more power vis-à-vis the central government. By the spring of 1990, however, they

had moved toward outright seccession and independence from the Soviet Union.

Reformed Government in Eastern Europe

The revolutions of 1989 and the elections of 1990 have brought fundamental change to traditional methods of government in the Second World states of Eastern Europe. Communist Parties in these states mostly have collapsed, and the levers of state power have been passed to reformed and reconstituted governments. These governments have been freely elected and largely are composed of multiparty coalitions that span the spectrum of political thought.

Although the path to reform government in the states of Eastern Europe has been unique to each of the countries in the region, there have been some similarities among the countries in what has taken place. There has also been an underlying set of factors at the international-system level that has impacted Eastern Europe as a whole.

For these reasons, the first part of this section of the chapter will focus on the Second World states of Eastern Europe as a whole. Drawing on the individual reform stories of the various states, as well as regional factors produced by the international system, we will try to develop a general model that lays out the different stages through which the Second World states have had to pass on the road to reform.

Our model will serve as a comparative guide for us when we examine in the second part of this section the reform route that one specific Eastern European state—Hungary—has taken. We will take a closer look at Hungary and describe how its processes of reform have been both similar to and different from any general post-communist norm.

Confederation of Anarcho-Syndicalists

Founded: May 1989	
Membership: 1,000	
Leaders: None	

Wants total abolition of the state. In favour of co-operatives, but anti-capitalist

Democratic party

Founded: January 1989	
Membership: 2,000	
Leaders: Lev Ubozhko, Rastislav Semenov	

Centre-left breakaway from Democratic Union (see below). Mr Ubozhko modestly describes himself as "the only leader who, standing at the head of the state, can pull it out of catastrophe"

Orthodox Constitutional Monarchy party

Founded: May 19 1990 (birthday of Nicholas II)	
Membership: unknown	
Leaders: S. Yurkov-Engelgardt, Neliya Milovanova	

Wants to unite the Russian Orthodox church, the army and KGB under a restored constitutional monarchy. Members swear allegiance to the grand duke Vladimir Kirilovich Romanov. Other monarchist groups want the tsar to be elected by a nationwide assembly

Constitutional Democratic party

Founded: May 1990	
Membership: 500	
Leader: Leonid Podolski	

Centre-left. Based on an organization called the Union of Constitutional Democrats, which is in turn a revival of the pre-revolutionary anti-tsarist Cadets party

Liberal Democrats

Founded: March 1990	
Membership: 3,000-4,000	
Leader: Vladimir Zhirinovsky	

"No ideology, our theory is common sense." Pro free market. Split away from the Democratic Union. Described by former allies as "trash" and "an arm of the KGB"

Party of Free Labour

Founded: February 1990 (but not yet a formal party)	
Membership: unknown	
Leader: Igor Korovikov	

Pro-business. The party of the co-operatives, it has money but limited popularity. Will not admit Communists

Christian Democratic Union

Founded: April 1989	
Membership: 2,500	
Leader: Alexander Ogorodnikov	

Centre-right. Implacably anti-Communist, it has close links with western Christian Democrats. Wins respect because its founder is a long-time religious dissident. Plans to set up an umbrella group called the Russian Democratic Forum

Russian Communist party in the CPSU

Founded: January 1990	
Membership: 2,000	
Leaders: Boris Gidaspov, Nina Andreeva	

Neo-Stalinist, in favour of strict central planning and Russian imperialism. The fundamentalists of the Communist party hostile to President Gorbachev and *perestroika*. The faction is not recognized by the national Communist party but has won the acceptance of the local Leningrad party

Socialist party

Founding congress planned in June	
Membership: 1,000	
Leaders: Boris Kagarlitsky, Vladimir Makhonov, Lev Volovik	

Socialist. Connected with the strike committees of the unofficial trade-union movement. Wants to give state property and economic control to local governments

Democratic Union

Founded: May 1988	
Membership: 2,000	
Leaders: None (very democratic)	

Uncompromisingly anti-Communist. The earliest and bravest of the informal political parties, determined from the beginning to behave as if the Soviet Union were a proper democracy. Its pioneer demonstrations were broken up by the KGB. It continues to boycott elections as insufficiently free, but its influence is falling as the country becomes more democratic and members leave to set up other parties

Russian Popular Front

Founded: December 1988	
Membership: Up to 40,000	
Leaders: Vladimir Ivanov, M. Skurlatov	

Favours the free market, democracy and the spiritual rebirth of Russia. One of the largest of the new parties, it attempts to do in Russia what the Popular Fronts are doing in the Baltic and TransCaucasian republics. Oddly mixes western democratic and Russian Orthodox values. It is split between the liberal Ivanov faction and the social democratic Skurlatov wing

Social Democratic Party of Russia

Founded: May 1990	
Membership: 5,000	
Leaders: Oleg Rumyantsev, Nikolai Tutov	

Centre-left. Well-organized, with good links to West European social democratic parties. Linked also with the reformist wing of the Communist party, but rules out a coalition with Communists. It is part of the Social Democratic Association, founded in Estonia in January. It failed to attract better-known social democratic deputies, who are drifting towards the Russian Peoples' party. Split between Muscovites (who want a centralized party) and Lengingraders (for a decentralized one)

Marxist Platform of the Communist party

Founded: April 1990	
Membership: unknown	
Leaders: Yegor Ligachev, Vadim Bakatin	

Conservative Communists, the mirror image of the Democratic Platform (see below). Likes some elements of *perestroika*, but dislikes the party's loss of monopoly power

United Workers' Front

Founded: October 1989	
Membership: more than 5,000	
Leader: Veniamin Yarin	

Marxist-Leninist. Stands for central planning, guaranteed full employment and a minimum wage. Closely allied with, and often indistinguishable from, the Marxist Platform of the Communist party. It has strong support in the large but polarized industrial cities of Leningrad, Moscow and Sverdlovsk. Its leader is a populist working-class hero in the Peronist mould

Democratic Platform of the Communist party

Founded: January 1990	
Membership: 500,000	
Leaders: Vyacheslav Shostakovsky, Gavriil Popov, Boris Yeltsin	

Social Democratic. The "left-radicals" (ie, reformers) of the Communist party. They want to turn the party in to a Socialist one, encouraging free enterprise and ending Communist control of factories, the army and KGB. Target of attack by party conservatives. Embraces many of Russia's most respected reformers, but they seem unlikely to take over the party, so many (but how many? and how coherently?) will split away

Russian People's party

Organizing committee exists, but party not yet formally founded	
Membership: –	
Leaders: Nikolai Travkin, Yuri Afanasyev	

Centre-left. Intended to be the home for disaffected Communist reformers if or when they leave the Communist party. Mr Travkin urged the new unofficial trade-union organization, the Confederation of Labour, to affiliate but it turned him down. The army trade union, Shield, and April, an influential reform group of the Soviet Writers' union, may, however, join

Figure 5.4 Communist Party factions and independent parties in the Russian republic, ranked on a scale of importance from one to ten. [From *The Economist* (May 26, 1990), p. 52.]

The Rejection of Traditional Methods of Communist Rule

Traditional Eastern European Communist Party leaders witnessed the emergence of increased opposition to their rule throughout the 1980s. This opposition was represented in such diverse forms as independent trade union movements; underground religious and human rights organizations; national, cultural, and environmental conscious groups; secret student and literary clubs; demonstrations; strikes; the dissemination of non–Party-sanctioned publications (samizdat); and the ever-growing sense of frustration among society at large, reflected in declining worker productivity and mass apathy. The pursuit of communism via a single-Party socialist system became an exercise in futility.

With the rise to power of Mikhail Gorbachev and the advent of his reform programs in the Soviet Union, the traditional communist leaders in Eastern Europe began to face opposition to their methods of rule not only from their societies at large but also from reform factions within their own Communist Party.

Historically in Eastern Europe, if a Party member toed Moscow's line, his chances for enhanced power within the Party were far greater than if he did not. With the advent of Gorbachev's reformist line and the refusal of old-line communist leaders in Eastern Europe to accept it, a good number of Gorbachev's newly converted Eastern European protegés in the mid-1980s probably did not truly believe in his reforms, but rather saw in them an opportunity to enhance their own power once any decision came down from Moscow that the hard-line, traditional Communist leadership must go.

Those who sought Moscow's intervention to remove traditional Communist Party leaders in Eastern Europe gradually learned, however, that the Kremlin of Gorbachev did not operate in the same manner as the Kremlin of his predecessors, relative to the domestic affairs of Eastern European states. The Gorbachev regime had publicly hinted on numerous occasions early on in its rule that it simply had too many other problems to worry about than the internal politics of Eastern European states. On the basis of 1956 Hungary and 1968 Czechoslovakia, however, few in Eastern Europe were willing to give Gorbachev's pronouncements the benefit of the doubt. Because of a belief that a sudden policy reversal in Moscow was possible, reform communists in Eastern European Parties and opposition groups at large within these Second World societies initially remained cautious in their calls for change in their country's traditional communist political system.

Unlike the past, however, the liberalized line in Moscow was not reversed when the call for change in Eastern Europe reached the point of the dissolution of traditional Party rule. This time, Party officials in Moscow had told the truth. They really were not going to intervene militarily, economically, or politically to prevent the dissolution of Party dictatorships in Eastern Europe.

By early 1989, the communist reformers and opposition groups in various Eastern European states had become convinced that what Gorbachev had been saying for years was indeed true, and with the promise of economic rewards being offered by the United States and countries of Western Europe for accelerated movement toward a pluralist, democratic political system, they began to make their respective assaults on state power. Without the support of Moscow to which they had grown so accustomed throughout the Cold War period, the traditional Communist Party dictators and their loyalists stood little chance of survival once they were exposed to an angry populace.

153

Alexander Dubcek and Vaclav Havel confer during a 1989 demonstration that led to the end of Communist Party rule in Czechoslovakia.

Initially, the reform communist faction of the Party and the opposition at large within Eastern European societies worked together to remove traditional Communist Party leaders from their positions of power. This was done by a reform communist bid for power from within the Party, which was reinforced by expressions of support from influential opposition forces outside the Party. These two factors, coupled with Moscow's ambivalence, resulted in a swing in the balance of power within the Party in favor of the reform communists, who, once they held a majority in the Central Committee of the Party, proceeded to purge the traditional communists from their positions of power.

For the most part, the purging of the traditional communist leaderships was done peacefully, without much loss of life. The exception to the rule, however, was in Romania. In Romania, the traditional communist dictator, Nicolae Ceausescu, refused to gracefully step down in the face of popular and intra-Party opposition. Rather, he ordered his secret police force, the Securitate, and the Romanian Army to engage in a slaughter of his opponents. The Romanian Army balked at such orders and instead sided with the opposition. After a series of bloody battles between the Securitate and the Romanian Army, which was aided by bands of civilian militants, the Army and the opposition prevailed, and the Ceausescu regime was overthrown.

The Implementation of New Governments in Eastern Europe

Once the Eastern European reform communists had gained control of their Parties, they soon realized that the opposition that had once supported them now increasingly wanted them to share their Party's reins of power. The opposition did not want just a reformed communist system; they wanted an entirely new system, based on the pluralist democratic systems of the West.

Confronted with this challenge to their newfound rule, the reform communists agreed to

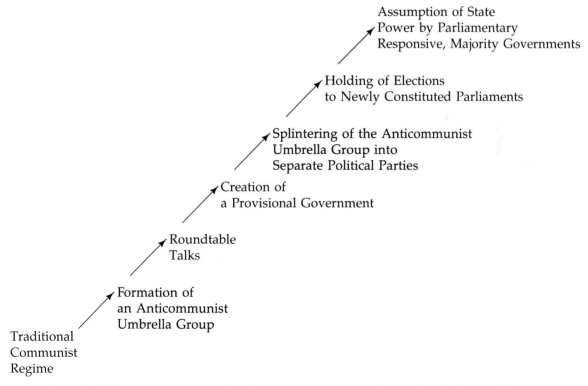

Figure 5.5 The process of transition from communist to pluralist regimes in Eastern Europe.

155

enter into roundtable negotiations with the opposition to hammer out reform methods of government that would be acceptable to both sides. The reform communists had little if any choice but to propose and enter the roundtable process. For example, the reform communist leaders in Poland found that the popular support commanded by Solidarity made it impossible to govern without recognizing and working with the free trade union movement.

A reform communist refusal to negotiate or to release the reins of dictatorial control would have been an adoption of the the same line that had supposedly been done away with by the purging of the traditional communists. The reform communists were too attuned to the increasing importance of popular support in governing within the region since the exit of dominant Soviet influence to make such a mistake. They recognized the need to command mass support and were, therefore, willing to allow the growth of independent political movements, more powerful assemblies, and more competitive elections. By so doing, reform communist leaders hoped to win enough acclaim from their populace to enable them to hold onto some of their power once their state's traditional political system had been reformed.

During the roundtable negotiations, the opposition parties won major concessions from the Party: The Party agreed to rescind state constitutional provisions granting it a monopoly of power; legalize opposition parties; have competitive, multiparty, free elections to a reformed national parliament based on Western European lines, which would assume state power from the Party once elected; and include noncommunists in a provisional government that would rule the country until parliamentary elections could be held.

The institutions of the provisional government were those of the traditional communist government with two major differences. First, the provisional government no longer took orders from the Party Politburo and Secretariat. Second, many of the seats and ministerial positions in the government were occupied no longer by subservient communists, but rather by leading figures of the umbrella opposition group.

During the provisional government phase of reform, most leaders of both the Party and the umbrella opposition were more concerned with positioning themselves for the upcoming parliamentary elections than with governing the country via the provisional government. In preparation for the elections, both the Party and the umbrella opposition split into various new parties representing all points of the spectrum of political thought. In Czechoslovakia, for example, almost forty new political parties were formed after the creation of the provisional government in that country. There now are parties throughout Eastern Europe in competition with each other, standing on such diverse platforms as traditional communism, reform communism, socialism, social democracy, lib-

This March 18, 1990 voting in East Berlin represented the first free election in East Germany since the 1930s.

eralism, religious conservatism, environmentalism, nationalism, populism, and even fascism.

The elections to the new national parliaments that have taken place in Eastern Europe have been conducted on the basis of secret ballots with universal adult suffrage. They have to a large extent been patterned after parliamentary elections in Western Europe. Elections in Western Europe differ from those in the United States in that there is more emphasis on the vote a party gets rather than the vote a particular individual gets. For example, in the United States, if an individual wins a majority of the votes in a Senate race, that individual occupies the Senate seat for which he has competed. In most European countries, however, that individual may or may not occupy the seat for which he has contested, depending on the desire of his party and the rank of his name on a party list.

In Europe, the number of seats a party is assigned in the parliament is based on the percentage of the total vote it receives in an election. In most cases, parties draw up lists of candidates that they consider once the number of seats allotted to them has been determined. The number-one candidate on the list fills the first available party seat, the second on the list the second seat, and so on down the line. Because the parties make out their lists under assumption that a clean sweep of all the seats in parliament is possible, inevitably, some candidates on the party list are not awarded seats because the party does not, in fact, win all of the seats available. Because of this fact, the ranking of the names on the party lists becomes very important.

Once the elections have taken place in Eastern European states and the seats in parliament have been allotted to the various deserving parties, the next step in reform has been for the majority party in parliament to form a government under the direction of one of its leaders, who assumes the title of prime minister. If no party has been awarded a majority in parliament by the electoral process, a coalition government consisting of a major party and one or two minor parties in alliance with one another has had to be formed. This coalition government controls the majority of seats within the parliament but is less stable than a single-party majority government because it is made up of different parties that often have very different platforms. They have aligned out of mutual self-interest to share power.

The prime minister of the coalition government typically comes from the party with the most seats in the parliament within the government coalition. The minor parties generally are rewarded by the prime minister for their participation in the coalition by the appointment of leaders of their party to ministerial positions within the government.

In addition to a prime minister who heads the legislative body of the government, most Eastern European states have made provisions for the election of a chief executive, or president. The office of president in most Eastern European countries appears to most closely resemble the office of president in France, in that the presidents in Eastern Europe will have strong state powers to handle national emergencies and state crises, to choose the prime minister, to veto legislation, and to dissolve parliament.

The Hungarian Reform Experience

Unlike the situations in some other Second World states of Eastern Europe, organized opposition to traditional communist rule in Hungary was not that strong before the cataclysmic events of 1989 and 1990. The Hungarian people, after all, had already been burned once by attempting to reform their traditional communist political system. The Soviet invasion of their

Election results are for the lower house of parliament, and percentages of the vote are for the first round of voting in 1990.

Bulgaria

Elections on June 10th and 17th, 1990, for a 400-seat, single-chamber two-year parliament.

	% of vote	seats
Bulgarian Socialist party (formerly communists)	47	211
Union of Democratic Forces (anticommunist alliance)	36	144
Agrarian Union (farmers)	8	16
Movement for Rights and Freedom (ethnic Turks)	6	23
Other	3	6

Czechoslovakia

Elections on June 8th and 9th, 1990, for a two-year federal parliament with 150-seat House of the People (101 from Czech republic, 49 from Slovakia) and 150-seat House of the Nations (75 from each).

	% of vote	seats
Civic Forum/Public Against Violence (Czech/Slovak anticommunist alliance)	47	87
Communists	14	23
Christian Democrats	12	20
Moravian and Silesian Autonomists	5	9
Slovak National party	4	6
Coalition of other minorities	3	5

East Germany

Election on March 18th, 1990, for a single-chamber, 400-seat parliament.

	% of vote	seats
Alliance for Germany (Christian Democratic coalition)	48	193
Social Democrats	22	87
Democratic Socialists (formerly communists)	16	65
Liberals	5	21
Others	9	34

Hungary

Election on March 25th and April 8th, 1990, for a single-house, 386-seat, four-year parliament.

	% of vote	seats
Democratic Forum (center-right)	25	165
Free Democrats (center-liberal)	21	92
Independent Smallholders (farmers)	12	43
Socialists (reform communists)	11	33
Young Democrats (center-liberal)	9	21
Christian Democrats	7	21
Hungarian Socialist Workers (unreformed communists)	4	0
Social Democrats	4	0
Other	7	11

Figure 5.6 Elections in Eastern Europe 1990. [Adapted from The Economist (June 23, 1990), p. 46; and *Report on Eastern Europe* (July 13, 1990), p. 41.]

<table>
<tr><td colspan="3">

Poland

This is a special case. The last general election was in June 1989 for a parliament with 460-seat lower house and 100-seat upper house, the Senate. In the free election for the Senate, the anticommunist movement, Solidarity, won 99 seats. Elections for the lower house were semi-free. There, Solidarity could compete for only 35% of the lower house seats.

</td></tr>
</table>

Poland	% of vote	seats
Solidarity...............	35	161
PUWP (Communists)......	37	173
Polish Peasant Party	16	76
Democratic Party..........	5	27
Former procommunist Christian Groups	5	23

Romania

Election on May 20th, 1990, for a two-year parliament with 396-seat lower house and 190-seat upper house.

Romania	% of vote	seats
National Salvation Front (ex- and not-so-ex-communists, military officers, former dissidents)	66	233
Democratic Hungarian Union....................	7	29
Liberals (center-right)......	6	29
Greens....................	3	12
National Peasants (farmers)................	3	12
Others	15	81

Figure 5.6   (Continued)

country in the fall of 1956 and the subsequent crushing of the revolutionary Nagy regime had killed thousands of Hungarians.

In the years after the 1956 revolution, the Hungarian people reached a sort of tacit agreement with their communist overlords. The people agreed to tolerate traditional communist rule if the regime provided them with a better standard of living than their communist brethren in the rest of the Soviet bloc.

The traditional Hungarian communist regime in the post-1956 era was headed by Janos Kadar. Kadar ruled Hungary with an iron hand. He was intolerant of dissent, yet he was willing to experiment with reform of the traditional Stalinist economic model to attempt to pacify his people with an above-average socialist standard of living.

In the late 1960s, Kadar and his Party designed the New Economic Mechanism for the Hungarian economy. The New Economic Mechanism

reduced the burden placed on workers by the central planning bureaucracy by transferring some management decisions to managers at the local-enterprise level. The workers initially responded to this plan by producing more and better-quality goods. The NEM also allowed Hungarians access to Western consumer goods not available anywhere else in the Soviet bloc.

When Mikhail Gorbachev and his reform programs came along in 1985, the imagination of the Hungarian people did not run wild, but the imagination of many mid-level, technocratic, young Communist Party members did. Reform communism was attractive to them because they recognized that the aging policies of the New Economic Mechanism no longer were able to generate the standard of living to which the Hungarian people had grown accustomed. In an effort to preempt political unrest, these reformers recognized that the Hungarian economy needed an infusion of new thinking. They turned to Gorbachev-styled reforms in both the economic and the political arena to solve their problems. They also saw in the Gorbachev line an opportunity to launch a challenge to Kadar's age-old grip on state power.

The enthusiasm the reform faction of the Hungarian Communist Party developed toward perestroika and glasnost soon outdistanced the Soviet Party itself in terms of its daring and boldness. Before long, the Hungarian people began to take notice of what was going on in their suddenly not-so-monolithic Party. The Party was splitting along reform and traditional lines. The traditional faction was being led by Party leader Janos Kadar. The reformist wing was being led by men such as Imre Pozsgay, Gyula Horn, Miklos Nemeth, and Rezso Nyers.

In May 1988, Kadar, via an intra-Party coup, was removed from his position as Party leader after thirty-two years in power. His replacement, Karoly Grosz, was a compromise choice between the reformist and traditional factions of the Party. Over the next year, a tug of war took place within the Party over its future direction. The reformists radicalized their programs in an effort to win increasing popular support. The traditional communists used their positions within the apparat to scuttle the implementation of new reforms.

By January 1989, the reformist faction of the Hungarian Party had succeeded in gaining a majority within the Party's Central Committee and traditional Hungarian legislature. It had successfully purged many old-line communists from the Party rank and file.

During January 1989, the traditional Hungarian legislature approved bills legalizing freedom of assembly and freedom of association for the Hungarian people. In February 1989, the Hungarian Communist Party Central Committee approved the creation of independent political parties in the country. In May 1989,

the Central Committee forced the former Party leader Janos Kadar into retirement from his ceremonial position as President of Hungary. In June, the reformists in the Central Committee replaced Karoly Grosz as Party leader with one of their own, Rezsos Nyers. Miklos Nemeth, another reformer, became Prime Minister.

Throughout the summer of 1989, the political scene in Hungary was in a state of flux. The Communist Party was disintegrating over factional battles between reformers and traditionalists, and between different leading personalities within the reformist faction itself. Opposition to communist rule, long dormant because of severe repression, had been reborn and rejuvenated. More than sixty parties (including one called the Winnie the Pooh Party!) had been formed in rapid succession since the approval of the February 1989 Party decree that allowed for opposition parties.

On September 19, 1989, roundtable negotiations between the Party and an umbrella opposition group concluded. The two groups reached an agreement allowing for the creation of a multiparty political system within Hungary. In exchange for the promise of free elections to parliament, the reform communists supposedly were reserved the right to provide the country's head of state. The new president was expected to be directly elected by the people before the new parliament was chosen, thereby giving the Party's likely candidate, Imre Poszgay, a good chance of winning.

Also at the roundtable talks, it was agreed that the Party's militia, the 60,000-strong Workers' Guard, would be turned over to a provisional government, which would hold sway over the country until the parliamentary and presidential elections could be held. The provisional government was to be led by the standing Prime Minister, Miklos Nemeth, and was to include representatives from both the

Party and the opposition. Seats were to be opened in the traditional legislature and were to be competed for by both members of the Party and the opposition in special elections.

In October 1989, the Hungarian Communist Party, officially the Hungarian Socialist Workers' Party, renounced Marxism and renamed itself the Hungarian Socialist Party. The leaders of the new Socialist Party, largely the same people that controlled the reformist wing of the traditional Communist Party, committed themselves to the creation of a market economy and a multiparty, democratic political system in Hungary. Shortly after the conclusion of the October Party Congress that had ratified the name change of the Party, the traditional communist faction within the new Socialist Party broke away and re-formed the Hungarian Socialist Workers' Party.

On October 23, 1989, on the thirty-third anniversary of the 1956 uprising, Hungary was proclaimed a free republic and the provisional government approved at the roundtable talks in September, under the leadership of Miklos Nemeth, took control of the state. The special elections to the open seats in the traditional legislature resulted in a string of defeats for the Socialist Party and inclusion of opposition leaders in the provisional government.

On November 26, Hungarians decided by referendum not to choose a president until they had chosen their new parliament. This was a real blow to the leaders of the Socialist Party because they thought an agreement had been struck at the roundtable talks that would allow the presidential elections to take place before the parliamentary elections.

The Socialists believed that their candidate for president, Imre Poszgay, would win in a presidential election held before the parliamentary elections because of his popularity as the Party man who peacefully negotiated away the Party's monopoly of power in Hungary. They thought he could not win in a presidential election held after the parliamentary elections. The Socialist Party was not expected to fair well in the elections for parliament (because they were the former Communist Party), and it would be difficult for a candidate from a minority party in parliament to win a national office such as the presidency.

Once the provisional government set March 25, 1990, as the date for parliamentary elections in Hungary, a flurry of Western-style campaign activity took place. A bitter campaign evolved between two leading parties once loosely linked to the anticommunist opposition. One of the parties, the Democratic Forum, emphasized traditional Christian values and conservative social policy in a manner similar to the center-right Christian Democratic Parties of Western Europe. The Democratic Forum also advocated a careful transition from socialism to a free-market economy and a convertible Hungarian currency; favored integration with Western Europe and a continued American role in Europe; and took up a nationalistic stance concerning the protection of Hungarian minorities living abroad, particularly those living in the Transylvania section of neighboring Romania.

The other leading party, the Alliance of Free Democrats, accused the Democratic Forum of being both overtly nationalistic and chauvinistic on the basis of its stance on the Hungarian minority issues. In addition to the two parties' differences on the minority issue, there were differences between the two relative to the pace at which Hungary should be integrated into the rest of Europe. The Free Democrats advocated a much more rapid shift away from the traditional methods of communist rule than the Democratic Forum. The Free Democrats called for radical moves toward a free market, laying out plans to privatize 35 to 40 percent of Hungary's business assets within two to three years after the elections, and 70 to 80 percent before ten years passed.

The Hungarian multiparty parliamentary elections held on March 25, 1990, were conducted on the basis of a two-tiered voting system. The two-tiered system allowed voters to vote on two ballots, one giving party preference and the other selecting individual local candidates. Any candidate receiving 15 percent of the vote qualified for a runoff, which was held on April 8, 1990.

The two big winners in the March 25 elections were the Democratic Forum and the Alliance of Free Democrats. The Democratic Forum won 24 percent of the total vote, and the Alliance of Free Democrats 21 percent. Of the other sixty parties that desired seats in the new Hungarian parliament, only six achieved the necessary 4 percent of the total vote to be granted representation. (No, the Winnie the Pooh Party was not one of these six!) Sixty-four percent of eligible Hungarian voters voted in the March 25 elections.

Following the runoff elections of April 8, seats in the first freely elected parliament in Hungary since the imposition of communist rule were distributed. No single party held a majority of seats in the new parliament; therefore, a coalition government had to be formed. The Democratic Forum, the party that won the most seats in the elections, was able to form a majority government by entering into an alliance with two smaller parties, the Smallholders and the Christian Democrats. Together, the three parties in the governing coalition in Hungary controlled 229 of the 386 seats in parliament.

The Socialist Party, primarily consisting of the reform communists responsible for the abolition of the Party's monopoly of power in Hungary, received only 11 percent of the total vote in the parliamentary elections. The traditional Communist Party, the Hungarian Socialist Workers Party, failed to earn 4 percent of the total vote in the election and was denied representation in the new parliament. By the spring of 1990, one could safely assume that communist rule had effectively come to an end in Hungary.

In May of 1990, Arpad Goncz, a founder of the Free Democrats and writer jailed for six years during the 1956 uprising, was selected by the Hungarian parliament to serve as the interim President of Hungary until national popular elections could be held. The Democratic Forum, the dominant party of the majority coalition within the new Hungarian parliament voted for Goncz, a member of the opposition Free Democrats, as interim President after securing promises from the Free Democrats that Goncz would call on the Democratic Forum to form a government and that they would supply the needed votes when legislation required a two-thirds majority. Shortly thereafter, Jozsef Antall, the leader of the Democratic Forum, was named Prime Minister of Hungary and called upon by Goncz to form a government. Peaceful bargaining and compromise between rival political parties had come to Hungary.

Suggestions for Further Reading

Barnett, A. Doak, *Cadres, Bureaucracy, and Political Power in Communist China* (New York: Columbia University Press, 1967).

Bialer, Seweryn, *The Soviet Paradox: External Expansion, Internal Decline* (New York: Knopf, 1986).

Bialer, Seweryn, and **Thane Gustafson,** eds., *Russia at the Crossroads: The 26th Congress of the CPSU* (Winchester, Mass.: Allen & Unwin, 1982).

Brown, J.F., *Eastern Europe and Communist Rule* (Durham, N.C.: Duke University Press, 1988).

Carter, April, *Democratic Reform in Yugoslavia: The Changing Role of the Party* (Princeton, N.J.: Princeton University Press, 1982).

Cocks, Paul, *Controlling Communist Bureaucracy* (Cambridge, Mass.: Harvard University Press, 1977).

Colton, Timothy J., *Commissars, Commanders, and Civilian Authority: The Structure of Soviet Military Politics* (Cambridge, Mass.: Harvard University Press, 1979).

Harding, Harry, *Organizing China: The Problem of Bureaucracy, 1949–76* (Stanford, Calif.: Stanford University Press, 1981).

Hough, Jerry F., and **Merle Fainsod,** *How the Soviet Union Is Governed* (Cambridge, Mass.: Harvard University Press, 1979).

Knight, Amy W., *The KGB: Police and Politics in the Soviet Union* (Winchester, Mass.: Allen & Unwin, 1988).

Lane, David, *Elites and Political Power in the USSR* (Brookfield, Vt.: Edward Elgar, 1988).

Little, D. Richard, *Governing the Soviet Union* (New York: Longman, 1989).

Lovenduski, Jean and **Jean Woodall,** *Politics and Society in Eastern Europe* (Bloomington, In.: Indiana University Press, 1987).

Nelson, Daniel and **Stephen White,** eds., *Communist Legislatures in Comparative Perspective* (London: MacMillan and Albany: State University of New York Press, 1982).

Pye, Lucien, *The Dynamics of Chinese Politics* (Cambridge: Oelgeschlager, Gunn & Hain, 1981).

Pravda, Alex and **Blair Ruble,** *Trade Unions in Communist States* (Winchester, Mass.: Allen & Unwin, 1988).

Ra'anan, Uri and **Igor Lukes,** eds., *Inside the Apparat: Perspectives on the Soviet System from Former Functionaries* (Lexington, Mass.: Lexington Books, 1990).

Sharlet, Robert, *The New Soviet Constitution of 1977: Analysis and Text* (Brunswick, Ohio: King's Court Communications, 1978).

Starr, Richard F., *Communist Regimes in Eastern Europe,* 5th ed. (Stanford, Calif.: Hoover Institution Press, 1988).

Vanneman, Peter, *The Supreme Soviet: Politics and Legislative Process in the Soviet Political System* (Durham, N.C.: Duke University Press, 1977).

Notes

1. V.A. Vlasov, *Sovetskii gosudartvennyi apparat* (Moscow: Gos. idz-vo i urid. lit-ry, 1959) p. 361, cited in Darrell P. Hammer, *USSR: The Politics of Oligarchy* (Hinsdale, Ill.: Dyrden, 1974), p. 278.

2. For an analysis and the text of the 1977 Soviet constitution, see Robert Sharlet, *The New Soviet Constitution of 1977* (Brunswick, Ohio: Kings Court, 1978).

3. I.N. Ananov, *Ministerstva USSR* (Moscow: Gos.

idz-vo i urid. lit-ry, 1960) p. 22, Ibid., p. 277.

4. For a description of the duties of the traditional state defense council, as told by former Party insiders, see Uri Ra'anan and Igor Lukes, eds., *Inside the Apparat* (Lexington, Mass.: Lexington Books, 1990), pp. 84–95.

5. Alexis de Tocqueville, *The Old Regime and the French Revolution*, trans. Stuart Gilbert (New York: Doubleday Anchor Books, 1955), p. 277.

CHAPTER 6

THE POLICY PROCESS AND ECONOMIC REFORM IN SECOND WORLD STATES

For decades, Second World states were described as Communist Party dictatorships. Political scientists generally referred to the policy process as totalitarian, meaning that the Communist Party and the elites who sat at the top of the Party hierarchy had almost total control over the making and implementation of policy. Was this an accurate description of the policy process in Second World states? And what about the present and future?

This chapter will examine and discuss different models and concepts that can be used to better understand the creation and implementation of policy in the Soviet Union, China, and selected East European states.

An Overview of the Policy Process

To simplify and aid in the understanding of something as complicated as politics and the policy process, political scientists use models, that is, simplified representations, to help capture important elements of reality.

Until the 1960s, the totalitarian model guided most studies of communist systems. This model drew attention to a highly organized, dictatorial process where individuals and groups outside of the top Party leadership had no significant political power. Two early proponents of this model, Carl Friedrich and Zbigniew K. Brzezinski, noted that the totalitarian system involved an unavoidable compulsion on the part of the rulers to absorb or destroy all social groups obstructing its complete control.[1]

Certainly, there was a considerable amount of totalitarian rule in the Second World during the Stalinist period. The Soviet political system was a dictatorial state in which the Communist Party dominated social, political and economic life. Stalinist totalitarianism was exported to communist China and the East European states after World War II and remained dominant in most Second World states throughout the 1950s and 1960s.

Although the widely used totalitarian model drew attention to some very important features of communist political systems, an increasing number of scholars in the post-Stalin era began to feel that it also obscured some equally important aspects of the policy process. H. Gordon Skilling, for example, contended that the totalitarian model focused too much attention on outputs (the decisions made by the Party leadership) and too little on inputs.[2] Skilling argued that groups and actors outside the formal Party leadership could make inputs (e.g., demands) that affected the political process in traditional communist systems.

This viewpoint resulted in new concern with the input side of the policy process and brought increasing attention to the competing interests and bargaining that went on prior to the formal making of decisions in the post-Stalin era. Scholars with these interests began to use group, or pluralist, models to study power and policy in communist systems—that is, by the 1970s, many Western analysts felt that increasing numbers of groups and political actors both inside and outside the Communist Party hierarchy were becoming influential in the policy process. With the decline of terror tactics following Stalin's death, the increasing complexity of social, political, and economic decisions, and the growing expertise of different sectors of society, the conditions were set for a more open, sometimes pluralistic process. Jerry F. Hough contended, for example, that these tendencies had become so prevalent that a new pluralist model of communist politics was needed.[3] Although some were critical of the group and pluralist models,[4] these newer approaches brought attention to the presence of interest group competition and to some measure, at least, of political pluralism in communist-run societies.

The introduction of this text called attention to different phases in the policy process—the setting of goals, taking action, and producing outcomes. The models of totalitarianism and pluralism help us to better understand these phases. We want to know, for example, who sets the goals and formulates policy objectives and proposals. Who makes the decisions and takes the actions? Who implements the policy and produces policy outcomes? To help answer these questions, we will now examine the policy process and the issue of economic reform in the Soviet Union, China, and Eastern Europe.

Politics, Policy Making, and Economic Reform in the USSR

When Lenin and his associates took over after the Bolshevik revolution in 1917, they were ill prepared to create and manage a socialist economy. When setting goals for the new socialist state, Lenin was guided by both Marxist ideals and the political exigencies of the moment. Believing that private ownership and capitalism were the roots of much evil, Lenin nationalized heavy industries, land, and the means of production. He and his associates hoped to rationally and comprehensively make economic policy and were willing to resort to totalitarian means to do so. Private ownership of land and industry was strictly forbidden.

However, during the 1918–21 period of civil war (the so-called war communism period), economic output fell to 20 percent of what it had been before the outbreak of World War I. The Soviet economy was in shambles. This forced the Bolshevik leaders to back away from their idealistic goals for building communism. Although large-scale industries and the banking systems remained nationalized, decisions were made to allow agriculture and small businesses to be run by private entrepreneurs. This phase of Soviet economic policy, the so-called New Economic Policy (NEP) of 1921–28, illustrated the presence of both totalitarian and pluralist incremental modes of decision making. Lenin and the Communist Party would have liked to have moved decisively in putting together a new socialist economic system. Social, economic, and political realities, however, forced them to pay attention to other groups and centers of political power in the system and move incrementally toward their goals of socialism and communism.

With Lenin's death and Stalin's assumption of power, the USSR moved far in the direction of totalitarianism. Stalin and the Communist Party leaders dominated the economic planning and policy-making processes. Agriculture was collectivized, businesses and industry were nationalized, and private labor and ownership were strictly outlawed. Communist Party planning and control were carried out through Five-Year Plans. Stalin and other Party leaders set the goals; the Party-dominated governmental organizations such as GOSPLAN, the Council of Ministers, and Supreme Soviet took action; and the various ministers and ministries were expected to produce the outcomes that would fulfill the Five-Year Plans. Although the Stalinist policy model and political system brought about the industrialization of the Soviet state, it did not do so without problems. In fact, the Stalinist system was repressive, wasteful, and inefficient.

In the post-Stalin years, leaders such as Khrushchev, Kosygin, and Brezhnev sometimes tried to address the problems of waste and inefficiency in the Stalinist command-administrative system. However, unwilling to consider all of the information, alternatives, and cost-and-benefit analyses available to them, they largely proceeded on the basis of totalitarianism to pursue the Stalinist economic model. They were unwilling to consider reform that would give workers, firms, and regions more economic autonomy, and they were loathe to reduce the

role of the Communist Party and the central government in the economic policy process. Although they attempted to control economic policy making and rationally and comprehensively proceeded on the basis of Five-Year Plans, they increasingly were bogged down in what many have called bureaucratic pluralism and its consequent incrementalism.[5]

By the 1970s, the Soviet political process was marked by a diversity of interests, which resulted in clashes and compromises among the different leaders and agencies. Under these conditions, in the words of Jerry F. Hough, incrementalism became the "hallmark of the system."[6] As a result, the Soviet system entered a period of stagnation.

What happened? How did the highly centralized, totalitarian leadership of the Soviet Union under Stalin evolve under Brezhnev into a group of political brokers who mediated the competing demands of different government and bureaucratic sectors? With the death of Joseph Stalin and the deconcentration of power that Khrushchev's rule ushered in, some political power devolved from the highest Party bodies to different bureaucratic and state organs. Although Khrushchev was an impulsive policy maker who would often take adventurous action to attain high-priority goals, his policies of liberalization and decentralization dispersed considerable autonomy and policy-relevant authority throughout the Soviet system.

Khrushchev's successors, Leonid I. Brezhnev and Aleksei N. Kosygin, moved the USSR even further in the direction of pluralism and incrementalism. Basing their leadership on a system of collective rule, these leaders provided the specialized state, Party, and scientific complexes with considerable policy-making autonomy in their fields. To avoid the loss of support that had led to Khrushchev's ouster, Brezhnev and Kosygin tried to keep their subordinates happy by giving the various departments an incremental budgetary increase each year.[7]

When Gorbachev came to power, some facets of the policy-making process began to change. Gorbachev proved to be a bold and decisive leader and wanted the system to break with the past and adopt the radical reforms embodied in glasnost and perestroika. Although he attempted to move radically, rationally, and comprehensively, many remnants of the old incrementalism remained.

It was clear by the time Gorbachev came to power in 1985 that the period of rapidly accelerating economic growth had ended and the command-type, Stalinist economic model had outlived its usefulness. The Soviet economy was now characterized by decelerating growth; although the economy was still growing, it was growing at a slower rate than before and much more slowly than the Soviet leaders desired. Under such economic conditions, it would be difficult for the Soviets to achieve their high-priority goals. Most observers believed that although the Soviet economy would not collapse, it would deteriorate even further in the future, in view of labor shortages, low productivity, and increasing energy prices. These economic pressures confronted Gorbachev with some very difficult challenges. What could be done to improve the Soviet economy?

A leading American economist outlined four alternatives that confronted the Soviet leaders in the 1980s.[8] The "conservative" alternative represented preserving and carrying on into the future the existing economic system with minor incremental changes. The "reactionary" approach represented a return to the highly disciplined economic system of the Stalinist period. This alternative would place a high priority on discipline and order and mean an even greater assertion of centralized CPSU control of the economy. The "liberal" alternative would

maintain traditional planning methods while liberalizing restrictions on private initiative and competition. Finally, the "radical" approach would represent the most significant change and emphasize decentralization of planning and management and utilize elements of private enterprise and competition.

Although considerable evidence suggested that fundamental changes—that is, the liberal or radical approaches—were required to right the Soviet economy, Brezhnev and Kosygin opted for the conservative alternative. The choices made and changes pursued in the Soviet Union under their leadership tended to be incremental and ad hoc rather than comprehensive and rational. Why was this so? Berliner argued that it was because they let short-term politics rather than long-term economics dictate their choices.[9] The pre-Gorbachev leaders opted for the conservative strategy because it would not rock the boat and was in line with their short-term political interests. Scientific, rational analysis might have suggested radical solutions, but short-run political considerations in the USSR ruled them out.

When Gorbachev entered office in 1985, some of this began to change. The Soviet economy required innovative and fundamental reform. Gorbachev and his associates began to move in the direction of liberal and even radical reform. Although most agreed that such reforms were necessary, they faced a fundamental dilemma in how to proceed. They could use totalitarian methods and try to force through radical reform. If they did so, however, they could be seen as dictators, a fact that would be in conflict with their goals of glasnost and democratization. Furthermore, they would risk losing both the ideas and the involvement of the people, on which economic reform ultimately depended.

On the other hand, Gorbachev and his associates could move more democratically and cautiously, step by step, in line with the principles of pluralism. This alternative also had costs. Allowing full debate and democratic pluralism could result in deadlock and delay. This would provide time for the opposition to organize. The reforms could become mired in bureaucratic pluralism. The "muddling through" and stagnation so prevalent during the Brezhnev years could have continued under Gorbachev as well.

The Gorbachev approach has turned out to be a complex blend of totalitarianism and pluralism. When Gorbachev took office, he realized that to reform the economy and move the Soviet Union forward, he would need the support of the people, including those at the top of the Party hierarchy who made the decisions, those in the bureaucracy who implemented the reforms, and those in the factories and on the farms who carried them out.

Gorbachev began by giving attention to all of these groups. He brought reformers into the highest Party and governmental bodies and got rid of the "deadwood" that was standing in the way of restructuring and reform. He promoted economists and advisers who shared his visions of glasnost, perestroika, and democratization and got rid of those who resisted. He was willing to use totalitarian tactics to form his new team and shape up the stagnant Soviet society.

Gorbachev also took his reform program and ideas for change to the people. Adroitly using the power of his personality and the Soviet media, he sought to convince the Soviet people that change was in their interests. He tried to persuade them to support perestroika rather than to become cynical and take to the streets when progress seemed remote or when prices had to be raised. He told them to work hard and be patient. He had to convince students and pensioners, intellectuals and workers, that perestroika and economic reform would be in their interests and that their patience, sacrifice, hard work, and cooperation was vital. He appealed to tradition, patriotism, and pride.

While Gorbachev was assembling his team and launching the ideas of perestroika and change in 1985–86, relatively little reform was actually taking place. This was the goal-setting stage and an opportunity for Gorbachev to think through and illuminate his policy objectives. Skillfully using Party meetings and organized media campaigns, Gorbachev sought to mold support for the inevitable challenges that radical change would encounter.

In the winter of 1986–87, the Gorbachev reformers began to move ahead, to translate their goals into action. After having decided on a series of radical reforms introducing private labor and enterprise, independent cooperatives, greater autonomy for enterprises, and joint ventures and expanded economic relations with the West, Gorbachev went to the critical Party and governmental organizations to garner their support. The Central Committee of the CPSU ratified much of what Gorbachev and the reformers in the Politburo wanted in the way of economic reform. As you will recall from the chapter on the Communist Party, the Central Committee traditionally has had the power to elect and dismiss the Party leader, in this case, Secretary Gorbachev. Nikita Khrushchev and Party leaders in other communist states had been ousted when they lost the support of the Central Committee. In the mid- and late 1980s, many wondered if this would also be the fate of Gorbachev and his reform program.

Gorbachev used the power of his leadership to bring reformers into the Central Committee, demoting those who were ambivalent or opposed. He also used his strength in the Central Committee to bring his supporters into the Politburo and Secretariat. He promoted his close adviser, Aleksander Yakolev, to the Secretariat in 1986 and to full Politburo membership in 1987. He made his close friend Eduard Shevardnadze a full member of the Politburo and Foreign Minister in July 1985. Without the support of these and other high Party leaders, Gorbachev's radical reform program would have had little chance for success.

During the 1985–90 period, Gorbachev proved to be highly skilled and successful in consolidating his power and building his team in the key Party and governmental bodies. Without such support, he would have become increasingly vulnerable to all of the pluralistic forces that had a stake in the reform process. If the Party leadership did not move decisively to push the reform program forward, there was always the danger of becoming mired in the excessive bureaucratic pluralism and incrementalism of the Brezhnev period.

It should be noted here that although Gorbachev was adept, he was unable to win the unqualified support of all who were at the top of the Party and government organizations. Many observers saw Yegor Ligachev as a conservative reformer and opposed to some of Gorbachev's radical initiatives. Others called attention to the opposition of Vladimir Shcherbitsky, longtime Politburo member and Party chief of the Ukrainian Communist Party, and to Andrei Gromyko, longtime Foreign Minister and fellow Politburo member. Gorbachev adroitly dealt with these challenges. Gromyko retired quietly from the Politburo and active political life in 1988; Ligachev was reassigned the portfolio for Soviet agriculture which, in view of its great problems, was a no-win situation and would surely keep him too busy, Gorbachev hoped, to interfere with his reform program. Shcherbitsky was forced to resign.

However, a program as bold and far reaching as perestroika cannot be introduced without generating opposition within a conservative, traditional society like the USSR. In January 1988, Gorbachev himself called attention to the presence of this opposition by noting criticism from the left and right. He went on to note that voices from the right were saying that he was undermining the foundations of socialism. One of those voices came from the editor and pages of *Sovetskaia Rossia*. At a January 1988 meeting between Gorbachev and Soviet media representatives, the editor V. Chikin warned Gorbachev that the radical reforms could lead to the resumption of capitalism and "ideological homelessness."[10] Then in March 1988, a dramatic page-long article appeared in *Sovetskaia Rossia*. Supposedly written by a Leningrad chemistry teacher, Nina Andreeva, the article defended the honor of Stalin and went on to criticize much of the Gorbachev reform program, including glasnost, perestroika and democratization. Various theories abounded about the motivations behind the article, including one that linked it to Politburo conservative Ligachev.

The editorial signified the presence of a troublesome conservative coalition whose highest-ranking member in the late 1980s was Ligachev. This coalition included Party functionaries, some military and bureaucratic officials, writers, journalists, and intellectuals who remained wedded to more traditional Soviet policies. Some opposed perestroika and the reform program for philosophical reasons, and many feared it because of its implications for their personal self-interests. Having risen to comfortable positions and salaries under the old system, many saw a dimunition of their power and, in some cases, the loss of their jobs with the advent of the Gorbachev reform program.

This conservative coalition also commanded powerful support from large sectors of the working class. Preferring the predictability and stability of the stagnant past, many resented the new freedoms of expression, the outbreak

Gorbachev faced opposition from both the political right and left in the late 1980s. Here he calms a group of deputies from the Soviet Congress during the winter session of 1989.

of ethnic nationalism, and the growing entrepreneurship in Soviet society. Seeing important self-interests in jeopardy, members of the conservative coalition worked in various ways to obstruct the radical reform programs.

Although some individuals and groups thought Gorbachev and the reformers were going too far and too fast, others felt they were not going fast enough. Politburo member Boris Yeltsin criticized Gorbachev and his colleagues for these reasons and was dropped from the Politburo. This did not silence Yeltsin, as he successfully ran for the Soviet parliament and continued to criticize the timidity and slow pace of Gorbachev's reforms. Later, he was voted into an even higher office, becoming President of the Russian republic in 1990. Others, for example, in the Baltic republics of Estonia, Latvia, and Lithuania, demanded greater reform and wanted the central government to provide them far more power over their own affairs.

Both from within and outside of the Party, those who criticized Gorbachev's economic reforms as not going far enough to stimulate Soviet economic recovery increased their calls for the Soviet leader to radicalize his program in early 1990. The increased pressure on Gorbachev came as a result of both the persistent evidence that perestroika was not working fast enough to improve the Soviet standard of living, and the successful adoption of shock economic programs by several of the reformed noncommunist governments of Eastern Europe. Shock treatment advocates argued that only a rapid transformation toward the free market could cure the popular discontent within the Soviet Union and keep the country together in the face of growing centrifugal nationalist forces.

Responding to the demands for adoption of economic shock measures by the Soviet Union, in early 1990, Gorbachev dispatched Leonid I. Abalkin, Deputy Prime Minister, and a team of economic specialists to draft an economic program that might stimulate accelerated Soviet economic growth through free market measures. At a meeting of the Presidential Council in April 1990, the shock program was presented by Abalkin to Gorbachev. Gorbachev flatly rejected it, later stating:

> Let market conditions be put in place everywhere. Let's have free enterprise and give the green light to all forms of ownership, private ownership. Let everything be private. Let us sell the land, everything. I cannot support such ideas, no matter how decisive and revolutionary they might appear. These are irresponsible ideas, irresponsible.[11]

The reasons for Gorbachev's rejection of a shock economic program for the Soviet Union appear to have been more related to politics than a conviction by the Soviet leader that such

171

measures would not work. Gorbachev felt that by adopting a shock program he would lose the middle ground between left and right in Soviet politics that he so cherished. Any further destabilization and deterioration of the Soviet standard of living caused by radicalized reform efforts might provide ammunition for Party conservatives in an effort to dislodge Gorbachev from power. The conservatives might possibly point to the economic upheaval of a shock program as a harebrained scheme. Having recognized these factors, Gorbachev apparently saw any further radicalization of perestroika as simply too great a risk to take at the time.

In addition to those in the Party, many in the bureaucracy felt that Gorbachev was going too far in some areas and not far enough in others. Many were uneasy about the impact of perestroika on their jobs. In the fall of 1988, Gorbachev announced that 700,000 ministry jobs would be cut and that at some industrial enterprises and collective farms, half of the managerial positions would be abolished. Gorbachev also announced that 40 percent of Party secretaries at the primary level had been voted out of office and 60 percent of Party leaders on the shopfloor were being replaced. It was clear that Gorbachev and the reformers were taking actions that would affect people's careers and lives. Resistance was inevitable.

As Gorbachev's reform programs were promulgated, it became increasingly clear to Soviet workers that perestroika was going to raise the expectations and standards placed on them by the Party and state. At the same time, perestroika did not seem to be allowing them to buy more or to be raising their standard of living. Many workers wondered what good perestroika was if it meant they had to work harder and receive fewer benefits. As a result of worker concern, organizations like trade unions took a great deal of interest in Gorbachev's initiatives. Although

free and independent trade unions like those we know in the West, or like Solidarity in Poland, did not exist in the Soviet Union, "official" state unions became more outspoken during the late 1980s and less obedient to the powers that be in the Soviet Union. In the era of glasnost, official unions became genuinely concerned with the Soviet workers they represented and less afraid to speak out and protect their interests.

During the summer and fall of 1989, thousands of Soviet coalminers expressed their displeasure with perestroika by bypassing official unions altogether and organizing a series of wildcat strikes. For several months, informal groups of miners walked off their jobs in various regions of the country, from the Ural Mountains and Siberia to the Ukraine and the Donetsk Basin. The miners' actions triggered a national economic crisis, which had to be addressed by Gorbachev and other key Soviet leaders. Workers striking in a supposed workers' state was something new for Soviet leaders. Gorbachev, his associates, and the miners reached a compromise, which resulted in the striking miners returning to work in exchange for concessions by the Soviet state. Violence and severe economic hardship largely were averted in the 1989 labor unrest. Both Party and state leaders throughout the Soviet Union learned, however, that future labor crises loomed on the horizon if perestroika did not start improving the economic situation and raising the living standard. The power of organized labor and strikes was rediscovered by Soviet workers in 1989 after years of repression and subserviency.

Gorbachev and the reformers also had to contend with powerful institutional groups like the Soviet military. Although the military leaders recognized that a strong economy was vital to maintaining a strong defense and were therefore inclined to support reforms that would strengthen the military, they were loathe to accept reformist policies that were likely to weaken or take resources away from the military sector. When Secretary Gorbachev announced military cuts late in the 1980s, including a unilateral cutback in Soviet military spending, he created considerable unease and resistance in the military. Groups like these lobbied hard to protect their share of the allocation of Soviet resources.

A Soviet economist described the complex planning and decision-making process surrounding Gorbachev's reforms as "bargaining between enterprises and ministries over . . . the allocation of resources" and noted that "the bureaucratization of the economy has taken on dangerous proportions."[12] Enterprises, ministries, and other pressure groups forcefully articulated their interests in a variety of ways to see their policy preferences served. Although Gorbachev and the reformers wanted to proceed decisively to do what they considered best for the country, various centers of power like the conservative political and bureaucratic opposition groups, the trade unions, the military, and so forth worked hard to see their interests served. In the age of glasnost and democratization, it was difficult for Gorbachev and his associates to avoid the pluralistic pressures and the sort of incrementalism that could stymie the reform program.

Perhaps the most powerful force driving the Soviet reformers in the direction of incrementalism was the sheer complexity of economic reform itself. With no master plan, Gorbachev and the reformers were experimenting without knowing what would ensure successful economic reform. Reality meant that they never had the time or information to consider all of the alternatives, costs and benefits, and likely outcomes. Gorbachev often expressed his frustrations about this reality. On the one hand, he wanted to move quickly and decisively and

introduce comprehensive reforms. On the other hand, he recognized the importance of what he called a "socialist pluralism of opinions," where people would speak out for what they thought was best.

When examining the setting of goals and the taking of actions surrounding economic reform in the Soviet Union, the political leadership in the form of Mikhail Gorbachev was a critical factor. Gorbachev and his associates led the reform movement. They wanted to pursue rational, decisive, and comprehensive reform. However, because of the complexity of the reform process and the plurality of opinions about what should be done, the Soviet reformers were often driven in the direction of incrementalism. This was not their preference, of course, because they wanted to reform the Soviet economy according to rational and comprehensive principles.

When Gorbachev proposed reform of the Soviet political system in the late 1980s, one had the impression that he was reacting to this fundamental dilemma, that is, how to promote rational, comprehensive decision making and yet allow the socialist pluralism of opinion and democratization that every modern society needs. The political reform proposals set forth during the period suggested that Gorbachev and his associates favored movement toward a bifurcated, two-tiered political system. On the top tier were Gorbachev and the ruling elite, who were to maintain strategic control of overall policy. On the second tier was the plurality of opinions—from groups, ministries, provincial and local governments, and informal groups—involved in a more democratic, competitive struggle over the allocation of Soviet resources. Such a political system was intended to help reconcile the forces of totalitarianism and pluralism very much present in contemporary Soviet politics and policy making.

Politics, Policy Making, and Economic Reform in China

The Chinese politics surrounding economic policy making and reform show both similarities to and differences from the Soviet case. Mao adopted important features of the Stalinist political and economic system. Like Stalin, Mao was the critical actor in Chinese economic policy making for decades. He played a major role in setting goals, initiating action, and producing outcomes. Mao fit the mold of the totalitarian leader. Michel Oksenberg describes Mao in the following terms:

> Mao was, to the end of his life, a revolutionary and a totalitarian ruler. He believed the only way to transform China was rapidly, violently, comprehensively; its elites and institutions would have to undergo continual transformation. China's problems were so vast that efforts to attain peaceful, gradual change would be lost in the morass of bureaucracy. In his view, to transform China required vision and extraordinary confidence that a politically involved Chinese populace—given no respite to cultivate individually-determined pursuits—could overcome their common plight of poverty and weakness. To unleash the masses in all their fury required leaders capable of interacting directly with the social forces in society unmediated by intervening bureaucracies. Mao saw institutions such as the Party, government, or army as having little intrinsic value. They were to be used instrumentally, as divisions in war, their credibility and authority expended in his larger efforts to make China a strong, prosperous, socialist China.[13]

In reality, however, Mao neither held total control nor was able to be completely rational

and comprehensive in the making of economic policy for China. Oksenberg goes on in his article to tell us that although Mao structured the Chinese political system to allow himself to intervene according to his idiosyncratic impulses, competing factional groupings had considerable influence on him. Oksenberg also suggests that the evolution of domestic policy choices was not based on careful analysis of the alternatives but more frequently on personal preferences and political exigencies.

Using case studies of various policy issues, we can see various blends of totalitarianism and pluralism at work in Maoist China. Examining five policy issues in China during Mao's reign—the Twelve-Year Agricultural Program, administrative decentralization, the commune movement, the Socialist Education Campaign, and the ideological rectification campaign—Parris H. Chang examined how policy was made and who was making it in the 1950s and 1960s.[14] Chang found a variety of important actors in the decision-making process in addition to Mao. Other actors included the Chinese Communist Party (CCP) Politburo; the CCP Standing Committee; the Party's Central Committee; Party officials at the provincial and local levels; the People's Liberation Army (PLA); the bureaucracy; and extraparty forces, such as the Red Guard and revolutionary rebels. The actors involved varied according to the policy area. For example, Chang noted that those institutions involved in setting goals, taking action, and producing outcomes in the area of rural policies included at the national level the Ministry of Agriculture; the Agricultural and Forestry Staff Office; the CCP Central Committee Rural Work Department; and the CCP Secretariat, Politburo, and Central Committee.[15]

How, then, was policy made in Mao's China? Chang answers this question by contending that:

Policy in Communist China was not made by a few leaders alone; actors possessing different political resources participated, directly or indirectly in each stage of the policymaking process and affected in a variety of ways, the decision-output of the regime.[16]

At the same time, Chang cautions, it is necessary to recognize the enormous power wielded by Mao. When Mao was most active—for example, during the second half of the 1950s—the policy-making process was more personalized and totalitarian. Mao used other institutions and actors to initiate, accept, and carry out the policies he preferred. For example, when other Party leaders favored a "go-slow" approach toward collectivization of agriculture in 1955, Mao vehemently argued for stepping up the tempo in a secret speech to provincial Party secretaries. By skillfully using others, Mao was able to overcome the go-slow opposition and launch an intense nationwide campaign to accelerate agricultural collectivization.[17]

The policy-making process became more open and less totalitarian in the post-Mao period. In the early 1980s, Oksenberg and Bush described China as having moved from "revolutionary totalitarianism" to "reformist authoritarianism."[18] They saw the Maoist "totalitarian revolutionaries" as having attempted a rapid, violent, and comprehensive transformation of China. In contrast, the "authoritarian reformers" of the 1980s were committed to more gradual and peaceful change within a more stable political framework. Although Deng, Zhao, and other reformers remained authoritarian and tolerated no organized opposition to their rule, they adhered to a more open, institutionalized form of collective rule. Decision making was more likely to involve the relevant Party and governmental bodies and to be based upon compromise and consensus. The authoritarian

reformers shifted the policy-making process away from Maoist totalitarianism to a more institutionalized process of governing through the Party and governmental bureacracies.

Oksenberg argues that whereas Mao was committed to revolutionary change, Deng was committed to reform. Whereas Mao was a totalitarian committed to a dialectic path of development, Deng was an authoritarian who sought to pursue a steady, persistent course. Whereas Mao sought to bypass the bureacracy, Deng sought to restore it.[19] Overall, Deng's major objective was to improve the standard of living of the populace. This required the setting of new goals and policies to achieve the desired outcomes.

Not everyone supported Deng's reformist ideas in the post-Mao period. With the death of Mao in 1976 and the ouster of the Maoist faction known as the Gang of Four, the new leaders soon polarized into two camps and held quite different goals to guide future Chinese policy. The traditional faction led by Mao's heir apparent, CCP Chairman Hua Guofeng, was composed of those who gained ascendancy under Mao's patronage. This faction favored continuity and opposed the comprehensive and radical reforms desired by Deng Xiaoping. The reformist faction, led by Deng and his more pragmatic associates, wanted to discard the Maoist model and implement a fundamental economic restructuring.

To build political support for their new goals, Deng and his cohorts initiated a "de-Maoification" campaign to rid Chinese society of its ideological inhibitions and lay the foundation for their new economic plans. The prelude to the campaign was a nationwide debate orchestrated by Deng and his faction on the theme "practice is the sole criterion of truth." Through such debates, this reformist faction wanted to convince the Chinese people that what works in practice, rather than Maoist ideology, ought to be the criterion guiding Chinese economic policy. The Deng faction won the struggle, and Hua and the traditionalists lost their positions of power in the early 1980s. Once in a dominant position, the reform faction of Deng Xiaoping, Zhao Ziyang, and the new Party leader Hu Yaobang announced the end of Maoism, with its emphasis on collectivism and self-reliance, and spelled out their new goals for building the Chinese economy. These goals were to reduce centralized control, emphasize the market mechanism, and open the Chinese economy to the world.

Although the reformers were now in power, there was continuing controversy within the leadership over such issues as the possible dismantling of central planning and state ownership and whether China should strive to become a full-fledged market economy. The more radical wing of the reformers argued for fundamental and far-reaching reforms, including significant constraints on centralized control and an expansion of market forces. The most zealous champions of radical reform were Deng's two protegés, Hu Yaobang and Zhao Ziyang. Hu had taken over the Party leadership and Zhao the governmental premiership from the defeated Hua Guofeng. This duo established their credentials as the primary goal setters and policy actors in the post-Mao reform period. These radical reformers spent the early 1980s outlining their plans for fundamental reform, a process referred to as "the destruction of the old and the establishment of the new."

Soon pitted against this more radical wing of reformers were a group of more conservative reformers in the Politburo and Central Committee. The leader of this faction was Chen Yun, a veteran leader and former Party vice-chairman whose forte was economic management and policy. In the 1950s, Chen figured prominently as China's premier economist. He was demoted during the Great Leap Forward because he was at variance with Mao and skeptical of his economic fanaticism. During the Cultural Revolution, he was for a time on the verge of being exiled by the Red Guards for his dissent from Maoist economics. Ironically, he emerged in the 1980s as the standard-bearer of economic conservatism.

Chen, other ranking leaders, and Party dignitaries were averse to the far-reaching economic changes proposed by the more radical reformers and wanted to safeguard the primacy of central planning and state ownership. Market mechanisms, they argued, should only serve as a supplement to the socialist economy. These more conservative and radical protagonists of post-Mao politics would be locked in a fierce fight throughout the 1980s over the orientation of economic reform.

Similar to Gorbachev in the Soviet Union, Deng Xiaoping played a critical role in the reform process by maintaining the middle ground and arbitrating disputes between the two competing reform factions. By staying above the fray, Deng was able to protect the power he had achieved in his victory over the Maoist traditionalists. He was the supreme leader during the reform period in China. Sometimes playing the role of dictator, sometimes calling for greater democracy, Deng frequently utilized his considerable political skills and power to manage political change and the policy process in China.

During the early 1980s, top priority was given to rural reform, the centerpiece of which was the introduction of the production responsibility system. The new policy stipulated that farmland and other means of production be allocated to households on a contractual basis, and that households supercede production teams and communes as the key economic unit in the countryside. This reform was tantamount to the decollectivization and privatization of Chinese agriculture.[20] Concurrent with rural reform in the early 1980s was experimentation with reforms in other sectors. The regime authorized some pilot schemes of enterprise autonomy in preparation for the more radical reforms to follow. However, even such a limited first step upset some hardliners. The emerging trends of social stratification and even polarization provided an impetus for expanding a campaign against "spiritual pollution." The campaign was launched to combat the Western ideology which was perceived by some Communist Party officials as getting a foothold in China and diluting Marxism and the Chinese cultural heritage. Disgruntled Communist Party cadres took advantage of this opportunity to vent their wrath and to obstruct the reform.

In spite of all this, rural reform turned out to be a success. Zhao Ziyang and Hu Yaobang were able to override the more conservative opposition. In their euphoria over success in the rural reform, the radical reformers announced in 1984 at the Third Plenum of the Twelfth Party Central Committee a broader industrial reform package encompassing enterprise autonomy, a tax-for-profit system, price reforms, expanded wage incentives, and a variety of other reform measures. It was evident from the blueprint that the radical coalition envisioned a more thorough reform in lieu of the previous piecemeal experimentation in the agricultural sector. If implemented in its entirety, this reform package would have meant the virtual decimation of the socialist economic system. Although the radical reformers still paid lip service to socialism, they could not allay the fear and opposition of conservatives headed by Chen Yun and Peng Zhen. Initially, Chen and the conservatives acquiesced primarily because success in rural reform had given the more radical reformers much leverage in influencing and

determining the orientation of the broader economic reform. They bided their time, and when the ill-designed and ill-fated broader reform program ran into trouble, they pounced on the radicals' mistakes and tried to scuttle the reform program.

From the outset, the more conservative reformers had serious reservations about radical economic reforms and were reluctant to give them their full support. Their opposition to and obstruction of extensive, rapid economic reform were not only ideologically and politically motivated but also associated with concerns for its social, economic, and cultural implications. Most of the conservatives were avowed communists who had strived all their lives to build a communist society. The economic reforms challenged many of the fundamental premises of Marxism that they had espoused. In addition, the institutional change called for in the economic reforms entailed the delegation of power to their subordinates and the recruitment and cooptation of new elements, which they considered an erosion of Party organization and authority.

Furthermore, to the conservatives, the idea of a market economy was akin to restoring capitalism. They saw the relaxation of state controls and price deregulation as engendering rife corruption, runaway inflation, and social stratification and polarization, which, in turn, fueled popular alienation and cynicism. They also saw the influx of "decadent" Western culture as a consequence of the radical reformers' open-door policy. Western culture, they argued, was polluting the minds of the people and causing a drastic increase in the incidence of crimes and other social evils. In the conservatives' opinion, economic reform was opening Pandora's box.

Criticism of the radical reformers also came from middle- and lower-level cadres and ordinary citizens. Economic reform threatened the role of the Chinese cadre corps. It threatened their ability to maintain their privileged positions because of the new emphasis on merit and the abolition of life tenure in Party positions. When local and regional leaders found the reform policies unpalatable, they criticized or tried to boycott or circumvent them. They argued laxity in discipline and growing regionalism had reached alarming proportions and raised the specter of the reemergence of fiefdoms prevalent during the turbulent precommunist period of warlordism.

The radical reform program of the 1980s also generated the opposition of many who were not materially benefiting from the reforms. In the course of the economic reforms, there were some who were well connected or blessed with business acumen who took advantage of the newly available opportunities for entrepreneurship and made a considerable amount of money. However, growing disparities in incomes and standards of living made many ordinary people feel deprived and therefore resentful of the reforms. Economic reform in the 1980s also brought an end to guaranteed employment, a system sarcastically referred to as the "iron rice bowl." It brought to an end the practice of equal wage remuneration irrespective of the significance of one's work contributions. As a result, less diligent and competitive personnel found their former positions and security threatened. The danger of unemployment, which never existed under Maoist communism, now loomed large. It goes without saying that many Chinese people had misgivings about the new reforms. Some of them preferred the Maoist period, when a secure livelihood was guaranteed despite the fact that many things were in short supply.

Economic policy making and the reform process were affected by a variety of political forces. For example, to justify and legitimize their goals and preferred policy actions, both the competing factions invoked the powers of ideology. Each side had at its disposal a brain trust composed of writers, researchers, and scholars steeped in Marxist and non-Marxist theories. Establishment theoreticians subscribing to orthodox economic doctrine congregated under the banner of conservatism, whereas the newly emergent, more Western oriented economic thinkers gravitated toward the radical reformers' camp. Writers in both camps couched their articles in the Marxist political jargon so as to give weight to their arguments, but some reform-minded researchers even incorporated non-Marxist theories and ideas into their writings.

The promotion, demotion, and recruitment of Party and government officials were utilized to influence the reform process. Expansion of factional representation and its reduction of the adversary in the various decision-making bodies was highly contested and served the purpose of increasing leverage in the competition for power. Appointment or dismissal of key figures like Hu Yaobang, Li Peng, and Deng Liqun had far-reaching repercussions. The proponents and opponents of reform also used demonstrations, protests, work stoppages and slowdowns to influence the policy process. Although we are unable to say that leaders in the competing camps instigated or abetted these activities, their policies often benefited and suffered from such events.

The reform process was also affected by nonpolitical forces. Soon after the inception of the urban reform, the Chinese economy encountered a number of difficulties. Starting in 1984, problems like uncontrolled economic growth; excessive increase in capital goods investment, credit, and consumption; price hikes; inflation; and depletion of foreign exchange reserves began to gain saliency. This development provided ammunition for the conservatives, who called attention to the potential costs of full-scale reform and pressed for modifications to the existing reform program. Due to opposition and economic difficulties, the radical reformers were forced to begin pulling back a bit in the mid-1980s.

A significant sign of conservative resistance and backlash was the removal of the reformer Hu Yaobang from the Party leadership in January 1987. Hu continually criticized and demeaned Mao's theoretical contributions to socialism while praising Western democratic theorists and freedoms. Hu's reformist inclinations had gone too far for the conservatives to accept. Finally, the Party conservatives gained enough strength to oust him, although they were forced to appoint another reformer, Zhao Ziyang, to replace him.

Another sign of conservative backlash and the struggle for control over Chinese economic policy during this period was the changing political slogans. For example, contrary to the radical reformers' exhortation in the early 1980s that "to get rich is glorious," the so-called No. 1 Directive of the 1987 Central Committee preached the "superiority of socialism" over capitalism and deemphasized material incentives to promote production. Attempting to redefine the goals of Chinese economic policy, the conservative faction attacked the threat of "bourgeois liberalization" and reemphasized more orthodox economic principles.

Although Zhao and the radicals had to consent to Hu's ouster as a way of placating the conservatives, they refused to compromise on the larger issues of economic reform. However, the reform program had brought unintended consequences and more ammunition for the conservative faction. Prices were soaring, and budgetary and trade deficits were on the rise. Government mints were operating at full capacity, and for the first time since the early period of Chinese hyperinflation in the late 1940s, new large-denomination bank notes went into circulation. Zhao Ziyang and the radical reformers diagnosed the problem as the inadequacy of reform. They remained committed to further reform and advocated stopping the practice of putting ceilings on the prices of thousands of commodities so that market mechanisms could play a larger role in the distribution of goods and services.

The freeing of prices from centralized control exacerbated the already very serious problems of inflation and corruption. China's financial system fell into disarray in the late 1980s. The inflation rate grew by leaps and bounds, jumping to 50 percent in 1988. The supply of goods faltered, and staple foods like meat, eggs, sugar, cooking oil, and even salt had to be rationed.

But Party leader Zhao and the radical reformers wanted to stay the course. They insisted that the decontrol of the pricing system would produce the desired effect in due course. At a succession of Politburo conferences held from June to September 1988, Zhao tried to enlist support for his ambitious price reform. Concerned by the magnitude of the crisis, even his followers became noncommittal, whereas his critics in the Politburo castigated him for his rashness in pushing for radical price reforms. There were heated debates at these meetings, but the conservatives overruled all of Zhao's proposals. Finally, Deng himself began to waver and indicated his readiness to scale back the bold restructuring. At the Third Plenum of the Thirteenth Central Committee held in late September 1988, the Party leadership decided to put a two-year moratorium on the radical reform program. In the late 1980s, much of Zhao's economic decision-making power devolved on Li Peng and Yao Yilin, who called for a slowdown of the reform. Though Zhao retained his General Secretaryship for the time being, his authority on economic issues had significantly declined.

In 1988–89, Li and Yao presided over a retrenchment and austerity program, with emphasis on controlling consumer demand, curbing inflation, doing away with economic overheating, and slowing down overly rapid industrial growth. The reversal was a heavy blow to Zhao and his radical reform program. Although Zhao and the radical group had not yet conceded defeat and were still trying to pursue their bold economic reforms, there was considerable uncertainty as China approached the end of the decade.

The events in Tiananmen Square of May and June 1989 brought about the defeat of the radical

Students put up a poster at Beijing University in April 1989 announcing support for a class boycott showing opposition to Chinese government policies.

reform faction. Zhao Ziyang was closely associated with the students' protest movement, and when Deng Xiaoping decided to crush the democratization movement, Zhao was ousted. The conservative hardliner Li Peng assumed control, and the course of radical reform and the possibility of growing pluralism in China suffered a major setback.

In summary, the Chinese policy process was the arena of intense competition between the conservative and radical reformers in the 1980s. The conservative faction approached the reform process cautiously and set limits on the extent and speed of the reform. The radical reformers, on the other hand, wanted to advance the reform and strove to do so rapidly and on all possible fronts. The continuing factional competition in the 1980s pushed China through periods of reform and retrenchment, or what some have referred to as a cyclical, experimental pattern of Chinese reform.[21] China had no comprehensive plan and therefore was forced to experiment. Harding quotes Deng Xiaoping as saying, "We are engaged in an experiment. For us, [reform] is something new, and we have to grope to find our way."[22]

Harding argued that the 1980s brought a reduction in the scope and role of the Chinese state and an increase in popular participation.[23] He also observed, however, that all of the opportunities for political participation were limited. When it came to reform, restrictions remained on what could be said and who could say it. Accordingly, the debate over Chinese economic reform primarily took place among elites and within Party and state organs. Although the process was not one of complete totalitarianism, neither was it one of democratic pluralism.

However, the Tiananmen Square massacre in 1989 signaled a return to more totalitarian rule in China. The Party leaders, including Deng

Xiaoping, were frightened by both the student movement in China and the revolutionary changes in Eastern Europe. Their response was to protect communism through repression and a return to more dictatorial rule. By 1990, China was clearly out of step with the political change that had come to Eastern Europe and the Soviet Union.

Politics and Economic Reform in Eastern Europe

As a result of the export by the Red Army of the traditional Soviet communist political system to many of the Second World states of Eastern Europe, and the indigenous rise of such traditional systems in Yugoslavia and Albania, Stalin's totalitarian command-administrative economic model was largely copied and implemented in the East European states after World War II. At that time, the East European leaders took strides to nationalize industry; collectivize agriculture; develop and implement five-year production and distribution plans; set and subsidize fixed prices; achieve complete employment of the work force through the assignment of individual citizens to specific jobs; and insulate their domestic economies from the free markets of the West via inconvertible currencies and inconsequential, bartered foreign trade.

The original Eastern European version of the totalitarian command-administrative model was virtually identical to the Soviet prototype, in that the economy was controlled almost exclusively from the center. The central planning ministries, under directions from the Party hierarchy, controlled all aspects of the economy. Enterprises and the individual workers were merely supposed to carry out the orders coming from the center; they were not to make their own economic decisions.

Many of the problems associated with the command-administrative economic model that arose in the Soviet Union in the post-war period also became evident in Eastern Europe. Irrational pricing, supply bottlenecks, overemphasis on heavy industrial production, quota-induced production of inferior and useless goods, excessive autarchy, and worker apathy all took their toll on the economies of the communist states of Eastern Europe.

The orthodox command-administrative economic model did not remain intact in Eastern Europe for very long after its introduction. For a variety of factors, both economic and political, Eastern European leaders attempted to modify and reform the traditional Stalinist model. Yugoslavia was the first communist state to do so. In 1948, Stalin expelled Yugoslavia from the Cominform. This action isolated Yugoslavia from the rest of the Eastern European communist states and their economic resources. Without economic assistance from the Soviet Union, in particular, the Yugoslav economy faced a grave crisis in the late 1940s. To receive economic help from the West, the Yugoslav leadership had to moderate their totalitarian decision making. Part of this moderation involved reform of the Stalinist economic model that Tito and the other Yugoslav communists had advocated before their dismissal from the Cominform.

The Yugoslav leadership reformed their economic system by introducing principles of self-management. Under self-management, instead of the workers and managers of individual enterprises being solely directed by central planners, they were allowed a larger say in what and how much they had to produce. The workers and managers were to some extent given control over the operation of their enterprises.

By introducing self-management reforms and including new actors in the process, the Yugoslav communists served to pluralize state economic decision making. They did so in hopes of jump-starting worker incentives by giving them a measure of control over their own destiny and in hopes of appeasing free-market advocates in the West who refused to sponsor assistance to the isolated communist state unless they backed away from economic totalitarianism. It was believed in Belgrade that adoption of self-management reforms would lead to economic recovery and would prevent civil unrest.

Although the other communist states of Eastern Europe ignored the process of reform in Yugoslavia while Stalin was alive, once the dictator was dead and his policies had been criticized by Khrushchev, other Eastern European communist leaders took a closer look at the advantages economic reform could offer them and their states.

After Gomulka had achieved power in Poland in 1956, he initiated decentralizing economic reforms in that country. Gomulka was a Polish nationalist, and by pluralizing decision making and distancing his economic policies from Moscow, he sought increased legitimation for his regime in the eyes of the Polish people. He thought by developing a Polish brand of socialism he could escape the puppet label attached to so many of the communist leaders in Eastern Europe and win support and assistance from the West. A similar rationale served as the basis for economic reforms in Czechoslovakia in the late 1960s under Alexander Dubcek.

In Janos Kadar's Hungary, the New Economic Mechanism, a decentralizing and liberalizing economic reform program, was introduced in the late 1960s to pacify a populace that had suffered through the brutal suppression in 1956 of the Hungarian Revolution by Soviet armed forces. For a brief moment in Hungary in 1956, the traditional communist political system had been overthrown. When Kadar was put in power by the Soviets, he had little if any le-

gitimacy in the eyes of the Hungarian people. When the Prague Spring in Czechoslovakia got out of hand in 1968, Kadar recognized that such unrest and antagonism of Moscow could erupt in Hungary as well. The New Economic Mechanism was designed to prevent such an occurrence by creating a better standard of living for the Hungarians than was enjoyed by their communist brethren.

The reforms undertaken by Second World states in Eastern Europe to traditional Stalinist economic systems during the Cold War can best be described as attempts to develop hybrid economic systems combining elements of both capitalism and socialism, pluralism and totalitarianism, market and command-type economic systems.

The resulting "market socialism" economic systems of communist Eastern Europe allowed for some private ownership of property, some decentralization of economic decision making to the firm and managerial level, some increased emphasis on the production of consumer goods and services, and some wage differentiation among workers. At the same time, however, price setting, state firm monopolies, centrally planned distribution, inconvertible currencies, and bureaucratic oversight and intrusion continued unchanged. State firms did not have to face competition or bankruptcy; central planners still set overall, if not micro-, policy; and workers and farmers still had little incentive for hard work because personal rewards from the system were miniscule.

By the late 1980s, the economic stagnation and malaise that the people of Eastern Europe had suffered through under both orthodox and market socialism contributed to the overthrow of traditional communist regimes throughout the region. With the rise of noncommunist regimes to state power in Eastern Europe by the start of the 1990s, new institutions, policies, and decision-making processes were being created to replace those of the former communist regimes.

As this book went to press, the economic institutions, policies, and decision-making processes of the various Second World states of Eastern Europe were in a considerable state of transition. Their final nature, composition, and structure were uncertain. The apparent trends, however, were that the new governments in Eastern Europe were moving away from centrally planned or even hybrid market-socialism economic models and decision-making processes, and toward First World models based more on pluralism and the free market.

Competing factions, spanning the spectrum of economic and political philosophy, were being allowed to participate in the policy-formulation processes in many of the new Eastern European regimes. Although advocates of orthodox communism no longer held a monopoly of power over economic policy and decision making, within the new noncommunist, pluralist regimes, even their opinions were allowed to be heard in policy debates. This was in stark contrast to the anticommunists' predicament when traditional communist economic models and decision-making processes were dominant throughout Eastern Europe; under those models, opponents of the Communist Party were not allowed to participate in policy debates or decision-making processes. In most of the new regimes in Eastern Europe, every group or party is afforded the opportunity to put forth policy alternatives and to engage in pluralistic politics to determine what state policy will be.

There is a popular adage in the West that trying to move gradually from a planned economy to a market economy is like trying to ask a nation to shift gradually from driving on the right hand side of the road to driving on the left hand side of the road. Based on the steps

An early meeting of the Hungarian Stock Market in February 1989, a clear example of the economic reform that has come to Eastern Europe.

its noncommunist government took as the 1990s commenced, Poland seemed determined not to let its economy crash! The reformed Polish government, on January 1, 1990, commenced a rapid economic conversion program designed to make the difficult transition from a command economy to a market economy in a little more than a year's time.

In Poland, numerous plans were drawn up, bills proposed, and laws passed, calling for privatization of industry, agriculture, banking, equity and bond markets, and property. The noncommunist Polish government moved to rapidly dismantle state-planning bureaucracies, end state subsidies, free up prices, and make their currency, the zloty, convertible on Western markets. They sought investment, information, and advice—but not necessarily outright loans or grants—from the First World. They hoped for integration into the European Common Market but, at the same time, did not desire to end their historical trading ties with the Soviet Union.

Polish leader General Woyciech Jarulzelski and Solidarity leader Lech Walesa, sit together at the first meeting of the newly created Polish Senate on July 3, 1989. The Senate is an important institution in determining Polish economic plans for the future.

The relatively high level of consensus for rapid economic conversion to free-market systems in Poland was not as clear-cut in other Eastern European states at the start of the decade. In Hungary, for example, the two dominant political parties in the new noncommunist government, the Democratic Forum and the Alliance of Free Democrats, were split over the pace and scope of reform of the Hungarian market socialist economy. The Free Democrats advocated a rapid push toward a free-market economy, with privatization programs and conservative social policies that would make Margaret Thatcher or Milton Friedman proud. The Democratic Forum, on the other hand, was not so eager to cast aside social welfare programs and state intervention in the economy. The Forum increasingly looked toward the social democracies of Western Europe, particularly the Swedish model, for ideas as to how they would like Hungary's

economy and economic policy processes to take shape in the future.

In some Eastern European states, the long shadow cast by traditional Communist Party supporters in the bureaucracy, the military, the government, and even society at large continued to interfere in movement toward pluralist economic decision-making processes and in adoption and implementation of free-market reforms. In Czechoslovakia, for instance, many members of the provisional, noncommunist government were hesitant in early 1990 to push forward plans for rapid economic conversion to a market economy before national elections could be held. They feared potential voter backlash at the polls over any economic crises that rapid conversion policies might produce, and they were afraid of the communists' ability to pounce on and manipulate such social dissatisfaction in attempts to subvert the new government.

By the start of the 1990s, Bulgaria and Romania had not moved as far away from traditional communist economic models and decision-making processes as some of the other Eastern European states. Opposition parties, groups, and factions were finding it difficult to gain access to the economic policy process in these two states. The communists in Romania and Bulgaria, while paying lip service to economic and political reform, largely retained control over the state economy and really sought more to reform the existing economic system along incremental, hybrid market socialist lines than to pursue adoption of a true free-market economic system and pluralist economic decision-making processes.

Conclusion

This chapter has attempted to apply totalitarian and pluralist models to the processes of economic decision making in Second World states. We have focused on the Soviet Union, China, and several Eastern European countries. Through our study, we have discovered that as the decade of the 1990s began, there was considerable variance among Second World states in the way they set their economic policy. No one particular model of decision making applied across the board.

China, for example, experimented throughout the 1980s with liberalization of their traditional command-administrative economic system. The policy-making process seemed to become a bit more pluralistic. Actors outside of the Party hierarchy and central bureaucracy increasingly were allowed to participate in economic decision making. Following the events in Tiananmen Square in the spring of 1989, however, China put its economic reform program on hold and reverted to its more traditional, totalitarian methods of making economic policy.

Economic policy making in the Soviet Union in early 1990 was caught up in the reforms of Mikhail Gorbachev. Gorbachev and his associates in the Communist Party of the Soviet Union were engaged in a balancing act, attempting to placate Party traditionalists while trying to please radical free-market reformers.

Gorbachev was calling for a complicated hybrid economic system—somewhere between socialism and capitalism. He recognized the need for privatization and market competition in the Soviet Union but had yet to free the economy from the guise of intrusive planners and bureaucrats. Gorbachev was holding the middle ground, and by 1990, the Soviet approach to economic reform appeared to be mired in pluralist incrementalism.

Various states in Eastern Europe, particularly Poland, Hungary, and Czechoslovakia, had moved beyond acceptance of a hybrid command economy by the start of the 1990s. Most parties in the new noncommunist leaderships desired free-market economic systems based on Western models; however, there were significant differences of opinion over the nature and pace of the transition process. Some wanted to make the move rapidly, as evidenced in the "shock treatment" pursued in Poland. Others preferred to make a slower, less abrupt transition. Still others appeared reluctant to make the transition at all. The differences and resulting debates in the reformed governments of Eastern Europe were a clear indication that totalitarianism had declined and pluralism was growing in the former Soviet satellite countries.

Suggestions for Further Reading

Aslund, Anders, *Gorbachev's Struggle for Economic Reform* (Ithaca, N.Y.: Cornell University Press, 1989).

Barghoorn, Fredrick C. and **Thomas F. Remington,** *Politics in the USSR* (Boston: Little, Brown, and Co., 1986).

Chang, Parris H., *Power and Policy in China*, 2nd

enlarged ed. (University Park, Pa.: Pennsylvania State University Press, 1978).

Chung, Han-ku., *Interest Representation in Soviet Policy-Making: A Case Study of the West Siberian Energy Coalition* (Boulder, Colo.: Westview, 1987).

Colton, Timothy J., *The Dilemma of Reform in*

the Soviet Union (New York: Council on Foreign Relations, 1986).

Dawisha, Karen, *Eastern Europe, Gorbachev, and Reform: The Great Challenge* (Cambridge: Cambridge University Press, 1988).

Falkenheim, Victor C., ed., *Chinese Politics: From Mao to Deng* (New York: Paragon House Publishers, 1989).

Friedberg, Maurice and **Heyward Isham,** eds., *Soviet Society under Gorbachev: Current Trends and Prospects for Reform* (New York: St. Martin's Press, 1987).

Gross, Susan, *Pluralism in the Soviet Union* (New York: St. Martin's Press, 1983).

Harding, Harry, *China's Second Revolution: Reform After Mao* (Washington, D.C.: Brookings Institution, 1987).

Hewett, Ed A., *Reforming the Soviet Economy: Equality Versus Efficiency* (Washington, D.C.: Brookings Institution, 1988).

Hoffman, Erik P., and **Robbin Laird,** *The Politics of Economic Modernization in the Soviet Union* (Ithaca, N.Y.: Cornell University Press, 1982).

Hough, Jerry F., and **Merle Fainsod,** *How the Soviet Union Is Governed* (Cambridge, Mass.: Harvard University Press, 1979).

Lampton, Michael D., ed., *Policy-Implementation in Post-Mao China* (Berkeley: University of California Press, 1987).

Lieberthal, Kenneth and **Michel Oksenberg,** *Policy Making in China: Leaders, Structures, Processes* (Princeton, N.J.: Princeton University Press, 1988).

Reynolds, Bruce L., *Chinese Economic Policy: Economic Reform at Midstream* (New York: Paragon House Publishers, 1989).

Rusinow, Dennison, *The Yugoslav Experiment, 1948–1974* (Berkeley: University of California Press, 1977).

Skilling, H. Gordon, and **Franklyn Griffiths,** eds., *Interest Groups in Soviet Politics* (Princeton, N.J.: Princeton University Press, 1971).

White, Stephen and **Daniel Nelson,** eds., *Communist Politics: A Reader* (New York: New York University Press, 1986).

Notes

1. Carl Friedrich and Zbigniew K. Brzezinski, *Totalitarian Dictatorship and Autocracy* (Cambridge, Mass.: Harvard University Press, 1956). The authors outlined the five essential features of a totalitarian system as: an official ideology, a single mass party, a monopoly of control of all means of armed combat, a monopoly of control of mass communication, and terroristic police control.

2. H. Gordon Skilling, "Interest Groups and Communist Politics," *World Politics* 18 (3) (1966): 435–451.

3. Jerry F. Hough, "The Bureaucratic Model and the Nature of the Soviet System," *Journal of Comparative Administration,* 5(2) (1973): 134–167; and "The Soviet System: Petrification or Pluralism?," *Problems of Communism* 21 (2) (1972): 25–45.

4. William E. Odom, "A Dissenting View on the Group Approach to Soviet Politics," *World Politics* 28 (4) (1976): 542–568; and Andrew C. Janos, "Interest Groups and the Structure of Power. Critique and Comparisons," *Studies in Comparative Communism* 12 (1) (1979): 6–20.

5. Incremental policy making, often called the process of muddling through, deals with policy matters, as they arise, on a more or less ad hoc basis and results in decisions that deviate from present policy only marginally. This form of policy making essentially is short term, or remedial, and does not place much emphasis on long-range planning and analysis or on the foresight necessary to promote future social and ideological goals.

6. Jerry F. Hough, "The Brezhnev Era: the Man and the System," *Problems of Communism* 25 (2) (1976): 1–17.

7. Hough, "The Soviet System": 29.

8. See Joseph S. Berliner, "Managing the USSR Economy: Alternative Models," *Problems of Communism* 22 (1) (1983): 40–56.

9. Ibid.: 54.

10. *Pravda*, January 13, 1988: 38.

11. May 14, 1990, *The New York Times*, p. A1.

12. *Kommunist* (3) (February 1988): 75–76.

13. Michel Oksenberg, "Economic Policy-Making in China," *China Quarterly* (90) (1982): 165–194.

14. Parris H. Chang, *Power and Policy in China*, 2nd enlarged ed. (State College, Pa.: Pennsylvania State University Press, 1978).

15. Ibid., pp. 186–187.

16. Ibid., p. 181.

17. Ibid., p. 189.

18. Michel Oksenberg and Richard Bush, "China's Political Evolution: 1972–82" *Problems of Communism* 31 (5) (1982): 1–19.

19. Oksenberg, "Economic Policy-Making in China": 170.

20. Not surprisingly, some resistance to the imposition of household farming occurred. Rural Communist Party cadres greatly resented the weakening of their privileged positions resulting from the decollectivization of agriculture and disbandment of the commune system. The replacement of the egalitarian distribution system by the one favoring competition and differential rewards offended many farmers accustomed to the life of collectivism and equality.

21. See, for example, Harry Harding, *China's Second Revolution: Reform After Mao* (Washington, D.C.: The Brookings Institution, 1987), p. 93.

22. Ibid., p. 87.

23. Ibid., pp. 174–183.

C H A P T E R 7

POLITICAL PERFORMANCE IN SECOND WORLD SYSTEMS

One year after Karl Marx's death in 1883, Friedrich Engels, using Marx's research notes and materials, wrote:

> Democracy in government, brotherhood in society, equality in rights and privileges, and universal education, foreshadow the next higher plane of society to which experience, intelligence and knowledge are steadily tending. It will be a revival, in a higher form, of the liberty, equality and fraternity of the ancient gentes.[1]

After many difficult decades of trying to build this higher form of society, it is clear that the ideals represented within it are more remote than ever. On May Day 1990 in Red Square, Moscow, a placard borne aloft during the unofficial parade read "Seventy Years on the Way to Nowhere!" What went wrong? Why didn't the Marxist-Leninist experiments result in democracy, respect, well-being, and enlightenment? This chapter will focus on these four values to summarize and assess the records of political performance in the Second World states.

Power: Democracy or Dictatorship?

Power relationships are of central importance in our examination of Second World rule. Mikhail Gorbachev began his address on political reform at the November 29, 1988 meeting of the Supreme Soviet by noting, "The question of power is the most important question in any society." He went on to say that the question "acquires a special significance in revolutionary periods when the old political system is being broken down and a new one established, when the orders and rules by which society will have to live and develop for a whole historical epoch are being instituted."[2] This is the sort of period in which the Soviet Union and many other Second World systems find themselves today. We will begin our examination by focusing on *goals*, *actions*, and *outcomes* in the Soviet case and will divide the Soviet experience into the pre-Gorbachev (1917–85) age and the more recent period.

A number of goals motivated the Soviet leaders concerning the distribution of power in the pre-Gorbachev period. Although Lenin once went so far as to say communism would not be achieved until full democracy was implemented, he and subsequent Soviet leaders were obviously not guided, at least first and foremost, by democratic goals. Rather, the primary goal was to see that the Communist Party of the Soviet Union (CPSU) maintained a monopoly of power. This was such an important goal that it was written into the Soviet constitution.

The Soviet leaders undertook many actions over the years to achieve this primary goal. They prohibited any organized opposition to their power and structured the political system to facilitate their authoritarian style of centralized one-party rule. On occasion, they encouraged mass involvement in the political process and requested the advice of experts outside of the formal Party and governmental hierarchy. But although there was some mass and expert involvement in the Soviet system prior to the Gorbachev period, it was strictly within the bounds prescribed by the CPSU.

In the Gorbachev period, the Party leadership finally confronted the costs of centralized Communist Party rule and began to recognize the need to reform the political system and to broaden the distribution of power. On the first point, Gorbachev rhetorically asked the delegates to the historic 19th Party Conference in June 1988 why the Soviet Union required a radical reform of its political system. He answered his question by noting:

First and foremost, comrades, it is a fact— and we have to admit this today—that . . . the political system established as a result of the [1917] revolution underwent serious deformations. This made possible the omnipotence of Stalin and his entourage, and the wave of repressive measures and lawlessness.[3]

Gorbachev went on in his speech to outline a new set of goals regarding political reform and the distribution of power in Soviet society:

First, everything must be done to include millions upon millions of people in administering the country in deed, not in word.

Second, maximum scope must be given to the processes of the self-regulation and self-government of society, and conditions must be created for the full development of the initiative of citizens, representative bodies of government, party and civic organizations, and work collectives.

Third, it is necessary to adjust the mechanism of the unhindered formation and expression of the interests and will of all classes and social groups, their coordination and realization in the domestic and foreign policies of the Soviet state.

Fourth, the conditions must be created for the further free development of every nation and nationality, for the strengthening of their friendship and equitable cooperation on the principles of internationalism.

Fifth, socialist legality, law and order, must be radically strengthened so as to rule out any possibility of power being usurped or abused, so as effectively to counter bureaucracy and formalism, and reliably guarantee the protection of citizens' constitutional rights and freedoms, and also the execution of their duties with respect to society and the state.

Sixth, there must be a strict demarcation of the functions of party and state bodies, in conformity with Lenin's conception of the Communist Party as a political vanguard of society and the role of the Soviet state as an instrument of government by the people.

Finally, seventh, an effective mechanism must be established to assure the timely self-rejuvenation of the political system with due consideration for changing international and external conditions, a system capable of increasingly vigorous development and of introducing the principles of socialist democracy and self-government into all spheres of life.[4]

On this and numerous other occasions, Gorbachev outlined his goals for what he called "the democratization of our society."

By the end of the decade significant actions were taken and efforts made to reform the Soviet political system. Gorbachev pushed through measures to give more power to the Soviets; to separate Party and government responsibilities, to place more emphasis on secret ballot, multicandidate, competitive elections; to give more power and responsibilities to the regions and national minorities. In 1990, the Soviet leaders went so far as to repudiate Article 6 of the Soviet Constitution, which formally guaranteed the Communist Party's monopoly of power.

No one can deny that historic changes were being made in the Soviet political system and in the distribution of power in the late 1980s and at the turn of the decade. Although it is too early to evaluate all of these changes and their consequences, the following observation should be made. Gorbachev and the Soviet Party leaders were willing to experiment with reforms that were beginning to bring about significant power redistributions within the broader society. This period was clearly an opportunity for the expansion of democratic processes in what had traditionally been one of the world's least democratic states. As we will note later, however, this democratization has begun to undermine the very existence of the Soviet state.

Even more revolutionary redistributions of power came to the states of Eastern Europe during the same period. After initially resisting the democratization that was taking place in the Soviet Union, the pace of political reform began to pick up in Eastern Europe in the late 1980s and finally exploded with the historic transformations of 1989. Poland started first, when the communist authorities entered in direct talks (the so called roundtable talks of 1989) with Solidarity, the Catholic church, and other noncommunist forces. These talks brought about the elections that resulted in a mandate for the noncommunist forces and the first clear use of the ballot box to vote communist governments out of power.

The redistribution of power away from the traditional ruling Communist Parties and into the hands of opposition groups and parties then unfolded in stunning and rapid succession. Within months, the prevailing power relationships within the East European states had been radically transformed. Traditional Communist Party rule was out and multiparty democracy was in. The goal of a Communist Party monopoly of power was being replaced by a serious but perilous movement toward democracy.

The Chinese Communists also considered political reforms in the 1980s but turned out to be much more reluctant about democratization than their Soviet and East European counterparts. From Mao's time to the present, the Chinese leaders have remained wedded to the primacy of Communist Party rule. During Mao's reign, the Party dominated in an intrusive and arbitrary way all aspects of Chinese society. The Party, and its top leaders, clearly were the power elite within the Chinese system. Of course, there were some efforts to build democratic participation—for example, through such concepts as the mass-line and activities like mass demonstrations during the Cultural Revolution. However, these activities were controlled by Mao and/or the Communist Party and had little to do with democratic rule. The mass-line idea, one of Mao's so-called democratic inventions, was supposed to provide a two-way flow of communication between Party members and the masses. In reality, however, the Party reserved almost complete decision-making autonomy and the masses had very little impact on the policy-making process. Overall, the Maoist period was one of arbitrary Communist Party and personalized (i.e., Mao and his associates) rule.

Although the primacy of Communist Party rule remained in China in the 1980s, some important changes began. Convinced that the overcentralization of power impeded economic development, engendered corruption, and contributed to the malaise among the people, Deng Xiaoping and his fellow reformers made some moves toward a limited diffusion of power. For example, many veteran Party officials were urged to retire and open up jobs for younger, better-educated people. There also was a rejuvenation of the government and bureaucracy, providing opportunities for better-trained, more technically competent people to play a role in decision-making processes. Greater separation of Party and government was also seen, which allowed people who were not Party members to play increasing roles in social and economic activities, particularly at the lower levels. The Chinese even began to experiment with direct and multicandidate elections, allowed greater decentralization of power to the regions, and implemented economic reforms that took some power, however limited, away from the central Party leaders. In 1987, Harry Harding observed that:

The Party no longer interferes in the detail of the daily lives of most citizens. A system of law, which guarantees the Chinese people certain substantive and procedural rights, increasingly constrains the exercise of political power. Greater opportunities have been opened for Chinese outside government, particularly intellectuals, to express their views on national policy. Discussion of political issues, both in private occasions and in public forums, is more lively, frank, and detailed. And the tone of political discourse is less charismatic, more secular, less ideological, and more rational. On balance, the political system is more open and relaxed than at any time since 1949.[5]

Harding went on to caution, however, that China was still not characterized by political pluralism and had not fundamentally transformed the basic features of a one-party Leninist political system. He emphasized that although the Communist Party leaders consulted with a larger number of people in the making of policy, it still allowed "no independent political parties, no autonomous mass media, no independent social or professional associations, and no true contest for political power."[6] The Communist Party's crackdown on the reform and democratization movements in the late 1980s and in 1990 confirmed that the Chinese authorities would try to resist the revolutionary changes that had come to the Soviet Union and Eastern Europe.

Yugoslavia's experience with the question of political power has been particularly interesting and is deserving of special consideration. The Yugoslavs began their experiment with communist rule in the dictatorial Stalinist tradition. When Tito and the Yugoslav communists took over power after World War II, they imposed a one-party dictatorship similar to the ones found in the Soviet Union and other East European states. In 1947, however, the Yugoslavs broke with the Soviet bloc and began to develop their own model of communism. Compared with its Soviet, East European, and Chinese counterparts in the 1960s and 1970s, it featured a number of democratic innovations that suggested movement toward a broader distribution of power.

The earliest and perhaps most significant reform involved the Yugoslav experiment with industrial democracy and what has often been referred to as self-managing socialism. The Yugoslavs began this experiment in the 1950s when they set up workers' councils to encourage workers to participate, along with management and Communist Party officials, in the process of industrial decision making. Subsequently, workers' councils and other participatory decision-making bodies were established in all social, economic, and political organizations within the society. The Yugoslav constitution was rewritten to require that schools, factories, and all other organizations manage their own affairs. The Yugoslav leaders boldly spoke about their desires to make Yugoslavia a more democratic, self-managing society.

Other democratic trends seemed to be developing in Yugoslavia in the 1960s and 1970s under the broad rubric of self-managing socialism. Considerable power was decentralized from the federal government in Belgrade to the regional governments in the constituent republics. The republics—Croatia, Slovenia, Serbia and so on—took on considerable power and could challenge and sometimes defeat the federal government on important matters of policy. The federal government hoped that the decentralization of power in a truly federal system could ensure "unity through diversity" and have a better chance of commanding the support of the multinational Yugoslav people than a highly centralized system as existed in the Soviet Union at that time.

The Yugoslavs also experimented with the fundamental principle of Communist Party rule. They undertook both symbolic changes—for example, renaming the Communist Party the "League of Communists of Yugoslavia" (LCY)—

and significant reforms. They decentralized considerable LCY power to the regional Party organizations, leading some observers to speak decades ago of a Yugoslav multiparty system—that is, a country with regional Communist Parties that were often at odds with one another. In the 1960s, Yugoslav communist leaders talked about "divorcing" the Party (LCY) from power, by establishing a greater separation of Party and government. What they had in mind was a Party that would still be very much involved in guiding and, in reality, controlling the country but would turn over increasing power to the government and self-managing institutions. The Party also experimented with rules requiring greater circulation and rotation of Party officials. This was intended to allow more people opportunities to assume leadership roles and avoid the personalized and centralized rule of the traditional, Stalinist Communist Party state.

Yugoslav leaders were guided by two primary and conflicting goals concerning the distribution of power in their political system. Although attempting to pursue, on the one hand, the democratic ideals of self-governing socialism, they were unwilling until recently to relinquish the Party's leading role. Yugoslav leaders wanted both self-government and Party rule and undertook actions to pursue both of these principles. The outcomes in Yugoslavia reflected these competing and conflicting goals. Self-management made some inroads into the traditional power relationships within the society. Some of the authoritarian arrangements of the past were replaced with more democratic processes, involving large and varied groups of people. But the process of democratization was still incomplete and was likely to remain that way as long as the LCY maintained its dominant role. Divided deeply along republic (i.e., national) lines, the LCY could develop neither the democratic consensus nor the totalitarian power to move the country forward. Although Yugoslavia also moved toward greater democratization and away from Communist Party rule in recent years, the challenges of stable democracy in this divided Balkan state are exceedingly great.

Respect: Community or Conflict?

To what extent did Second World systems create political communities of love and friendship? And to what extent were they divided by class and conflict? An examination of the value of respect will give us a clearer idea.

Soviet leaders long ago realized that the class divisions and ethnocentrism that plagued and contributed to the collapse of tsarist Russia would have to be resolved if they were to be successful in developing a unified Soviet commonwealth. Social and national cleavages were deeply cast in the old Russian state; radical goals and policies were required to overcome them. The initial goal that guided the postrevolutionary leaders was state survival, which Lenin, Stalin, and others pursued through the repressive policies of centralized rule in hopes of promoting societal cohesion and political integration. The Soviet leaders also sought to establish respect and a spirit of comradeliness among the diverse Soviet peoples. These traits, the leaders hoped, would contribute to the goal of a unified Soviet state.

To encourage the development of these traits, the leaders emphasized the common struggles of the Soviet peoples, the bonds that united them, and the importance of cooperation and friendship among the different ethnic and national groups. At certain times in the past, some might have thought that these efforts had reduced ethnocentrism and discriminatory rela-

tions among the Soviet peoples. However, recent research and experience suggests that interethnic differences persist, and the Soviet leaders have been unable to create what Soviet leaders traditionally referred to in the past as a "fundamentally new social and international community" of Soviet people. What social harmony existed in Soviet society was imposed by suppression. It did not emanate naturally from social and ethnic relations in the society. Anti-Semitism among large sectors of the Soviet people continues, and strong ethnonational tensions have exploded into full view. There appears to be little community of shared interest among the diverse Soviet peoples. The destructive disputes between the Armenians and Azerbaijans and the assertion of national pride and demands for independence among the Baltic nationalities are among the numerous examples indicating that the Soviets have not solved their nationality problems. Gorbachev has pleaded with the Soviet people, telling them that "we are one family." As we enter the 1990s, destructive feuds continue, indicating serious differences within the Soviet "family."

Another traditional shortcoming in the USSR concerned the system's disrespect for human rights and the personal freedoms taken so seriously in the Western democracies. Past Soviet constitutions elaborated in great detail the citizens' economic guarantees that formed the centerpiece of the Soviet's traditional definition of human rights: the right to housing, education, work, leisure, medical care, and maintenance in old age. Less prominent and heavily qualified were the political rights, including freedom of speech, press, assembly, demonstration in the streets, religion, and privacy. The constitution diluted these rights by declaring that they were granted only "in conformity with the interests of the working people and for the purposes of strengthening the socialist system." An explicit limitation aimed at dissidents noted, "The exercise of rights and freedoms shall be inseparable from the performance by citizens of their duties."

We should note, however, that Soviet human rights policy has considerably improved during the Gorbachev period. Many political prisoners have been set free; many minorities and former "refuseniks" have been allowed to emigrate. Dissidents, such as the late Andrei Sakharov, were returned from exile and allowed to speak out and even run for political office. Magazines and journals are addressing sensitive issues and themes that were strictly forbidden in the past.

But along with the opening of Soviet society and improvements in human rights problems come new challenges and difficulties for the Soviet people. During the present period of change and transition in the Soviet Union, the social contract on which order, respect, and trust are based is changing. In this environment of change and uncertainty, some Soviets have called attention to a disintegrating social and moral order. Some make references to a dead, sick, or corrupt society. There has been a rise in organized crime in the USSR. Many reports call attention to bands of disciplined, organized criminals who bribe officials to achieve desired ends such as protection from the law, prized apartments or property, raw materials for business projects, and so on. They also use their organization to exploit prostitutes, black-marketeers, and law-abiding citizens who are trying to start cooperatives and private enterprise. It has never been easy to promote love and respect, brotherhood and unity, among the Soviet peoples, and it has become no easier under glasnost, reform, and perestroika.

Other Second World states have encountered similar problems when trying to achieve a secure and supportive community from their diverse nationalities and ethnic groups; the Yugoslav policy makers also wanted brotherhood and unity but pursued rather different policies than the Soviets. Traditionally, Yugoslav policy actions showed greater respect for human rights and local autonomy. Yugoslav socialization policies were less coercive, more respectful of the people, and more patient concerning the considerable time required to bring about the desired changes. Government actions in the area of federalism and self-management granted high levels of political and economic autonomy to the various ethnic groups and local organizations, reflecting more respect for the interests and concerns of the diverse Yugoslav peoples.

Although Tito and the Yugoslav policy makers may have tried to do more to allocate respect to all groups and regions on the basis of universalistic norms and principles, the regional groups, such as the Albanians, Serbs, and Croats, often have been unwilling to accord respect and trust to one another. When faced with difficult political choices that critically affect the national republics and provinces—such as whether to take the profits of the richer republics to subsidize the development of the poorer—Tito tried to decide in the collective, or Yugoslav, interest. Many contemporary regional leaders, however, are unwilling to place Yugoslav interests before the interests of their own national or ethnic group. As a result, political decisions often degenerate into nationalistic squabbles pitting one nationality against another.

The value of respect in Yugoslavia dropped to a postwar low in the late 1980s along with the declining economy and deteriorating interethnic relations. The people of Yugoslavia were angry. Their standard of living was plummeting and they vented their frustrations on any convenient target. Often it was the government, and at other times, neighboring ethnic groups. No matter who was the target, antagonistic ethnic and social relations in Yugoslavia had reached a critical and dangerous stage. There is more conflict than community in contemporary Yugoslavia.

As a result of the deep social and regional cleavages of traditional China, the value of respect and the goal of societal integration also commanded high attention from its postrevolutionary leaders. To unify the society, Mao and the communist leaders hoped to transform the Chinese populace by developing a new socialist person. Emphasizing the themes of respect, equality, and comradeship, the Mao leadership once was thought to have achieved considerable success. But with the benefit of hindsight and more information, we now know that Maoist China was far from the paradise of harmony, love, and mutual respect that the leaders sought to convey. Large segments of the population discriminated against others on the basis of class background, family connections, social status, and geographic origin. People of the privileged classes, such as the political, economic, and cultural establishment, were often unwilling to associate with those considered to be inferior. Overall, the Maoist regime did little to promote the values of comradeship it so deeply desired to instill.

Perhaps the most significant outcome of Mao's policies was the level of equality—at least *income* equality—evident in the Chinese system during the 1960s and 1970s. In a society with a long and strong tradition of elitist, hierarchical relations, Mao's actions altered a social characteristic that many observers had thought impossible to change. However, along with this trend toward increased income equality came reductions in economic efficiency and development.

In the post-Mao period, egalitarianism was deemphasized to promote higher productivity and economic efficiency. The post-Mao reforms emphasized initiative, competition, and "getting rich" as being more important to China than equality. Increased corruption, however, followed. In the 1980s, corruption among Party officials, new entrepreneurs, and government bureaucrats became a problem of unprecedented dimensions. Some observers have said the country was turned into a "kleptocracy," where the values of greed and materialism replaced the former superficial commitment to comradeship. The economic reforms expanding entrepreneurship provided opportunities for profiteering, which generated resentment among sizable sectors of the Chinese people. Social relations declined, and gambling, prostitution, and crime were on the rise.

What about human rights in China? Interestingly, considerably little has been said and written in the West over the years about Chinese human rights policy, compared with the considerable attention given this problem in the Soviet Union. In fact, Mao's record on human rights was at times as dreadful as that of Stalin's. For example, shortly after the communist takeover in 1949 and during the Cultural Revolution in the late 1960s, the Maoist regime put due process in abeyance and utilized what we would refer to as kangaroo courts to mete out capital punishment for millions of people. There were also thousands of political prisoners who suffered under the harsh and arbitrary strictures of Maoist rule. Friendship was to give way to "comradeship," a euphemism for interpersonal relations based on mutual suspicion. People were reluctant to confide with their former friends. Respect and trust had disappeared.

The 1980s witnessed considerable improvement in the regime's performance with respect to human rights and civil liberties. Although the new regime continued to incarcerate some political dissidents, such as Wei Jingsheng, there no longer were reports of mass imprisonment and mass execution for political reasons. Another significant change in the 1980s was that ordinary people were emboldened to voice their grievances against the regime's policies in public, a felonious offense punishable by death or stiff prison terms in the Maoist past. Although there were conservative backlashes and the movement toward human rights liberalization was slow and limited, the Chinese people in the 1980s enjoyed much more freedom of speech and press than in the past. During this period, the mass media began to carry out vigorous investigative reporting and exposed corruption and incompetence.

The democratization movement and confrontation in Tiananmen Square in 1989 and the convulsive events that have brought dramatic change to much of the Second World place new challenges on the Chinese authorities in the 1990s. The leaders' initial response has been conservative and repressive. They have dug in their heels and denied the changes taking place around them. They lied to the Chinese people and to the world about the massacre in Tiananmen Square. They lied about the yearning for democracy and human rights in their society. Such an approach shows little promise for promoting trust and respect in Chinese society.

Traditional social and elite-mass relations in Eastern Europe showed some of the same negative consequences of repressive, dictatorial rule. The leaders lied to the people, and the people lost respect for the leaders. In the repressive and economically deprived environments, people worried first and foremost about themselves. Values of love, respect, and true comradeship were lost in the struggle for survival. The social contract was no longer viable. The societies became morally ill. No one spoke more eloquently about this problem than the new Czechoslovak President Vaclav Havel in his 1990 New Year's Day address to the Czechoslovak people (see excerpts from address).

'The Great Moral Stake of the Moment'

Perhaps not since Abraham Lincoln's Second Inaugural has a head of state delivered a speech as searching as Vaclav Havel's New Year's Day address to Czechoslovakia. The new president challenged his compatriots to face their past collusion with communist rule and their future responsibility for their own freedom. Excerpts:

For the past 40 years on this day you have heard my predecessors utter variations on the same theme, about how our country is prospering, how many more billion tons of steel we have produced, how happy we all are, how much we trust our government and what beautiful prospects lie ahead. I do not think you put me into this office so that I, too, should lie to you.

Our country is not prospering. The great creative and spiritual potential of our nation is not being used to its fullest. Whole sectors of industry are producing things in which no one is interested, while things we need are in short supply.

The state, which calls itself a state of the working people, is humiliating and exploiting the workers. Our outdated economy is squandering energy . . . A country which could once be proud of the standard of education of its people spends so little on education that today it ranks 72nd in the world. We have laid waste to our soil and the rivers and the forests our forefathers bequeathed us, and we have the worst environment in all of Europe today. . . .

The worst thing is that we are living in a decayed moral environment. We have become morally ill, because we have become accustomed to saying one thing and thinking another. We have learned not to believe in anything, not to care about one another and only to look after ourselves. Notions such as love, friendship, compassion, humility and forgiveness have lost their depth and dimension, and for many of us they represent merely some kind of psychological idiosyncrasy, or appear as some kind of stray relic from times past, something rather comical in the era of computers and space rockets. . . .

The previous regime, armed with its arrogant and intolerant ideology, denigrated man into a production force and nature into a production tool. In this way it attacked their very essence and the relationship between them. It made talented people who were capable of managing their own affairs . . . into cogs in some kind of monstrous, ramshackle, smelly machine whose purpose no one can understand. It can do nothing more than slowly but surely wear itself down, along with all the cogs in it.

When I talk about a decayed moral environment . . . I mean all of us, because all of us have become accustomed to the totalitarian system, accepted it as an inalterable fact and thereby kept it running. In other words, all of us are responsible, each to a different degree, for keeping the totalitarian machine running. None of us is merely a victim of it, because all of us helped to create it together.

Why do I mention this? It would be very unwise to see the sad legacy of the past 40 years as something alien, handed down to us by some distant relatives. On the contrary, we must accept this legacy as something which we have

brought upon ourselves. If we can accept this, then we will understand that it is up to all of us to do something about it. We cannot lay all the blame on those who ruled us before, not only because this would not be true but also because it could detract from the responsibility each of us now faces—the responsibility to act on our own initiative, freely, sensibly and quickly. . . .

Throughout the world, people are surprised that the acquiescent, humiliated, skeptical Czechoslovak people who apparently no longer believed in anything suddenly managed to find the enormous strength in the space of a few weeks to shake off the totalitarian system in a completely decent and peaceful way. We ourselves are also surprised at this, and we ask where the young people, in particular, who have never known any other system, find the source of their aspirations for truth, freedom of thought, political imagination, civic courage and civic foresight. How is it that their parents, the generation which was considered lost, also joined in with them? How is it possible that so many immediately grasped what had to be done?. . .

Of course, for our freedom today we also had to pay a price. Many of our people died in prison in the '50s, many were executed, thousands of human lives were destroyed, hundreds of thousands of talented people were driven abroad. . . . Those who resisted totalitarian government were persecuted, [as were] those who simply managed to remain true to their own principles and think freely. None of those who paid the price in one way or another for our freedom today should be forgotten. . . .

Neither should we forget that other nations paid an even higher price for their freedom today, and thus also paid indirectly for us, too. The rivers of blood which flowed in Hungary,

Poland, Germany and recently in such a horrific way in Romania, as well as the sea of blood shed by the nations of the Soviet Union, should not be forgotten . . . it was these great sacrifices which wove the tragic backdrop for today's freedom or gradual liberation of the Soviet-bloc nations, and the backdrop of our newly charged freedom, too. . . .

This, it seems to me, is the great moral stake of the present moment. It contains the hope that in the future we will no longer have to suffer the complex of those who are permanently indebted to someone else. Now it is up to us alone whether this hope comes to fruition, and whether our civic, national and political self-confidence reawakens in a historically new way.[7]

The new East European leaders and their societies are now facing tremendous challenges. Among other things, they must establish a new social contract that brings out the best in their people. In their efforts to transform their economic and political systems, they must build civic cultures that will promote private initiative and public cooperation, personal integrity and social respect. They are swimming in uncharted waters and will find this a challenging task.

Well-Being: Welfare or Poverty?

The value of well-being represents an area of social policy of considerable importance to Second World states. In his speech to the 24th CPSU Congress in 1971, General Secretary Leonid I. Brezhnev claimed that the country's principal goal was raising the standard of living. At the 25th Congress in 1976, he reemphasized that goal by pledging:

"a further increase in the Soviet people's well-being, the improvement of their living and working conditions, and significant progress in public health, education, and culture."

At subsequent Party congresses, similar pledges were made.

When examining the actions and outcomes, we encounter a mixed picture. It is apparent that some things were done in the area of social services. The Soviet Union is a welfare state. Housing is exceedingly cheap although always in short supply; medical care, health services, and education are free; employment is guaranteed. Yet, when comparing the average Soviet citizen with his or her West European counterpart, he or she clearly is deprived of many goods and services associated with a higher standard of living. For example, housing is exceedingly scarce, forcing many families to share apartments or to wait for years to be provided an apartment suited to their needs. Second, medical care generally is of poor quality. Third, consumer goods are in critically short supply. Soviet department stores show a limited variety of modern appliances, clothing, and other consumer goods that we take for granted in the West. True, the Soviet leaders continue to speak of altering this situation, but the extent to which change is possible, at least in the short term, is a matter of some contention.[8]

The Soviet economy is having severe problems, and there is not nearly enough money in the Soviet budget to bring about necessary improvements in the social and consumer sectors. Like the United States in the late 1980s, the Soviet Union during that period also was running a huge budgetary deficit. Although figuring the USSR's size and comparing the Soviet deficit with the American one are difficult, one leading Soviet economist and deputy prime minister, Leonid Abalkin, estimated the Soviet deficit at $165 billion in 1989 and called it the most important economic problem facing the country.[9] A $165 billion deficit would be about 11 percent of Soviet GNP, which would suggest that the Soviet deficit was considerably larger than the American deficit, which was about 4 percent of the American GNP in the late 1980s.

Because perestroika was unable to bring about a rapid turnaround in the economy—Albalkin predicted it would be at least six years before perestroika produced a significant improvement in the standard of living—the Soviet leaders faced hard choices as they approached the 1990s. What would it be: guns or butter? Social programs or military spending? There was not enough money to bring about necessary improvements in health care, old-age pensions, child care, food and housing, and all of the other services of a welfare state. Gorbachev and the Soviet people knew that they would have to do better. Perestroika was the plan, but even in the most optimistic scenario, the relief would be neither immediate nor guaranteed. Albalkin said cuts would have to be made in both military and civilian spending; in addition, the government would be forced to shift many government projects to private financing, something previously heretical in the Soviet state. By the end of the decade, the Soviets had

Antiaircraft missiles on display in Moscow's Red Square at the anniversary celebration of the Great October Revolution. Although heavy spending in the military sector moved the USSR into "superpower" status, it meant considerable deprivation for the consumer.

announced a 14 percent cut in the military budget, a 20 percent cut in capital investment related to civilian construction, and an expansion in the role of private and cooperative financing and building of housing.

In an April 1990 report to the U.S. Congress, the Central Intelligence Agency (CIA) and the Defense Intelligence Agency (DIA) confirmed the bleak assessments on the state of the Soviet economy.[10] Among other things, the report noted that the:

1. Production of energy and industrial materials had fallen and that industrial production had registered its worst performance since World War II.

2. The combination of inflation and shortages had made daily life extremely difficult for all but the most privileged segment of the population; according to Soviet sources, 15 percent of the population was living below the poverty line.

3. Shortages in consumer goods and inequalities in their distribution had contributed to a growing number of strikes and ethnic clashes.

Heavy Soviet spending on the military left little money for environmental protection, as indicated by the pollution from this Estonian phosphate plant.

To deal with these and related economic stringencies, the CIA and DIA reported that the Soviet leaders had reduced defense spending by 4 to 5 percent; military procurement was cut by 6 to 7 percent; the production of tanks was halved; uniformed military manpower was reduced by 200,000; military deliveries to Third World countries were reduced by nearly $2 billion; and substantial military withdrawals were made from Eastern Europe. Although these were important steps designed to redress the traditional "guns and butter" imbalance, few believed that they would have a significant impact on improving the social well-being of the Soviet people in the short run.

Because of the lower level of economic development and the much greater number of people, the problem of providing all citizens with a reasonable level of well-being has been even more severe in China. Accordingly, the primary goal guiding the Chinese policy makers in the postrevolutionary period was the provision of a minimal level of economic security.

These provisions in a historically underdeveloped area like China require high rates of economic modernization and industrial production. Although there have been notable achievements, China remains a colossus mired in poverty and economic backwardness. In terms of GNP per capita, it still trails behind more than a hundred countries in the world. Although the mass of Chinese people are better fed, better clothed, and enjoy a longer life span than ever before, they are not keeping up with the advances of other parts of the Far East.

To encourage economic growth, the post-Mao Chinese leaders undertook dramatic economic reforms in the 1980s. In the agricultural sector, they broadened the rights of peasants to farm on their own and to engage in profitable activities. In the industrial sector, they reduced governmental control and placed greater emphasis

Chinese factory workers' flats usually consist of one room inhabited by parents and child. Kitchens and bathrooms are generally shared with other families. Although this space seems inadequate by Western standards, it is an improvement over the prerevolutionary period in China.

1987. He claimed that the first goal involved a doubling of the 1980 GNP and the solution of food and clothing problems. The second step involved another doubling of the GNP by the end of the century, and the third was to reach the per capita GNP level of an average developed country by the middle of the next century. These long-term goals did little to assuage the concerns and improve the living standards of the Chinese people. Expectations and feelings of deprivation among the masses were rising in China. To avoid the dangerous consequences of excessive deprivation, frustration, and cynicism in the future, the Chinese leaders must be able to demonstrate progress toward their goals.

on competitive market forces. The overriding goal in both agriculture and industry was to promote initiative, competition, and efficiency. By so doing, the leaders hoped to promote modernization and social well-being in China.

Like the Soviet Union, China's economy has been unable to support all of the social needs of a welfare state. And with the post-Mao deemphasis on equality, the gap between the haves and have nots began to rise. Successful entrepreneurs were able to provide for their needs, while those dependent on the state often suffered from the provision of minimal services. While the standard of living for a minority rose, the masses were struck by rising prices and a decline in the quality of life.

Former Party leader Zhao Ziyang recognized the problems confronting China in the 1980s and outlined three basic goals for improvements in an address to the 13th Party Congress in

Contemporary China is a blend of the new and old.

The former Communist Party states of Eastern Europe were overthrown for a variety of reasons, but one of the most important was their inability to provide the levels of social well-being so long promised their societies. The people of East Germany had been told that they were building a workers' paradise, yet when the Berlin Wall came down, they found the paradise (at least in terms of standard of living and social well-being) on the other side. The people of Romania had been forced to live in extreme deprivation under the dictator Nicolae Ceausescu and had one of the lowest standards of living in Europe.

The peoples' well-being in Eastern Europe also was affected by the deteriorating physical environment. Because the governments could not afford the high cost of environmental protection, many people were forced to live in environs of sticky soot, carbon monoxide, nitrogen oxide, sulphur, heavy metals, and other unhealthy materials spewed from industrial plants. Much of Eastern Europe had become an ecological disaster, and the governments could not afford to address the growing problem. Overall, the highly centralized command economies had not produced sufficient resources, and much of the meager resources produced was invested in programs (e.g., military) that did little to improve the living conditions of the people (see Table 7.1 for indicators of some of these conditions in the 1980s). Such conditions generated considerable resentment in these societies, fueling the explosions of discontent that characterized the 1989 revolutions.

Well-being is one of the values that is more amenable to quantitative evaluation and comparison. A useful way of examining and comparing government actions, for example, is to see where they spend their money. Table 7.2 gives us some idea of how much money each Second World government spent per capita in the mid-1980s on the military, education, and

health. Before examining the data, we should remember that because of their weak economies, Second World states did not have very much to spend. Second, of what they did have, far too much was spent on the military. Examining military spending as reflected in Table 7.2, we see that the USSR spent far more per person (and overall) than any other Second World state. Although it spent somewhat less per person than the United States, it spent far more as a percentage of its gross national product (GNP). The USSR was clearly the big spender in the defense sector in the 1980s. Observing the domestic consequences of military spending, Soviet leader Gorbachev announced cuts in Soviet military expenditures by the end of the decade. China had comparatively little to expend and invested less per capita in the military sector than any of the East European states.

Turning to education expenditures listed in Table 7.2, the USSR and East Germany were the clear leaders, although both spent substantially less than the United States. The education and health expenditures of the Laotians, Vietnamese, and North Koreans were extremely low and explain the low quality of health care and schooling found in these countries. When combining health and education expenditures and comparing them with military expenditures, some interesting facts appear. Whereas the United States, for example, spent $1,002 per person a year on defense and $1,445 on health and education, the Soviet Union spent $816 and $559, respectively.

Actions in terms of government expenditures are, of course, related to policy outcomes. Table 7.1 provides a number of indicators of such outcomes, describing levels of health care, nutrition, and so forth in the Second World states in the 1980s. Examining in the first column the number of people per physician, we find that the Soviet Union purportedly had the best ratio

Table 7.1   Health and Nutrition Indicators, 1986

Country	Population per Physician	Population per Hospital Bed	Infant Mortality* Rate per 1,000	Life Expectancy	Calorie Supply† per Capita	Protein Supply† per Capita	Percent of Population with Safe Water
Albania	671	170	39	72	na‡	na	92
Bulgaria	339	110	16	72	3,634	106.3	96
Cambodia	14,404	410	130	48	na	na	3
China	1,673	460	32	69	2,628	62.0	na
Cuba	455	190	15	73	3,107	78.9	82
Czechoslovakia	327	80	15	71	3,673	103.3	74
East Germany	424	100	9	73	3,800	112.7	90
Hungary	304	100	20	70	3,561	101.7	84
Laos	6,353	370	110	47	na	na	21
Mongolia	401	90	45	64	2,829	92.5	100
North Korea	na	740	24	69	3,199	93.6	100
Poland	497	180	18	71	3,298	101.8	67
Romania	475	110	22	70	3,396	106.3	77
Soviet Union	235	80	24	69	3,396	105.6	100
Vietnam	3,233	430	64	61	na	na	41
Yugoslavia	549	160	25	72	3,542	101.5	68
USA	462	190	10	75	3,692	106.5	100

* Deaths of infants under one year old per 1,000 live births.
† Per capita supply of food, in calories, and of grams of protein per day; the figures of caloric supply relate to 1984–1986 average.
‡ Not available.
(*Source*) Adapted from Ruth Leger Sivard, *World Military and Social Expenditures, 1989* (Washington, D.C.: World Priorities, 1989), pp. 50–55; and *Production Yearbook; 1988* (Rome: Food and Agricultural Organization of the United Nations, 1989), pp. 293–294.

in the world (235 people for every physician). However, we must be cautious about the use of such statistics. Although the Soviet Union may have an impressive quantity of doctors, it also has many glaring deficiencies in the quality of its health care system.

With the exception of the Albanians, the East European states also do very well on the people-per-physican indicator. The Asians, on the other hand, do very poorly. The second column, de-scribing the population per hospital bed, reflects the same trend. When examining the three indicators of nutrition in Table 7.1, the Soviets and Europeans do quite well once again, whereas the Asians lag far behind. Cambodia (Kampuchea) and Laos are among the few states in the world with calorie-supply-per-capita levels below 2,000 per day. Cambodia (Kampuchea) suffered tragic losses in the 1970s through star-vation and war. In 1975, the country had a

**Table 7.2 Public Expenditures per Capita:
Military, Education, Health in 1984**

Country	Military (US $)	Education (US $)	Health (US $)
Albania	56	na*	32
Bulgaria	179	219	160
Cambodia	na	na	na
China	18	8	4
Cuba	148	124	64
Czechoslovakia	272	241	278
East Germany	432	335	228
Hungary	146	234	196
Laos	na	3	na
Mongolia	93	na	11
North Korea	123	na	12
Poland	167	228	201
Romania	62	73	75
Soviet Union	971	442	270
Vietnam	na	na	na
Yugoslavia	146	140	157
USA	1,164	928	783

* Not available.
(*Source*) Adapted from Ruth Leger Sivard, *World Military and Social Expenditures, 1989* (Washington, D.C.; World Priorities, 1989), pp. 50–55.

population of approximately 8 million; by 1980, as many as 4 million had died. No nation on earth suffered more during the last two decades than this once tranquil and fertile land.

Enlightenment: Erudition or Ignorance?

Policy choices concerning the nature and distribution of enlightenment—what one should know about oneself, one's work, and one's world—have been the focus of considerable controversy and debate in political systems throughout the world. Should the goal be the development of a citizen broadly trained in the humanist, liberal tradition, or the development of a more narrow, ideologically trained zealot? Should enlightenment be determined by the people, or controlled by the state? These and other choices confronted policy makers in Second World states as they attempted to mold populations that contributed to the construction of communism.

Past Soviet policy emphasized the molding of a new socialist person through a social and educational system tightly controlled by the

Communist Party. Enlightenment was what the authoritarian and ideologically motivated Party leaders wanted it to be. Education, the mass media, the arts, and all opportunities for access to information were carefully monitored and controlled by Communist Party authorities. What largely resulted was a passive, bored, and stagnant society that was conducive to neither the building of communism nor the general development of Soviet society.

Soviet policies and performance concerning enlightenment changed significantly during the Gorbachev period under the theme of glasnost. In his book *Perestroika*, Gorbachev spoke about glasnost in the following terms:

> We want more openness about public affairs in every sphere of life. People should know what is good, and what is bad, too, in order to multiply the good and to combat the bad. . . . Glasnost, criticism and self-criticism are not just a new campaign. They have been proclaimed and must become a norm in the Soviet way of life. No radical change is possible without it. There is no democracy, nor can there be, without glasnost. And there is no present-day socialism, nor can there be, without democracy.[11]

The content of newspapers changed considerably under glasnost and served as a good indicator of the opening of Soviet society. By the end of the 1980s, Soviet citizens were reading daily about shortcomings in their society, including the problems of perestroika, bureaucratic inefficiency, and the Stalinist heritage. In a break with tradition, the media were allowed to report on Soviet disasters, and newspapers began to give fuller accounts of such events as the nuclear power accident in Chernobyl, the tragic earthquake in Armenia, and the independence movements in the Baltic republics.

Letters to newspaper editors, long a safety valve in the Soviet Union allowing citizens to let off steam, began in the 1980s to print letters that addressed much more sensitive issues. Letter writers complained about all sorts of things, including glasnost and the Communist Party itself. Typical letters read, "All we have is glasnost—but you can't eat glasnost, you can't clothe yourself in it." The KGB and other formerly taboo topics came under scrutiny. Some letters raised questions about the KGB and its role in a modern society. Some letters denounced Stalin as a murderer and tyrant, whereas others praised him as a great leader and the architect of the Soviet state. Soviet editors came to brag about the number of letters received, considering them a barometer of public trust. The government newspaper, *Izvestia*, boasted that it had received more than 450,000 letters in 1988. The outspoken weekly magazine *Ogonyok* announced that it had received 600,000, a tenfold increase since 1985. And *Literaturnaya Gazeta*, a weekly newspaper read primarily by intellectuals, was pleased to announce its receipt of 110,000. Although still a tiny minority in Soviet society, people expressing opinions can be found more and more.

The Soviet press also began to publish articles and statistics showing some of the darker sides of Soviet life. In February 1989, Soviet authorities released detailed crime statistics for the first time in more than fifty years, calling attention to a sharp increase in Soviet crime. "Perhaps this will shock many people," *Izvestia* commented, "but it is better to know the reality of things. . . ." General Anotoly Smirnov, chief of the Interior Ministry's information center responsible for releasing the statistics, reported specific numbers in specific categories. For example, he reported that there had been 16,710 murders and attempted murders in 1988, 37,191 cases of aggravated assault, 17,658 rapes and attempted rapes, 67,114 holdups and burglaries, and 165,283 thefts of state and public property. Overall, these and other crimes showed a 17.8-percent increase over the previous year. Smirnov went on to say that his ministry would regularly publish such statistics in the future, to give the society a clearer picture of Soviet crime, a topic that had been classified as a state secret since 1933.

The Soviet people also began in the 1980s to learn more about their leaders. A Soviet youth paper revealed that members of the ruling Politburo were paid 1,200 to 1,500 rubles a month and that Mikhail Gorbachev got a bit more, or about $30,000 a year. The highest salaries, however, went to leading Soviet military figures, who received as much as $2,000 rubles a month. The article also revealed that Gorbachev had given his $600,000 in royalties from his book *Perestroika* to the Soviet Communist Party Central Committee. In the pre-Gorbachev period, such personal information about Soviet leaders was tightly controlled.

Included in the printed media's new openness were direct attacks on the Communist Party's policies and Gorbachev himself. As noted in an earlier chapter, the Soviet periodical *Sovetskaia Rossia* published an article in 1988 defending Stalin and questioning Gorbachev's reform policy. In 1989, the Leningrad literary and political monthly *Neva* published a scathing attack of the Soviet Communist Party and of Gorbachev. The article asserted that the Party had become an interest of the "new class" and was ignoring the needs and interests of the people. The article argued that "we have to admit that it was the Party leadership that brought the country to economic crisis and moral decline." Publications like these represented a significant broadening of the boundaries of Soviet debate and fundamental changes in Soviet society. As fear diminished, and education and glasnost

increased, people were prepared to criticize their leaders and the communist values they represented.

Another change related to the jamming of foreign radio broadcasts into the Soviet Union. Since the early 1950s, Soviet authorities had gone to considerable expense to interfere with foreign broadcasts of the British Broadcasting Corporation (BBC), the U.S. government's Voice of America, and Radio Liberty, an American-financed station. The Soviets stopped jamming these stations in 1987 and 1988. Not only were the Soviet leaders broadening the boundaries of their domestic debate, but they were allowing Western broadcasters to contribute to it.

Glasnost also had significant consequences for the arts. Soviet films and books addressed topics that were strictly forbidden in the past. The authorities allowed the publication of formerly banned books like *The Foundation Pit*, a brutally irreverent fable by Andrei Platonov about the building of Soviet communism. They also allowed films and theater that addressed controversial themes. "Repentance" was a film made for television in the republic of Georgia but which was shown throughout the Soviet Union and worldwide in the late 1980s. Although Stalin is not mentioned by name, the film portrays the brutality of the Stalinist dictatorship and suggests that Soviet society still has not adequately dealt with the terrors of Stalinism.

Perhaps the most important development relating to enlightenment in the USSR concerns what began to happen in Soviet schools in the 1980s. Glasnost was carried into classrooms at all levels, and there was a refreshing openness in the study of history, politics, and economics. Students began to discuss the Stalinist heritage, the problems of perestroika, and the differences between communism and capitalism in ways that were unheard of in the past. The conservative American president, Ronald Reagan, was allowed to go before students at Moscow State University and lecture them on human rights and Western democracy. People were exposed to a broader range of opinions than had ever existed in the Soviet past.

Although we should not ignore these and other developments related to glasnost and enlightenment in the Soviet Union, we also should not overstate them or underestimate their fragility. Communist Party leaders remain in control of the instruments of political socialization in 1990, and they could close the opening of Soviet society even faster than they opened it. However, significant changes have taken place in the Soviet Union that will make it difficult to return to the closed society of the past.

Chinese policy and performance in the area of enlightenment has also changed considerably from what it was during the Maoist past. As indicated earlier, Mao thought all Chinese citizens should be selfless, imbued with a collective spirit, and willing to endure personal hardships in service to the public good and the building of communism. Mao and the CCP leaders undertook a variety of actions to develop these new minds, new outlooks, and new behaviors. They adopted a strategy of political socialization that utilized fanatic and heavy-handed indoctrination in the schools, the mass media, and the arts. The printed and spoken word was to serve the revolution, and a politically conscious populace was thought to be necessary for victory.

Although all of the consequences of Maoist fanaticism, such as the Cultural Revolution, are not yet clear, the apparent reverence to Mao's word has all but disappeared in contemporary China. The 1980 reformers under Deng Xiaoping deemphasized Mao's teachings and political conformity and emphasized pragmatism and productivity. There also was a broadening of

As illustrated by these three students at the Technical University of Jiaotang, Chinese education is trying to stay abreast of the computer age.

the boundaries of political debate and opinion. The Chinese Communist Party in the 1980s was no longer above criticism, and dissidents were allowed to enter the public debate. China went through a period of great change in the 1980s and so did the values of its people.

Illustrative of the changes were the value orientations of some sectors of the younger generation. In the late 1980s, more and more people had lost interest in both politics and education. Many were more interested in money and pleasure. A highly materialistic and even hedonistic generation had emerged. College degrees were devalued and considered not worth the time and energy invested because they could not make people rich. At the same time, an increasing number of Chinese made a cult of Western-style consumerism. Some of them would go to any length to go to the West, in their opinion the paradise of opportunity and affluence. It is clear that enlightenment in contemporary China was coming to mean something quite different than it had during the Maoist period.

Beginning with the crackdown in Tiananmen Square in 1989, the Chinese Communist Party attempted to reverse the tide. Whereas they engineered a liberalization of the conservative Maoist policies in the 1980s, in 1989 and 1990 they began a return to a more conservative line. "Redness" was again emphasized over expertise; ideology was stressed in the schools and workplace; revolutionary heroes and models were brought back into the lessons and textbooks. Chinese policy was undergoing a reversal that put it very much at odds with what was going on in the Soviet Union and Eastern Europe.

Without doubt, the most dramatic changes in the area of enlightenment at the turn of the decade took place in Eastern Europe. Still under conservative leadership in the mid- and even into the late 1980s, some of the states, such as Czechoslovakia, East Germany, and Romania, were slow to change. However, with the revolutionary transformations of 1989, East European enlightenment practices were radically altered. The teaching of Marxism-Leninism was taken out of the schools; ideology and the Communist Parties were taken out of the workplace. There was freedom of speech, press, travel, and religion. For the first time in forty years, East Europeans were free to inform themselves about their country and the world. It was a time of incredible change. Dissident writers and playwrights became presidents (e.g., Vaclav Havel in Czechoslovakia and Arpad Goncz in Hungary); noncommunists took over the ministries of education and culture; the press and mass media were suddenly free. It was indeed an historic change, a period of enlightenment.

When considering the changes that swept across Eastern Europe in 1989 and the already high state of education and communication in these societies, one realizes the great potential in these societies. One of the tragedies of the communist experiments was the repression of this human potential. Because of the heavy hand of the Communist Party and state, the proud and able people of Eastern Europe were unable to contribute fully to their societies. Although much remains uncertain about the East European futures, the recent expansions in enlightenment should help to contribute to positive political and economic change.

Conclusion

Our four-value framework has been useful in helping us review some of the important consequences of the Marxist-Leninist experiments and Communist Party rule. We found that the traditional communist states of the Second World did not allocate power in a manner that led to socialist democracies; they did not build unified societies where people respected and supported one another in pursuit of common goals; they did not generate economic abundance, a high standard of living, and equality; and they did not create a new, enlightened citizenry conducive to the building of communism.

Because of their inability to perform— whether measured by their own or Western standards—they were forced to reconsider what they were doing and to begin to do something about it. What was done, is being done, and will be done in the 1990s is of historic significance. Mikhail Gorbachev and Deng Xiaoping started the process in the 1980s by moving their societies in the direction of reform. While the Chinese backed away from the reform process in 1989 and moved toward a policy of retrenchment, the Soviets accelerated their reforms. Many of the East European states took an even bolder approach in 1989 and 1990 by attempting, through revolution, to move from Communist Party dictatorships to pluralist democracies in one radical stroke. But what is the future of reform, revolution, and retrenchment in the Second World? What are the factors that will influence these states' success in dealing with the tremendous challenges ahead? What will affect the allocation of values in the 1990s and into the next century? Although we should be modest about our ability to predict the future, the following factors will no doubt affect it. The first is the difficult challenge of actual reform and revolution. There are no precedents or blueprints for moving from communist dictatorships and state socialism to pluralist democracies and market economies. The leaders are forced to experiment, to try to reform through trial and error. This is exceedingly difficult and risky business.

The experiences of the Soviet Union and China in the late 1980s are indicators of the nature of the challenge. By 1990, most observers agreed that the Soviet reforms were in trouble. Perestroika and glasnost had not put food on the table, and the Soviet people's support for reform was wearing thin. One had an uneasy feeling that the Soviet experiment was in peril. One was reminded of Tocqueville's famous passage on the beginnings of the French revolution. Suffering is endured patiently but becomes intolerable the moment it appears there might be an escape. In China, the process of reform had also encountered problems and underwent a serious reversal in 1989. Reforming the two

giants of communism was not proving to be an easy task.

The possibilities for positive change in some of the other Second World states are more promising. The smaller, less heterogeneous, more governable East European states stand a better chance of meeting the challenges of revolution and reform in the 1990s. The people of East Germany will find their transition to be eased considerably by their fellow Germans in the West. The other East European states hope to have their economic situations eased by expanding economic relations with their neighbors in Western Europe. As we look to the 1990s, we should recognize that the challenge of reform, the allocation of values, and human dignity will be quite different among the Second World states. There no doubt will be both successes and failures.

Another factor that will affect the chances for success will be the quality of political leadership. Mikhail Gorbachev did a remarkable job bringing about change in the 1980s. It was a clear indication that a great leader could make a difference. Yet, as we have seen, there were challenges to his leadership from the right and from the left. Some thought he was going too far too fast and that he was being excessively critical of the Soviet past. Others thought that he was not going far and fast enough and that the reform process was becoming bogged down in incremental rather than radical reform. Overall, however, we should note that Mikhail Gorbachev provided strong leadership for the Soviet reform process and deserved much of the credit for what had been accomplished by the beginning of the decade.

Some thought that Deng Xiaoping would play a similar role in China. During the 1980s, Deng and other moderate leaders were able to push the Chinese reforms forward. However, Deng was frightened by the 1989 democratization movements in both China and Eastern Europe and brought a halt to what he had earlier referred to proudly as China's "second revolution." By 1990, the powerful leadership of Mikhail Gorbachev and Deng Xiaoping was affecting the reform movements in the two Second World giants in very different ways. The quality of leadership provided the East European states will also make a difference and have much to do with the allocation of values and the state of human dignity in these societies in the 1990s. If leaders can outline their visions, win the confidence of the people, and effectively govern these changing societies, their chances for success will be reasonably bright. On the other hand, the absence of leadership may be disastrous, as demonstrated in Yugoslavia in the late 1980s. Having adopted a highly decentralized, multinational system of collective and rotating leadership in the post-Tito period, the Yugoslavs in effect created a vacuum of leadership in their society. Because the collective presidency and Party bodies called for a sharing of leadership functions among representatives of the republics and provinces, and because the regional organizations were deeply divided on many important political choices along national-regional lines, the Yugoslav leaders were locked in a stalemate. Although most recognized that reform was important and necessary to save the Yugoslav union, and although radical reform programs were put forward, the Yugoslav leaders were unable to agree on and implement the most critical reform measures. Yugoslavia was in a state of crisis, and its leadership largely was paralyzed by the end of the decade.

A third factor involves the quality of government itself. We will be seeing increasingly different forms of governments in the Second World in the 1990s. Some of them will remain the traditional Second World governments controlled by the Communist Party. Others will enter into complicated new forms of coalition government that will include communists and noncommunists. Still others will completely break with communism and constitutionally elect new leaders to put together policies and programs emulating those of the West European democracies. In all the scenarios, the governments will be under tremendous pressure to enact and carry out policies that can bring progress to these societies.

Not only must policies be made, they must be implemented in ways that bring about necessary changes. This raises the issue of the incredible challenge of implementation facing Second World governments and their bureaucracies. Responsible for the implementation of reform policies, the bureaucracies have considerable influence in facilitating or impeding reform. The giant bureaucracies in the Soviet Union and China did more of the latter than the former in the 1980s. Finding much in the reforms that was threatening to their self-interests, important sectors of the bureaucracies tried to sabotage the reform process. Created to implement the policies, the Soviet and Chinese bureaucracies often acted as constraints to the leadership's reform initiatives. In other countries, such as Yugoslavia, the federal bureaucracy was unable to act and eventually lost the support of the people. The political leadership was excessively decentralized, the federal bureaucracy was divided and without sufficient power, and Yugoslavia was "muddling along" near the brink of disaster.

The fourth factor of considerable importance to the reform process concerns the people themselves. Ultimately, the reform process and the allocation of values depends on the people of the Soviet Union, China, and the other Second World states. If the people support the reforms, if they agree with the goals and actions of the leaders, if they contribute fully in their daily work settings to promote economic output within their societies, the prognosis for reform is much brighter. However, the situation is extremely complicated and less than ideal in all of the countries we are considering.

There is no national consensus behind the reform programs in many of the countries we are considering. In the Soviet Union, for example, Gorbachev and the reformers have gone to great lengths to get the people to support perestroika and glasnost. Although many people do, many more seem to be passive and reluctant, and some very much opposed. There is no common interest or vision in Soviet society today. Surprising as it may seem to us in the West, some sectors of Soviet society long for the Stalinist past and consider the reform policies of Gorbachev a threat to the more authoritarian and stable society they prefer. The Soviet people also are divided along national-regional lines. The non-Russian nationalities want to increase their power and promote their values in the Soviet state, whereas many of Russian origin are fearful of a crumbling of the Russian empire and of losing all of the values their dominance implies.

The people of the Second World societies will also have a considerable impact on the reform process, by the way they go about their work and daily lives. In many of these societies, people have grown accustomed to lax and unproductive work environments. Soviet people often say, "They [the government] pretend to pay us and we pretend to work." For perestroika and economic reforms in these societies to succeed, people will have to work harder and produce more. Soviet economic reform and competitiveness in the global economy will not succeed if the Soviet people continue to cling to the work ethic of the past. If the reformers can reorganize their economic systems to bring out the best in their workers, they will have tapped

a great reservoir of human resources that can contribute much to the reform process. On the other hand, if the people go about their work and lives as usual, they will prove to be a formidable constraint to the reform and development process.

All of the factors addressed above involve politics, what some have called the "art of the possible." If the leadership, the governments, and the people can coalesce around a viable reform process, they can bring about significant changes in their society. On the other hand, if the leadership and the governments are divided, if the bureaucracies are resistant, and the people opposed to or reluctant about the reforms, the likelihood for progress is low.

Economic forces will also be very much involved with what happens in the Second World states. If the leaders can adopt economic policies that stimulate economic growth and improve the level of well-being, they will win support from the people and buy the time needed to move forward with their reforms. The East Europeans' moves toward privatization and market economies are both dangerous and promising. Although the new pricing systems, austerity programs, and related changes will no doubt bring about increased economic hardship in the short run, they may establish the foundations for more competitive economies in the long term.

The last factor to be mentioned concerns the influence of external forces. Although the most powerful determinants of the reform process and the future of Second World societies are those domestic factors mentioned above, there are some powerful forces in the international system that will have some bearing on reform and the allocation of values in the 1990s. For example, the improvement in East-West relations begun in the 1980s may result in a significant dampening of the arms race, which will lead to considerably lower levels of military expenditures in Second World societies. This in turn would allow these systems to invest more of their resources in the civilian sectors and make more available for allocation to education, social services, and consumerism.

Finally, global and regional economic relations will have much to do with the outcome of the economic and political experiments in the Second World. The Marshall Plan had a tremendous impact on the postwar economic reconstruction and development of Western Europe. The European Community and East-West economic relations can have a similar impact on the East European countries in the 1990s. Significant economic forces involving trade, technological,

and monetary cooperation already have been set in motion and no doubt will influence the processes of change and development.

As we can see, there are many factors that can and no doubt will affect the reform processes and the allocations of values of the Second World states. Many important developments are taking place in these countries as this book goes to press. Because it is difficult to predict just what will happen in the years ahead, it will be important for you, the student, to follow these affairs carefully and to make observations and judgments of your own. With the opening of these societies, you have more information at your disposal and much more to study than ever before.

Suggestions for Further Reading

Bergson, Abram, *Planning and Performance in Socialist Economies. The USSR and Eastern Europe* (Winchester, Mass.: Allen & Unwin, 1989).

Brezezinski, Zbigniew, *The Grand Failure: The Birth and Death of Communism in the Twentieth Century* (New York: Charles Scribner's Sons, 1989).

Butterfield, Fox, *China: Alive in a Bitter Sea* (New York: Times Books, 1982).

Connor, Walter D., *Socialism's Dilemma: State and Society in the Soviet Bloc* (New York: Columbia University Press, 1988).

Curry, Jane Leftwich, *Dissent in Eastern Europe* (New York: Praeger, 1983).

Dawisha, Karen, *Eastern Europe, Gorbachev, and Reform* (New York: Cambridge University Press, 1988).

Garton Ash, Timothy, *The Polish Revolution* (New York: Schribner, 1984).

Harding, Harry, *China's Second Revolution: Reform after Mao* (Washington, D.C.: Brookings Institution: 1987).

Herlemann, Horst G., ed., *Quality of Life in the Soviet Union* (Boulder, Colo.: Westview Press, 1987).

Hewett, Ed A., *Reforming the Soviet Economy: Equality versus Efficiency* (Washington, D.C.: The Brookings Institution: 1988).

Karlins, Rasma, *Ethnic Relations in the USSR: The Perspective from Below* (Winchester, Mass.: Allen & Unwin, 1988).

Kaser, Michael, *Health Care in the Soviet Union and Eastern Europe* (Boulder, Colo.: Westview Press, 1976).

Lasswell, Harold, Daniel Lerner, and **John D. Montgomery,** *Values and Development: Ap-*

praising the Asian Experience (Cambridge, Mass.: MIT Press, 1976).

McFarlane, Bruce, *Yugoslavia: Politics, Economics, and Society* (London: Pinter Publishers, 1988).

Matthews, Mervyn, *Patterns of Deprivation in the Soviet Union under Brezhnev and Gorbachev* (Stanford, Calif.: Hoover Institution Press, 1989).

Miller, R. F., J. H. Miller, and T. H. Rigby, *Gorbachev at the Helm: A New Era in Soviet Politics?* (London: Croon Helm, 1987).

Moore, Barrington, Jr., *Authority and Inequality under Capitalism and Socialism: USA, USSR, and China* (Oxford: Oxford University Press, 1987).

Nathan, Andrew J., *Chinese Democracy* (New York: Alfred A. Knopf, 1985).

Roeder, Philip G., *Soviet Political Dynamics* (New York: Harper and Row, 1988).

Sacks, Michael Paul, and Jerry G. Pankhurst, eds., *Understanding Soviet Society* (Winchester, Mass.: Unwin Hyman, 1988).

Scalapino, Robert A., *Communism in Korea, Part I: The Movement* (Berkeley: University of California Press, 1972).

_____, *Communism in Korea, Part II: The Society* (Berkeley: University of California Press, 1972).

Skilling, H. Gordon, *Czechoslovakia's Interrupted Revolution* (Princeton: Princeton University Press, 1976).

Notes

1. Friedrich Engels, "The Origin of the Family, Private Property and the State," reprinted in Robert C. Tucker, ed., *The Marx-Engels Reader* (New York: Norton, 1972), p. 659.

2. *Pravda*, November 30, 1988.

3. As excerpted in *The New York Times*, June 29, 1988.

4. Ibid.

5. Harry Harding, *China's Second Revolution: Reform After Mao* (Washington, D.C.: The Brookings Institution, 1987), pp. 199–200.

6. Ibid., p. 200.

7. *Newsweek*, January 15, 1990; 42.

8. For details, see Mervyn Matthews, *Patterns of Deprivation in the Soviet Union under Brezhnev and Gorbachev* (Stanford, Calif.: Hoover Institution Press, 1989).

9. As reported in *The New York Times*, January 26, 1989.

10. "The Soviet Economy Stumbles Badly in 1989." Presented by the Central Intelligence Agency and the Defense Intelligence Agency to the Technology and National Security Subcommittee of the Joint Economic Committee, Congress of the United States, April 20, 1990.

11. Mikhail Gorbachev, *Perestroika: New Thinking for Our Country and the World* (New York: Harper and Row, 1987), pp. 75, 79.

PHOTO CREDITS

INDEX

A

Abalkin, Leonid I., 45, 171, 199
Afghanistan, 46
Aganbegyan, Abel, 120
"Agitprop," 74
Agriculture, 38; in China, 174, 176–177; collectivization of, 39; private farmers, 8
Albania, 2, 98, 104; Communist Party of, 128; communist victory in, 23, 28, 29
Albanians, in Yugoslavia, 61
Alexander, King of Yugoslavia, 23
Alia, Ramiz, 128
Alliance of Free Democrats (Hungary), 126, 161–162, 184
Almond, Gabriel, 68–69
Andropov, Yuri, 113–114
Anti-Semitism, 193
Area studies, 2
Armenia: Azerbaijani conflict with, 59, 83, 123, 193; earthquake in, 46, 49, 59
Army, role in communist systems, 140, 143
Arts, *glasnost* and, 206
Azerbaijan, Armenian conflict with, 59, 83, 123, 193

B

Baltic states, 60–61, 83, 151, 171
Barghoorn, Frederick S., 78, 96
Basic Provisions (1987), 45
Batista, Fulgencio, 26
Batmonh, Jambyn, 129
Bay of Pigs invasion, 26
Beneš, Eduard, 24
Berliner, Joseph S., 168
Berlin Wall, 126
Biryukova, Aleksandra, 115
Bogomolov, Oleg, 120
Bohme, Ibrahim, 126

Bolshevik Revolution, 8–9, 16–18
Brazauskas, Agirdas, 123, 124
Brest-Litovsk, Treaty of, 17
Brezhnev, Leonid, 73, 82, 85, 105, 113, 114, 119, 167–168, 198
British Museum, 13
Brown, Archie, 99
Brucan, Silviu, 127
Brzezinski, Zbigniew K., 165
Bulgaria, 2, 44, 104; Communist Party in, 126–127; communist victory in, 25, 28, 29; economic policy in, 184; elections in, 158; wages in, 53
Byelorussians (White Russians), 56

C

Cambodia. *See* Kampuchea
Capitalism, 13, 42
Castro, Fidel, 26, 28, 30, 71, 129
Ceausescu, Nicolae, 127, 129, 155, 202
Central Committee, of Communist Party, 110–111, 169
Chang, Parris H., 174
Chebrikov, Viktor, 112
Chen, T. H., 89
Chen Yun, 176, 177
Chernenko, Konstantin, 113, 114
Chernobyl nuclear accident, 46
Chetnik movement, 23
Chiang Kai-shek, 21
Chikin, V., 170
China, 2, 7, 38, 53; army in, 143; comradeship system in, 83–84; economic policy in, 39–40, 46–47, 175–181, 185, 200–201; education in, 72–73, 129; government structure in, 140–144; human dignity in, 3–4; ideological study in, 91–93, 129; Maoist period, 81, 82, 83–84, 89–94, 95, 175, 190–191, 195–196, 207; Mongolians in, 129; Nationalist, 20–22, 27; nationalities in, 61, 96; political culture of, 70, 76, 81–82, 83–84, 88, 89–93; political performance in, 190–191, 195–

Index

Index

Index

Index

Versailles, Treaty of, 19
Vietnam, 2, 26–27, 29, 104. *See also* North Vietnam; South Vietnam
Vietnam War, 27
Vogel, Ezra F., 83
Volgyes, Ivan, 77
Vorotnikov, Vitaly, 147

W

Wage differentials, 52–53, 85, 195
Walesa, Lech, 79
Wang Jie, 84
Wang Luoshui, 81
Wang Ruowang, 81, 95
War communism, 166
Warsaw Pact, 32, 44
Wei Jingsheng, 195
Well-being: as human value, 5, 7; political culture and, 85–89; political performance and, 198–204
"What Is to Be Done?" (Lenin), 16, 103
Women, discrimination against, 54
Workers' councils, 43
Work force: in Eastern Europe, 38; reward system and, 52–53, 85; "sending-down" campaigns, 93; women in, 54. *See also* Trade unions
World War I, 16, 17

World War II, 26; China in, 21; Eastern Europe and, 22, 23, 24–25; economic impact of, 40, 41
Wu Zhuguang, 81, 95

Y

Yakovlev, Aleksander, 112, 115, 122, 169–170
Yalta Conference, 24
Yanan period, 21
Yang Shangkun, 140, 143
Yao Yilin, 179, 180
Yeltsin, Boris, 110, 120–121, 147, 171
Young Pioneers, 73
Youth organizations, 73
Yugoslavia, 2, 104, 119; Communist Party of, 128, 192–193; communist victory in, 23, 28, 29; economic policy in, 40–41, 42–43, 181–182; expulsion from Cominform, 32, 41; nationalities in, 61, 98, 194; Party organization in, 108; political culture of, 70; political origin of, 22–23; political performance in, 191–193, 194–195, 210

Z

Zhao Ziyang, 110, 115, 116, 117, 128–129, 142, 143, 176, 177, 179, 180, 201
Zhivkov, Todor, 126
Zhou Enlai, 142, 143